# deckstyle

design, create and enjoy your deck

# deckstyle

## design, create and enjoy your deck

CONSULTANT: JOANNA SMITH

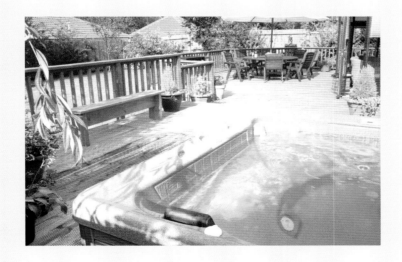

GREENWICH
EDITIONS

This edition published in 2005 by
Greenwich Editions,
The Chrysalis Building,
Bramley Road,
London W10 6SP
United Kingdom

© Salamander Books 2003

An imprint of **Chrysalis** Books Group plc

ISBN 0-86288-766-6

Printed and bound in China

**CREDITS**
Compiled, edited and designed by Joanna Smith
Commissioning Editor: Marie Clayton
Proofreader: Alison Leach
Production: Don Campaniello

Text written by Joanna Smith, Graham Quick, Jenny Hendy, Richard Bird and Sue Phillips.

# contents

# introduction

For more and more people around the world, a deck is proving to be more than just a level wooden surface in the garden, it is a way of life. Outdoor living is ever more popular, with designer furniture, patio heaters and hi-tech barbecues. And people are realising that the best place to spend their leisure time is on a stylish and sturdy deck. As well as its good looks, decking is relatively easy to lay, durable, and easy to maintain, provided you spend the money on a good hardwood which will need nothing more than an annual scrub with a stiff brush and some fungicide.

A deck can be just like an extra room – somewhere to relax with the family, a place for hobbies and pastimes, somewhere to enjoy leisurely meals with friends, a safe haven for the kids to play or simply a place to escape for time alone. And it can be as comfortable and beautifully designed as any room in the house, with matching furniture, soft cushions, perhaps an attractive parasol or awning and a chic water feature to soothe away the stresses of the day.

If you are keen on cooking al fresco, then add a barbecue or even a full-scale outdoor kitchen to the deck and start sizzling in style. With the use of subtle lighting, a small patio fireplace and a comfy chair, the deck can become an outdoor sitting

LEFT: *An enclosed gazebo with awning makes a delightful secluded dining area on this smart deck.*

RIGHT: *Use the basic deck-building technique to create a woodland walkway. Decking has a natural affinity with plants.*

room, an area of peace and tranquillity after the hustle and bustle of work. Now that hot tubs and spas have become more affordable, the deck also offers the perfect place for a relaxing soak. Even a sauna can be incorporated into a deck area. As with any living space the deck can be split into several levels and have steps leading to other areas, each for its own separate use – the small deck with the morning sun for breakfast, to the larger deck for entertaining friends.

Decking produces a wonderfully soft-looking surface, which can be left natural or stained in one of the good new colours now available – slate blue, silvery grey or a soft bottle green all make a good foil for the planting. It is warm and comfortable to walk on or even to sit on if you have a cushion to hand.

Another reason for its popularity is that decking will cope particularly well with an uneven site, saving you from spending a lot of money levelling it out. You simply adjust the height of the bearing timbers to take in any changes of level. In fact, you can use any changes of level to your advantage to build a tiered or stepped surface, which helps add interest to the garden. If you want to include a water feature in a small garden, decking is an ideal medium to use, as you can incorporate the pond into the decked area, building the decked surface over part of the pond to form a bridge.

As it is relatively light, decking is also one of the best surfaces for a roof terrace. The main concern here is not to pierce any damp-proof membrane covering the roof terrace in the construction of a new surface, but as the roof-top surface is already flat, you can simply 'float' the decking just above the asphalt on reasonably heavy load-bearing joists. Always check with a building surveyor when planning a roof terrace, or any work to it, to ensure that it will not only bear the weight of whatever you have in mind, but also that any drainage system that already exists will be adequate for the purpose.

LEFT: *This deck has been built around an existing tree which casts dappled shade over the handsome tree seat below.*

RIGHT: *Ready-made decking squares are smart and convenient and perfect for laying directly over an unattractive patio.*

LEFT: *Here the clean lines of decking have been combined with cool slate paving for an interesting contrast.*

RIGHT: *A stylish screen creates a warm and sheltered sunny corner for sunbathing, relaxation and lunch.*

In a small garden, decking can be used to cut down on the lawn area, thereby reducing time spent on garden maintenance. The greenhouse or shed can be put at the end of the deck to allow easy access in poor weather. Decking can be extended around the swimming pool to become a 'beach', more pleasant underfoot than hot paving.

The idea behind this book is to encourage you to plan, design and build your own deck without the need to go through garden design school or train as a builder. Even if you have not worked with timber and concrete before, this book will guide you through the necessary steps from the start to the finish of your dream deck. You will learn each step with practical information and confidence to visualize, plan and construct your outdoor living space so that it blends with your garden and your lifestyle.

As you look round garden centres and builder's merchants you will discover many decking components and ready-made units. Whether you buy ready-made or decide to custom-build to your own design, this book will guide you through the process. There are also plenty of ideas and helpful advice for furnishing your deck and enjoying it to the full, whether you want a space to lounge or a complete dining area for entertaining in style. The sooner you build your deck, the sooner you will be able to enjoy it.

# design

# initial planning

The process of designing a deck, selecting an appropriate site for it and deciding on its final use should take full advantage of what the garden has to offer. The deck should blend in with the home and garden, as well as be able to cater for the family's needs. A well thought-out deck will fit effortlessly into the site and not look like a bolted-on extra.

Perhaps the most daunting task for the amateur deck builder is the design process. This can be broken down into a number of stages and surveying the site to find the ideal location for the deck is the first and most important. One way to find the right place is to walk around the garden, pick two or three places to sit in and look at what your view would be if you built the deck in this position. Remember to walk away and look at the deck from the rest of the garden to see how it will fit in with the garden's overall design.

As you walk over your decking area, think about where people are going to walk and how doors are going to open on to it – there is no point having the table in the way of the door or having to climb over it to get to the garden. These small details will make the finished deck perfect for your needs.

## SIZE AND SHAPE
The deck needs to be appropriate for its intended use and the shape in which it is to fit. One of the greatest joys of possessing a garden is being able to sit in the open air surrounded by both plants and wildlife. The sound of water, birdsong or humming insects can be a great bonus, so it is worth ensuring that the deck is large enough to allow you to sit out in comfort when the weather allows.

As a guide, the deck should be the same size or slightly larger than an equivalent room indoors to allow for garden furniture which is normally larger than the indoor version.

Decking areas can be separated by introducing alternative patterns or changes in height or board direction or by creating an L- or T-shaped deck. Most important of all is that the deck should be in proportion to the house and its surroundings.

## PRIVACY
If you have neighbours close to the deck, it is preferable to construct it in a low position as you would not want to be perched high on a deck above your fence for all to see, and the neighbours probably do not want to see you either!

ABOVE: *Start by trying out your garden furniture in different parts of the area in which you plan to construct the deck. As you are rearranging the furniture, ask yourself a number of questions. Can you get out of the door? Is the table big enough for your needs?*

RIGHT: *The furniture fits well on the finished deck and there is plenty of space to get in and out of the door.*

## AMBITIOUS PROJECTS

If you are planning to build a raised deck over 60cm (24in) above ground level, it may be better to seek professional help in the design and building of it as important factors such as safety must be considered. You will, of course, still be the one to decide how the deck will look and what features you require.

## ACCESS

A deck should look inviting and a large doorway will encourage people to go out on to the deck. A small step may be needed to help the transition to the deck if it is much lower than the floor of the house.

As with any DIY project, concentrate on constructing a quality deck rather than an overambitious one which may lead to disaster. There will always be the opportunity to add to the project at a later stage.

# SUN OR SHADE?

A deck can be placed in a shaded spot if it is to be used mainly in the evenings when sun is not a priority, but a daytime deck would be better placed in the part of the garden that gets the most sunshine.

This does not necessarily have to be the part closest to the house, although it is obviously convenient if it is so that you can carry out drinks and food easily.

If, though, your garden faces north and the area behind the house is shaded, then why not site the deck at the far end of the garden, perhaps linking it to the house with a specially created and planted walkway?

In areas where the prevailing wind may cause problems, a fence or hedge will be needed to act as a wind break, but this can be added after the deck is built.

LEFT: *The sloping ground in this garden makes it difficult to see how high the deck will be when it is raised up to the bottom of the windows. Nonetheless, this is still the best place for the deck. The eucalyptus tree offers some privacy from the neighbours.*

ABOVE: *It is worth roughly outlining the size of the proposed deck to get an idea of size and proportion.*

RIGHT: *This deck was built in two stages – the main deck first and the octagonal extra section at a later date.*

# choosing a style

Your deck has the potential to become your own little bit of heaven, a sanctuary from the hurly burly of everyday life. Through television and magazines, we are bombarded with images of perfect 'designer' gardens and the prospect of designing our own private space can be daunting. But a garden is a personal place and all that really matters is that you make a deck to suit your needs and preferences – a garden you really like.

For many of us, the decision about the style of deck we should have is really out of our hands. As it is usually a major garden feature, a deck should blend in with its surroundings and become a natural part of the overall landscape of the garden rather than something that looks out of place. A stark, minimalist deck of black-stained wood would be far too modern for a stone cottage, and a natural wood deck with decorative handrail, wooden planters and a trel-lis pergola over the top would be far too fussy for a sleek roof garden. Choose the design carefully as it will be an expensive and time-consuming feature to change if you become bored with it.

That said, however, it is vital to choose a design you really want to look at every day, and create a space where you really want to spend time. It must reflect your likes and your personality so you feel relaxed and comfortable when using it.

## HINTS AND TIPS

● **DO** go through gardening magazines and cut out pictures of decks and plants which appeal
● **DO** look at deck manufacturer's brochures for ideas
● **DO** have a theme or style in mind to help you select specific features
● **DO** use plants, pots and other decorative touches to create the style you want
● **DON'T** try to cram in too many features. Simple designs work best
● **DON'T** ignore your surroundings. Choose a style and a design that blend comfortably with the local architecture and landscape
● **DON'T** forget colour can make a big impact on the overall style of a deck

LEFT: *The soft grey decking creates a sympathetic background for a picnic bench. Decorative screening makes this an intimate and private space.*

RIGHT: *A simple deck is all that is required in such a natural setting – a fussier feature would detract from the surrounding garden and countryside and simply look out of place.*

## DECK FEATURES

Extra features, such as raised areas, pergolas, handrails and built-in seats, can have a big impact on the style of the deck you create. By surrounding a deck with trellis, for example, and building a pergola over the top you will make an intimate space perfect for dining. By constructing a simple square of decking next to a pond in a wild area of the garden, you will create an understated feature with a natural feel.

Use areas of different heights to add interest on larger decks, and try laying the boards at different angles to define different sections.

## MATERIALS AND STYLE

The wood you choose will also affect the look of the finished deck. Flat planks create a less 'graphic' and stripy deck than grooved boards. Light and dark boards also provide different effects, which can be enhanced or obliterated with the use of woodstain or paint.

ABOVE: *A basic deck of pale boards can take on a whole range of different styles, depending on the furniture, plants and pots you use to furnish it. Because it is so plain, it will need decorative objects to soften the look, but these can be changed to create different styles as the mood takes you.*

LEFT: *Grooved decking really adds to the impact of laying the boards in two different directions and makes the raised area more of a feature in its own right.*

# ready-made decking

For an easy-to-build and flexible solution, consider using decking squares to build your deck. These create quite a different look to long planks as you get a chequerboard effect, rather like paving slabs.

Providing that additional maintenance is carried out, decking squares will produce an acceptable finish and will last. To avoid unnecessary cutting and rebuilding, the final design should stay within the sizes that the modules come in.

### FLEXIBILITY

The advantage of the ready-made system is that it can be a temporary surface, moved seasonally or extended without any major work to the original patio. If you fancy a new pattern this can be done with little effort and no cutting required. Another plus is the ease of installation – there is no cutting required if it is lying on an existing patio and estimating the number of units required is simple.

**ABOVE RIGHT:** *Decking squares can be laid in a chequerboard pattern with the boards running in alternate directions, as here, or alternatively with all the boards running in the same direction to create the look of traditional decking.*

**RIGHT:** *Easy-to-lay square panels are readily available and can be used to make a deck with a wonderful texture.*

Decking squares are perfect for surfacing areas that are difficult to build on, such as on a balcony or small roof deck, where access for long lengths of timber would be tricky.

### THE COST

As with any ready-made goods you are paying for the convenience – it will work out more expensive than a boarded deck, but if you are not too handy with power tools then this is a safe and easy choice. The only limit to decking tiles is that they are not really suitable for building raised decks.

# advanced decks

It is important to realize that the most expensive does not necessarily mean the best. A simple, well-designed, professionally built deck can often be a better way to spend your money than a not-so-well-built DIY deck. If for any reason you feel unhappy with a project that is beyond the methods shown in this book, look to a deck builder to do the work for you.

As with any garden feature, some of us want to build something just a little bigger and more ambitious. In any large-scale building project, such as constructing a deck, it is best to seek advice about its design and construction as a small mistake could be disastrous and dangerous to people – as well as the attached building.

## ALL-IMPORTANT PLANNING

Planning is even more important when the decks are more complex as rectifying mistakes can be very expensive once construction is underway. If you are going to build the deck in stages to spread the cost, or to allow extra work to be carried out in the meantime, explain to the builders what sections are to be constructed when. This will give them an idea of how to plan the deck in sections that can be easily completed and left in a

LEFT: *Decking makes an ideal alternative to paving around a pool – cooler and more pleasant to walk on and often more attractive too.*

ABOVE: *A good choice of colour has enabled this deck to blend in with its surroundings, without it overpowering the house. The raised section makes an additional, more intimate, seating area, surrounded by handsome handrails and a matching pergola. The furniture has been stained to match the deck.*

state that makes the deck not only usable, but structurally safe before the final sections are added.

Once the deck's use and position have been decided, a call to the decking company is required to allow them to come out and complete your design to local building regulations, if any apply in your area. Always get two or three quotes to make sure you are getting what you want, and ask to see samples of the timber before they start work.

CHOOSING A DECK

With a professional company building your deck, you will be able to have almost any type of deck shape or size that you can imagine.

Why not consider a multi-level deck from a first floor balcony with a stairway leading to lower levels for dining, and walkways to other areas of the garden such as the spa, hot tub or swimming pool?

There is no limit to design or size, providing the deck solves all your requirements for use and the cost is within your budget.

**LEFT:** *This magnificent deck has a summerhouse as its central feature, with space for sitting out front in comfort. This is an ambitious project which should be left to the professionals unless you have very good carpentry skills.*

**RIGHT:** *This brand new, well-designed deck has all the right qualities: it is well built, on a good site, and has enough space to be useful.*

DESIGNING YOUR OWN

You may want to design your own deck and then supply the drawings to the builders yourself for them to quote for. Remember to listen to their comments, as some of your ideas may be too complex or just not feasible, so do not ignore what they have to say. If you are sure that the design fits your requirements, get another builder to give you their opinion. If both builders agree that the design is not workable, you will have to think again.

If the deck changes the appearance of the house you will need to check to be sure that planning permission is not required. If it is, any building regulations are applied to the deck and its supporting structure.

## CHOOSING A DESIGNER

Before you choose a designer for your deck, it is preferable to check out two or three of their previous designs to see if you like the decks they have built in the past. A good designer will be able to judge exactly what you require from the style of your existing house and garden. Approach a few different designers and see who comes up with the best and most workable deck for your needs.

# designing the deck

The number of patterns that can be created with timber is endless but only a few will look acceptable on any given deck. A few general rules will help you select the right pattern for your deck. Decks with a plain border around them will have a more finished appearance, containing the pattern within.

The smaller the deck, the simpler the pattern should be as complex patterns tend to look untidy and fussy. Complicated patterns will make defects in the timber show up much more than simple ones. It is better to spend more money on superior timber and less on the time and labour needed to create complex patterns.

Long rectangular decks with the boards running away from you make the eye follow the boards to the far end, accentuating length. Boards running across the deck are more relaxing and make you want to stay on the deck.

Diagonal boards draw attention to a view or direct you to steps or a doorway. They can also be used to follow lines from the house or garden.

**RIGHT:** *A photograph of the house and garden makes visualization much easier.*

**FAR RIGHT:** *Grooved boards make the direction in which the planks have been laid even more obvious, so plan carefully to get the right effect.*

## CHOOSING BOARD WIDTHS

Whatever width you choose for your boards there are a few factors to consider. One is the span across your joists; narrow timber will only cover short spans and this must be decided before you start to build the deck. If you plan to use a diagonal pattern, the spans will be wider and the joists need to be closer together. Avoid boards wider than 15cm (6in) as they are prone to warping and drain poorly.

## TYPES OF JOINTS

In most cases the deck boards will be long enough for your deck, but if the deck is longer than a single board it will be necessary to use additional lengths to complete the run. It may be necessary to install extra joists to accommodate the board lengths, which is something to remember in the building stage.

The three most common joints are:
1. A continuous joint where all the joints run down or across the deck in one line, such as the centre line of a herringbone pattern.
2. Random joints where the joints occur at different, random, positions across the deck.
3. Pattern joints where the joints alternate positions but form a pattern across the deck. This is a similar pattern to overlaying bricks in a wall, where the joints are in a basic repeating pattern.

Small decks will look best with an intentional pattern – a random joint will look odd and create an uneasy feel on the deck. Large decks can tolerate any of the joints, but a long continuous joint can look obvious and may become the main feature of the deck – probably not what you would plan for.

# HINTS AND TIPS

- A deck for dining on should be close to the kitchen
- Fence or trellis around the deck can provide a screen from sound and wind and offer privacy
- A deck with some shade offers choice for sitting out – warm sun in cool weather or cool shade when it's hot
- When planning steps or raised sections in a decking system it is not ideal to step off or up a corner. Cutting the corner off makes for a better transition
- Steps can be wider than they are indoors to make them more inviting
- To highlight steps, change the direction of the boards to make them stand out. Grooved boards, running across the step, will make them safer when wet
- Avoid curved edges and round decks as the supporting structure will have to be complex
- If the deck is quite small, keep the design simple and arrange the boards in a basic pattern

## DRAWING PLANS

Drawing up an initial plan will help you visualize the deck and make estimating the materials easier. With a graph pad, go into the garden and measure fixed points such as the house and fence. This will give you a good idea of the shape and space available to you.

Another method is to take a photograph of the area and, with tracing paper over the top, draw in the intended design; you can then go back to the measured plan and work out if it will fit in. Once this has been done, lay a hose or rope out around the 'deck' and position tables and chairs to make sure everything has enough room to work. You can then finalize the plan and measure up for materials and fixings.

**ABOVE RIGHT:** *Due to careful planning, this deck has been laid with few joints.*

**BELOW:** *Always do a scale plan on graph paper to design your deck.*

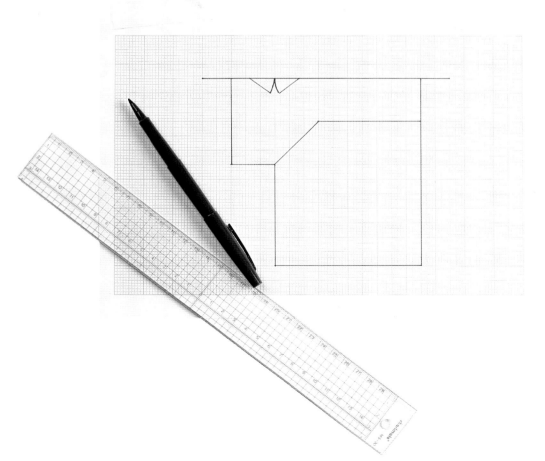

## THE PAPERWORK

With your plan drawn to scale you can then work out the amount of timber required to make the deck. Start by working out the number of posts needed – it is better to have a few extra than a springy deck. Then work out the number of beams required, if any, and then the joists. Deck board is often sold by the square metre so your supplier will work this out for you. Any extras such as hand rails and spindles can be added to the order at this point. As with any building project allow for an extra 10% of materials to cover damaged timbers or mistakes. It is also important to check whether planning permission is needed, particularly if the deck is likely to be especially large or high.

# themed decks

The smaller the space, the more it really needs a theme to define its personality, and few decks are very large features. The best way to stamp a style on a deck is to choose a definite theme. Decide from the start what you want and make sure every feature, however large or small, really says what you mean.

When space is limited, a deck needs a linking theme. Instead of planting and furnishing it with a random mixture of ideas, it pays to have a particular style in mind. That way, everything you do has a focus: the plants you buy, the pots, seating and decking boards all give out the same message. The result not only looks unified, but can also save you a great deal of money in plants and accessories that quickly lose their appeal when they do not look as good as you hoped once installed.

A deck does not have to be fashionable to be stylish. What is fashionable may not look right for your home or neighbourhood, or suit the way you want to use your surroundings. An Oriental style deck, for example, would look out of place in a rural area, but be quite at home in a minimalist town garden. But with thoughtful planning and good design you can often adapt unlikely styles to suit a range of different surroundings. For example, you could have a woodland deck in the middle of town or a colonial-style deck outside a city basement.

And if you are worried that you might get bored with one distinctive style, you could change part of the design or planting scheme every few years to give the garden a regular face-lift. Or even change the style completely, leaving only the decking itself and other permanent features as the common factor. It is only practical to consider making such sweeping changes to a small area, where plenty of style can be achieved with relatively little effort and cost.

RIGHT: *An Oriental theme is simple to achieve as it is inherently minimalist. Here, the defining features are the fence and the bamboos.*

# Mediterranean deck

A Mediterranean deck would be perfect for warm, dry climates, but most of the plants are adaptable. The essence of this style is colour, wall space and containers. Use warm shades of terracotta, yellow and red for walls, natural tones for the deck (rustic boards are best), and hot colours (as below) or cooler lilacs and lemons for the planting. Choose rustic wooden furniture if possible.

**FROM LEFT TO RIGHT: Hebe *'Sapphire'*, Anisodontea capensis *'Sapphire', red pelargonium,* Salvia officinalis *'Purpurea' (front),* pink potentilla *(centre),* Gazania *'Daybreak' (front),* Lotus hirsutus *(back), and* Portulaca *'Sundial Mixed'.***

Climbers, such as grape vines or jasmine, can be trained on typical Mediterranean pergolas, or on trellis or netting on a wall. Containers, including hanging baskets, wall planters and tubs and troughs, are the popular way of adding seasonal colour and changing interest to a garden of this type.

Grow drought-tolerant plants, such as *Acaena* (New Zealand burr), prostrate junipers, whipcord hebe, dwarf lavender, creeping thyme and *Rhodanthemum hosmariense,* all in terracotta pots mulched with gravel.

## HINTS AND TIPS

● *Good, compact shrubs for a Mediterranean deck include potentilla, cistus and hebe*
● *More unusual dwarf shrubs include* Lotus hirsutus *and* Convolvulus cneorum
● *Terracotta pots and natural, untreated wooden boxes complete the Mediterranean style; all team up well with plain, simple decking*
● *Drought-tolerant, sun-loving plants are best for containers in warm sunny places. Pelargoniums, anisodontea and portulaca all make a good show, and have the typical, bright flowers of Mediterranean gardens. Also try daisy-flowered marguerites*

# woodland deck

Decking has a natural affinity with trees, shrubs, ferns and other shade-loving plants and is the ultimate natural-looking surface. Build a deck among some established trees to create a shady hideaway, or plant small trees and shrubs around your deck for a similar effect.

Choose natural wood furniture and accessories, and build some raised beds from the same timber as the deck. Alternatively, use wooden half barrels for planting and mulch the surface of the compost with bark chips, cocoa shell or leafmould for that woodland feel.

Go for natural schemes of woodland plants in muted shades, relying on beautiful foliage for year-round and seasonal interest. Use small birch trees and ornamental cherries for dappled shade, and underplant with ferns, deadnettle (*Lamium*) and ajuga. Use pine cones, pieces of interesting bark and rustic wooden structures to enhance the theme.

FROM LEFT TO RIGHT: Polystichum setiferum *'Congestum'*, Corydalis flexuosa, Cornus controversa *'Variegata'*, Rubus calycoides *'Betty Ashurner'*, Blechnum spicant *(front)*, Luzula sylvatica *'Aureomarginata' and* Athyrium filix-femina.

## HINTS AND TIPS

● *Use bark chippings or cocoa shell to mulch beds and tubs*
● *Choose low-growing, spreading plants for ground-cover, such as* Rubus calycoides *and* Aegopodium podagraria *'Variegatum'*
● *Ferns are known for their delicate lacy foliage and love of woodland conditions. Choose a selection of different varieties*
● *Moist soil and light shade suits many beautiful woodland plants, such as cyclamen, hellebores, violets and epimediums. Use them in tubs and beds*

# Oriental deck

An Oriental-style garden contains characteristic ingredients: raked gravel, smooth stones and Oriental-style ornaments, such as a bamboo deer scarer (shown below), a stone bridge over a dry 'river' of pebbles or a stone lantern. All these features look at home on or near decking.

Added to these should be a few typically architectural plants, such as bamboos, grasses, Japanese apricot, craggy conifers, Japanese maples and irises. You might also add shelves of small potted bonsai-style conifers, half hidden behind a bamboo screen. Oriental themes are ideal for easy care gardens because, lacking any flower beds, they require little care.

True Oriental gardens are full of symbolism, and each individual rock or ornament is placed with great care and much thought, but the idea can be adapted to create an Oriental-style deck at home. Instead of adjoining flower beds, have areas of raked gravel with carefully positioned stones. Don't forget the weed block fabric underneath.

**FROM LEFT TO RIGHT:** Pinus leucodermis *'Blue Giant',* Sciadopitys verticillata, Pleioblastus auricomus, *and finely cut acer.*

- *Aim for romantic chaos. Try to make the plants appear as if they have seeded themselves*
- *Terracotta is a strong element. Use terracotta pots and even old tiles as decoration*
- *Wooden trugs make attractive containers for small pots of plants*
- *Old garden tools, such as hand trowels and watering cans, can also be handsome*
- *Choose wicker or wooden furniture for the right effect*

# country style deck

A country garden is deliberately intended to look very natural, almost as if the flowers had appeared randomly all by themselves, without having been planted. This effect is partly achieved by growing plants that look in keeping, and partly by the way they are grown. Typical cottage garden plants include hardy annuals (violas, calendula and cornflowers), wild-looking perennials, such as hardy cranesbills, and cultivated forms of wildflowers, such as coloured primroses and violets. Equally authentic are culinary, decorative and medicinal herbs, shrub roses, flowering fruit trees, old-fashioned shrubs, such as myrtle and flowering quince, spring and summer bulbs, such as daffodils and lilies, and chrysanthemums and dahlias.

Choose terracotta pots and a few decorative garden accessories to complete the picture – old watering cans and even discarded garden tools will do the trick.

**FROM LEFT TO RIGHT:** *Dendranthema 'White Gloss', variegated fuchsia (front), hardy fuchsia cultivar (back), old-fashioned pinks (front), lavender (back), Antirrhinum 'Liberty Cherry' (front), pansy (front) and tobacco plants.*

# family deck

A family deck must be immensely versatile to cater for the changing needs of a growing family. It must be inexpensive to create, quick and easy to look after, safe and tough enough to withstand family fun, yet also look attractive all year round and cater for outdoor entertaining.

The most essential ingredients of a family deck are a barbecue area and space for a table and chairs, and indestructible plants which will either bend over or recover quickly from damage. Good examples include shrubby willows, such as the *Salix alba* varieties, *Cornus alba*, *Ribes sanguineum*, philadelphus, buddleja and hebe. Planted around the edge of the deck, these shrubs provide shelter and privacy, as well as acting as a good barrier. Avoid potentially poisonous plants (ask at the garden centre), plus prickly plants like berberis or those with sharp-edged leaves like bamboos.

Extra features might include a built-in swing or slide, a sandpit or paddling pool incorporated into the deck, a small nature area to encourage wildlife, and a border or even a single container, where children can enjoy growing their own plants.

Don't forget to make provision for the adults to enjoy themselves too – set aside an area for lounging and install lighting or flares for evening parties and barbecues.

FROM LEFT TO RIGHT: Sorbus racemosa *'Sutherlandii', nasturtium 'Gleam' (front),* Cornus alba *'Elegantissima' (back),* Polygonum affine *'Darjeeling Red' (front),* Corylus avellana *'Contorta' (back) and* Spiraea vanhouttei *'Pink Ice' (front).*

# colonial deck

A colonial-style deck is a good way to fill a small space with big style. Instead of choosing plants in scale with their surroundings, do exactly the opposite to create a jungle look. There are plenty of exotic-looking shrubs and perennials that look the part yet are perfectly hardy. Foliage will play a big part – pick plants with large leaves and bold, architectural shapes, such as bamboo, phormium, *Fatsia japonica*, *Arundo donax* and *Trachycarpus fortunei*.

Add big terracotta pots of tender plants for exotic summer flowers, including plants like agave, bottle-brush (*Callistemon*) or abutilon and move them under cover or protect them outdoors during cold weather.

For seasonal flowers, fill containers with tropical-looking tender plants, such as castor oil plant (*Ricinus*), tithonia, cannas or any of the large tobacco plants (*Nicotiana tabacum, N. sylvestris* or *N. knightiana*).

Choose suitably tropical-inspired garden furniture – bamboo seats or slatted wooden painted tables and chairs. Add bamboo screens and vigorous climbers like *Campsis radicans* in a sheltered sunny spot.

**FROM LEFT TO RIGHT: Solanum crispum *'Glasnevin'*, Acacia dealbata *(back)*, canna *(centre)*, Phormium tenax *'Pink Panther' (front)*, Phygelius capensis, Callistemon citrinus *'Splendens'*, Abutilon *'J. Morris' and* Cordyline australis *'Atropurpurea'*.**

# water garden deck

## HINTS AND TIPS

- *Use large-leaved plants with strong architectural shapes*
- *Choose a mixture of foliage types and colours for added interest*
- *Combine with cobbles, pebbles and larger stones to contrast with the plants*
- *Grow moisture-loving plants in containers by lining the pots with plastic*
- *Mulch containers and bog gardens with bark chippings to retain moisture*

Decking has a natural affinity with ponds, bog gardens and moisture-loving plants, so why not transform your deck with a water garden theme? You don't have to actually have a pond to create the leafy effect – just some moist soil is all that is required. This can be achieved by creating a small bog garden beside the deck by digging out the soil to a depth of about 60cm (24in) and lining the hole with thick black plastic or pond liner. Poke a few small holes in the liner, then replace the soil, mixed with a good quantity of organic matter such as leafmould or garden compost to retain moisture. Water well, then plant up with handsome moisture-loving plants and keep the soil damp.

If you don't have a deckside bed for a bog garden, then use a container instead. Line it with black plastic and plant up as before, with plenty of organic matter mixed into the compost. Keep well watered.

Moisture-loving plants create a verdant, leafy effect and many have spectacular leaves and brightly coloured flowers. The only downside is that most of them die down below ground over winter.

**FROM LEFT TO RIGHT:** Gunnera manicata, Lobelia cardinalis *'Queen Victoria' (back),* Schoenoplectus *'Zebrinus' (zebra rush),* Mimulus luteus *(centre), red astilbe and* Hosta fortunei aureomarginata.

# using colour

The way you use colour in the garden can have a tremendous effect on the success of your design, and this is especially true of the area around the deck. Most people are happy to consider colour scheming indoors, but out in the garden they often jumble colours together and the effects can be far from relaxing. Unless you are confident and have a strong idea of what you want, stick to a limited colour palette for guaranteed success.

Colour affects our mood and can also give a certain look or feel to a deck area or whole garden. For example, the use of lots of grey and silver foliage, white, blue and a few yellow flowers can create a seaside feel, especially when it is combined with gravel and pebbles.

On the other hand, terracotta coloured pots, tiles and rendering suggest a hot climate even before the plants have been added. Bright reds, oranges and dayglow colours like magenta and cerise stimulate the senses, whilst soft mauves and purples will create a quieter, more contemplative atmosphere. Bear this in mind when you come to choose a scheme for your deck.

## CONTRASTING COLOURS

You can change the feel of the garden and make the various parts more interesting by contrasting the colour schemes used in different parts. This is particularly effective in a segmented garden consisting of a series of outdoor rooms. To lift schemes that use closely related colours, drop in spots of a contrasting or complementary colour. For example, in an all-yellow and cream border, use lavender-blue or purple highlights; and in a pastel pink planting consider adding deep velvety crimson.

## INTRODUCING COLOUR

Paints and stains can be used to highlight certain objects and structures in the garden and decks especially lend themselves to this treatment. Use the same colour as a linking theme running through the garden if possible. Take care not to use very bright or strong colours on the whole deck, though, as it can be too much over such a large area.

Colour can also be used to ease the transition between indoors and out with matching wooden furniture colours, pots and fabrics all helping to make the space feel connected and larger overall.

Making your own items of wooden furniture and garden structures around the deck creates all kinds of

## GREENS

Whatever other colours you choose, when plants are involved the main element of any garden colour scheme is green. There are a myriad shades and some incredibly tranquil gardens, such as certain Japanese styles, employ this colour very successfully, using other colours only very sparingly to add highlights.

ABOVE LEFT: *A dark brown woodstain creates a natural effect in a natural setting. It harmonizes well with the bark chips. A paler shade would have contrasted too much and looked artificial.*

ABOVE: *These decking tiles have been stained in slightly contrasting shades of pale blue to create a subtle chequer-board effect. The simple white planting and galvanized tubs enhance the style.*

design possibilities. Paint is useful for hiding imperfections and helps protect against moisture ingress. Consider picking out the detail of structures like a trellis gazebo, perhaps using a darker shade to highlight the main struts and a paler shade to colour the trelliswork. An uninspiring garden shed could be given a similar treatment to transform it into a feature!

DECORATIVE OBJECTS

Often quite ordinary objects or ones no longer in use can be given a new lease of life with a lick of paint or woodstain. These can be used as decorative objects around the deck to add interest. Use special paints for metal objects such as watering cans and wrought iron furniture, and microporous paints and special woodstains for woodwork.

Water-based acrylic paints can be used to paint pots and ornaments of terracotta, concrete or plastic. Look out for old items of furniture and traditional gardening implements in junk shops and car boot sales, such as wheelbarrows and metal flower buckets. Even wicker baskets can be painted in different shades to fit a particular colour scheme; plant them up with flowers to match.

LEFT: *Terracotta is a popular colour but should be used with care; choose plants which complement it.*

ABOVE: *Grey is a warm and neutral colour for decking and contrasts nicely with the natural tones of plain wood.*

## HINTS AND TIPS

- *DO use colour scheming to create different moods and effects in the garden, remembering that greens are neutral, hot colours stimulate, and cool colours relax*
- *DO use contrasting colours to highlight certain features or objects. For example, set a bright blue chair on a soft lemon deck*
- *DO link colour schemes indoors and out to create the illusion of space*
- *DO enjoy yourself with colour. After all, it's your garden and you are the one who will be living with it*
- *DON'T use too many different colours together, especially in a small space, unless the backdrop is neutral, for example a white wall or a soft blue-grey stained deck*
- *DON'T be too rigid with colour scheming – the effects can be rather flat*
- *DON'T overdo strong colour contrasts. They work best as occasional highlights*
- *DON'T use very bright, attention-grabbing colours like white and orange at the end of a small garden. It will make the space feel even shorter. To lengthen the garden, use soft blues, purples and greys*

# optional extras

Before you settle on a final layout for your deck, it pays to spend some time thinking about the finishing touches. These might be practical or decorative. Ask yourself who will be using the deck and what features will benefit them – children and older people need careful consideration. Also ask how it will be used – for dining al fresco, sitting out in the evenings, or simply as a children's play area?

Decks are often built on the side of a house or round a garden building, creating an extension of the living space. The impression of an outdoor room can be strengthened by linking the deck and building via some kind of overhead structure to form a 'ceiling'. Simple wooden pergolas fulfil this function admirably. If the deck is in a hot, sunny spot, the pergolas can be adapted to provide a little shade or offer a certain degree of seclusion.

Wooden pergolas can be bought off the peg from DIY stores and builder's merchants but you can also get your local timber yard to cut the necessary pieces to your own specifications. Getting the proportions right is the key to success. The uprights need to have substance and the height of the structure and spacing of the components should create a feeling of spaciousness rather than one of claustrophobia!

Plan it on paper and then stick to your guns. It may well look too big at first, but when covered with climbers it will blend in nicely. Don't forget to make provision for the plants, preparing the ground and planting holes before the deck is laid.

Once the basic framework is up, you can add decorative features such as specially shaped trellis elements. Interesting effects of light and shade can be achieved by laying patterned trellis panels over the crossbeams. For

an Oriental look or for maximum privacy or shelter from wind, consider fitting bamboo, heather or wicker panels between the uprights. Square-pattern trellis fencing panels create a feeling of enclosure and security but the deck still feels light and airy.

BELOW: *As well as the swimming pool, this deck features an attractive gazebo to provide a shady seating area, and built-in matching planters.*

## CHILD-FRIENDLY

Small children will love to play out on the warm dry boards of the deck and a sand pit could become a focus for their games. Match the timber and construction style and build a water-proof cover to keep the sand clean and dry when not in use. Built-in planters and furniture such as bench seating can really make a feature on the deck, especially when picked out

ABOVE: *If the deck is to be used by small children, safety is of utmost importance. Building a sand pit in one corner of the deck will help to confine the play area and make it easier to supervise.*

in a contrasting or complementary shade. Waterproof wooden lockers can also be incorporated, perhaps within a seating unit, to store cush-ions and toys for easy access.

# pergolas and arches

It pays to include some overhead structure to provide both privacy and shade on a deck, and a support for climbing plants. There is something wonderfully evocative about sitting beneath a canopy of foliage on a hot summer's day, the light filtering through softly. It is as though the garden is cocooning you. You can achieve this effect with trees, but there is not always room, especially on small decks. The other possibility is to build some kind of overhead structure, for example a decorative arbour erected over a seat, or a traditional pergola built over a dining area. Overhead structures effectively form the ceiling of your deck. They can consist of a very light framework but they still have that same psychological effect, making us feel enclosed, safe and secure, and therefore at the same time more relaxed.

There is a wide range of such supporting structures to choose from, from the highly ornate to the remarkably simple. How big and how grand you wish to make it is a matter of taste, and also of budget.

For a very basic structure, sink metal or wooden posts well into the ground next to the deck to give them strength, and tie, screw or nail overhead horizontal posts or rails to them. For a more rustic form you could use strong ropes as the horizontal elements, slotting them through eyes in the upright posts.

Often, some kind of seating is included beneath a pergola as the dappled shade makes such a pleasant environment to sit, especially in warm weather. If you prefer, you can create a smaller structure using one of the garden walls as the back support, so that you have shelter on one side at least. It will make an attractive frame similar to a bower, and if you grow climbers – ideally those that are scented as well as attractive – around it, it will be the perfect place to relax on a summer's day.

## ARCHWAYS

Archways are inherently romantic and can be used to mark passage into a different area of the garden and to create a sense of mystery. They can also be used in a theatrical way to frame the deck or a feature on it, such as a palm in a pot.

Arches built over an entrance point have a similar function and can also help to create a contrasting atmosphere – outside the arch, the garden feels open, warm and sunny; inside the deck area is cool, shady and enclosed.

Whatever kind of overhead structure you choose to construct on your deck, always ensure – as with any garden feature – that it will complement your existing deck design and tie in well with the house and any other structures nearby. Scale is the main consideration with an inherently tall, upright feature: too large a pergola or archway will look ridiculous towering over a very small deck, whereas a mini pergola will look equally out of place and inconspicuous in a large garden.

## HINTS AND TIPS

- *Do* use pergolas to create an easy transition between deck and garden
- *Do* build pergolas to create 'outdoor rooms' suitable for al fresco dining
- *Do* use archways to define different areas of the deck
- *Do* use archways to create vistas and highlight focal points on the deck
- *Do* make a secret sitting area beneath a climber-covered arbour so that you can escape now and then!
- *Don't* make pergolas and archways too low or narrow. Build vertical and overhead structures in the correct proportions so that the space they occupy feels comfortable and not claustrophobic. Build for a solid and substantial feel
- *Don't* place archways in isolation. Fit them into the deck layout in a meaningful and logical way
- *Don't* plant vigorous climbers on small structures; they will take over!

# fence and trellis

Fence or trellis around the deck can further enhance a feeling of privacy and seclusion, and can also be used to divide off one area from another, perhaps to create a separate dining area or a secret space for reading in peace and quiet.

Fences are obviously more solid than trellis panels, which allow light through and a view of the garden beyond, so choose according to how much privacy you want to create. Unless you have a large area and want a really strong division, then trellis is more sympathetic and a solid fence more suited to creating a garden boundary.

Both fence and trellis panels can be supported by the uprights of a pergola, if you have one. If you don't, you will need to install supporting posts.

BELOW: *A trellis screen makes a light, neutral backdrop for this deck.*

FIXING UP FENCE OR TRELLIS
Whatever type of screening you erect, you must ensure that the supporting posts are secure. Traditionally, part of the post was buried in the ground and anchored with a collar of concrete, but because the base of the post was below ground level, it eventually rotted, even if the wood was treated with preservative. On the other hand, a steel fence spike (and its close relative, the bolt-down fence support designed for use on hard-surfaced areas) keeps the vulnerable post completely above ground level. Both types have a square socket into which you fit the post end and come in sizes to accept 50mm (2in), 75mm (3in) and 100mm (4in) posts. Some have a socket with steel teeth that lock the post permanently in place as it is hammered in. Others have a bolt-operated clamping action reinforced by screws or nails. This system allows you to remove the post without disturbing the socket.

# steps

Without doubt almost every deck will need some form of step or stairway. These are easy to build and install, but a few basic rules will make the task simpler. Being outdoors, the steps can be larger and wider, creating a sense of space, and whatever your design, they should be inviting to use. Free-flowing steps can lead you around the deck to the garden.

There are three basic methods for building steps. The first is the box method (see page 73). It produces a very simple and strong structure but is best suited for just two or three treads. As the timbers used are normally 100mm (4in) or 150mm (6in) joists, which are commonly used riser heights for stairs, this makes the box steps easy to work out as the standard timbers do not need to be cut.

The second method is ideal for a greater amount of steps, such as in a stairway between decks, and is another simple technique. Two large timbers – known as stringers – 50mm (2in) by 250mm (10in) or 300mm (12in), can be set between the decks

**ABOVE:** *Posts with ornate tops and patterned panels turn these steps into an attractive feature. How plain or patterned is largely influenced by the style of the building.*

**RIGHT:** *A large flight of steps needs careful planning to ensure safety for the people using it and also to keep it in proportion with the deck and the adjacent building.*

and with stair hangers treads can be screwed between the stringers to produce a stairway. Treads need to be the right width for the riser height.

The last method, cut-out stringers, produces the best quality and neatest looking stairs, but requires more working out before you start the job. Cut-out stringers are available 'ready to use' but normally cover only three or four steps. You can always purchase a pre-made one and copy the pattern onto a larger piece of timber to increase the length of the stairs. If you have more than three steps a hand rail will be required for safety.

# built-in furniture

Tables, chairs and benches can be built into the deck structure as part of the overall design. The disadvantage is that they cannot then be moved around to benefit from the evening sun, perhaps, or be used for additional seating when guests arrive. However, there are many advantages. Built-in furniture gives the deck a more streamlined, fitted appearance than you can achieve with freestanding furniture. This is partly because you can use the same materials from which you have built

the deck itself, and partly because it can be made to fit perfectly into the design, using awkward corners into which you are unlikely to be able to buy furniture to fit.

You can also make built-in furniture to last, with stronger joints which will outlast anything you can buy. Try to keep it fairly elegant and attractive, however.

BELOW: *This handsome high-level deck features a built-in seat with an attractive curved back. It fits neatly into the design and takes up a lot less deck space than a freestanding bench.*

# bridges

As well as being used for its traditional purpose of crossing water, a bridge can also be installed as a link between two decks or could even create a short cut across a flower bed. A simple bridge can be built using straight timbers, but why not be more adventurous and build a visually more exciting arched construction to make a real focal point?

Building a bridge is the same as building a narrow deck and providing that the span to cross is short, decking joists can be used in the construction. The obvious disadvantage of decking joists is the lack of a curve to produce the small humpback bridge look; these shaped joists are available from specialist timber merchants.

The design should allow for the width of the crossing and an overhang either side for the starting point.

The smallest joists should be at least 150x50mm (6x2in) for a 2m (6ft) span, with ideally a 90cm (3ft) overlap onto the land either side. A larger overlap will be required if the soil is sandy or subject to erosion. Joist spacing should be closer than on a deck – 30cm (12in) will be enough. The treads should be wide enough for people to walk across without the feeling of a tightrope – 60cm (24in) is the minimum, but 90cm (3ft) will feel more comfortable. All grooves must go side-to-side across the bridge to ensure a non-slip surface. Keep the treads clean to avoid accidents, using safe cleaning products as they may fall into the waterway.

TOP: *A simple decking bridge can create a focal point to draw you to it and creates a convenient link to other parts of the garden.*

ABOVE: *This bridge allows a short cut to the other side of the garden. The deck offers a step up onto the bridge, which has an added railing for safety purposes.*

LEFT: *This handsome bridge joins two areas of deck and provides a walkway over the pond in between.*

# hand rails and balustrades

Not all decks need railings, but if required they should be planned for at the beginning of the project. The design may have to be changed to allow firm fixing points or posts moved to stop a clash of fixings. Other factors will need to be considered. These include the effect that the railings will have on the view and what practical purpose they are intended for.

The main reason for incorporating railings into a deck is for safety, but this need not affect the overall aesthetics of the deck. Most railings have to be of a minimum height and distance between the spindles or horizontal rails. It is a good idea to check with your local building regulations for these exact measurements. The rails must perform their number one role, which is the safety of people on the deck; they must be secure and be able to withstand people leaning against them. It is far better to over-design than under-design in this case and some thought must go into the structure and materials used in the construction of the rails.

As with other aspects of the deck there are many options for the type of rails used and the way they are constructed. Most decking suppliers will have at least one rail in their range, probably many more, but you can design and build your own very easily. From simple wooden rails to

copper tube or stainless steel wire running between the posts, the choice is endless. On a windy site you may require a wind break, in which case toughened glass could be used to preserve the view. In situations where the view is not important, solid panels are another alternative.

## planters

Many decks feature built-in planters and raised beds built from the same timber as the deck, and stained or finished in the same way. These create convenient places to grow a range of flowers and foliage plants to soften the look of the deck. Most built-in planters are larger than containers and so better suited to permanent plantings of shrubs, small trees and perennials. They also give a more 'designed' appearance than a selection of odd containers.

**ABOVE:** *This is an example of a ready-made rail. They come complete and just need to be painted and installed, with no assembly required.*

**BELOW:** *A stand-alone feature such as this angled trellis screen and planter could be positioned to give height and privacy.*

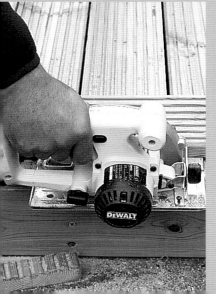

create

# preparation

Before you start building your deck, take the time to make sure you are well prepared. Having the right tools and materials to hand will make the job easier, and if you have mastered the basic techniques and prepared the site, little can go wrong.

## choosing materials

The most important choice in deck building is the timber you decide to use. There are five factors that require consideration when choosing timber: availability, appearance, life expectancy, strength and cost.

With the wide variety of timbers available, it is difficult to choose the most suitable. The majority of timber used in deck building is softwood such as pine. Hardwood is available but is expensive and the finish is not that much better; its resilience to decay is not such a major factor now that timber preservatives are so good.

Softwood from colder climates is the best as the growth rings are close together and give a stronger board, less prone to warping. Some of the most popular woods include western redwood, which is resistant to decay and need not be treated prior to use; cedar, which is noted for its light weight, great strength and durability; and red pine, a timber often sold as redwood but not quite as robust, though it is cheaper.

Always buy tanalized wood if you are using softwood as it is a far better way of resisting decay than trying to paint on a preservative. Look for a supplier who offers a guarantee – some will guarantee the timber for up to 15 years.

Deck boards come in a range of styles. Some have all the sides planed smooth, usually the more expensive types. Others have only one face planed and are much less expensive.

Some decking boards are grooved, others smooth. Grooved boards are better for steps as they don't become as slippery and will channel the water off the decking. Grooved deck boards can also be used to show a change in height or a step by laying them in a different pattern to draw your attention to the change and make the step more obvious.

ABOVE: *Deck boards come in a wide variety of widths, patterns and colours. The timber can also be ordered pre-treated if required.*

Your final choice of wood will be dictated by how far your budget will stretch – if you can only afford to buy pine rather than redwood, then so be it. You will still have a deck that, with the correct treatment, should last you 15 years or more.

# fixings

Fixing the timber is best done with screws as they have obvious advantages over nails. The most important is the 'draw strength' – the amount of energy needed to pull a screw out of the wood is much greater than a nail would require, therefore creating a far stronger joint.

Screw joints can be undone easily and moved if required and it is much easier to remove decking boards if you have screwed them down rather than nailed them. Screws will also stop the deck boards splitting when you are fixing them.

The screws must be corrosion-resistant otherwise they will rust and break over time.

When joining larger joists and posts together, it is essential to use coach bolts as large loads will be transferred to the posts through this very strong fixing.

LEFT: *The different types of timber used in the construction of a deck. From left to right: beam, supporting post, 175x50mm (7x2in) frame timber, 125x50mm (5x2in) frame timber, hand rail, and edge covering strip.*

## THRU BOLTS (RAWL BOLTS)

*Rawl bolts are used to fix the first joist or ledger board to masonry walls. They need to be spaced every 60cm (24in) along the ledger to support the weight of the deck and people on it.*

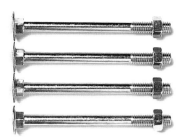

## COACH BOLTS

*Coach bolts are used for joining joists to posts and provide a very strong fixing. Use stainless steel as any corrosion will stain the wood. The length required is the thickness of the two timbers plus 25mm (1in) to allow for a washer and nut. Ideally use size M10 or M12.*

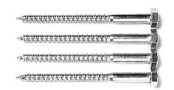

## COACH SCREWS

*As coach bolts except they screw in with a spanner. A very secure fixing which is good for larger timber where the use of an electric drill may be dangerous, for example near water.*

## DECK FRAME SCREWS (POZIDRIV)

*The main fixings for the frame will be 6x80 screws. A secure fixing and easy to undo. Pozidriv are best as they are less prone to slipping with a power driver.*

## DECK SCREWS (POSIDRIV/SQUARE SOCKET)

*The deck boards use 5x50 screws that are self-drilling and self-counter-sinking, making pre-drilling unnecessary. Again they must be corrosion resistant.*

## DECK NAILS

*Deck nails are not as good as screws or as secure, but are ideal for inserting noggins because appearance is not important. It is essential to use galvanized nails.*

# preparing the site

In any project, preparation is the key to a quick and efficient job. Once debris has been cleared from the site of the proposed deck and weeds have been removed, the deck can be started. Place all the required materials in a position that is easy to reach – this not only makes construction easier but allows for a smooth flow to the work rather than continually stopping and starting.

Although most modern timber is decay-resistant, it is best to avoid contact with soil as this will allow moisture to work its way into the deck and spoil the finish. With low-level decks some time spent on preparation will help save work in the long run.

The first job is to make sure the ground drains well, as the deck must not sit in water. Measure the deck area out and mark the site with posts. Remove any surface plant growth to 5cm (2in) below the ground level and cover the soil with weed block or thick black polythene (perforated every 30cm (12in) to help drainage) to prevent re-growth of weeds.

Cover the area with coarse gravel. This holds down the ground cover material and allows the joists to touch the ground but not the soil, letting air circulate freely around them. Dig out any live tree stumps as they could regrow and damage the deck.

On higher decks the ground underneath could well be visible and the combination of ground cover and gravel not only stops weeds but also looks neat and tidy.

ABOVE: *Dig out and conserve any plants you want to keep. Skim off annual weed growth or lawn grass with a spade or use a systemic weedkiller to remove perennial weeds.*

ABOVE: *Remove loose items – it is much easier to bolt the framework to a solid surface. It is also more secure. Removing any old steps like this will mean that the decking can go straight up to the doors.*

### REUSING AN OLD BASE

An old concrete or paved patio makes a perfect base for a new deck and requires little preparation before work can begin. The patio should fall away from the house to aid drainage. If not, the deck can be bolted to the house and raised to create a slope. If water sits on the existing patio, create a fall on the joists to stop water laying on the timber and soaking in. If the deck is to extend beyond the patio, use piers set on a gravel base to fix the additional decking. If the ground falls away from the deck you will need to build footings to rest the posts on; these will raise the deck to the current level.

## WHEN TO BUILD IT

Subject to weather conditions, timing is not really a factor that comes in to play, although obviously spring and summer often give the best weather for construction.

## TIMBER DELIVERY

If the deck is large, it is definitely worth getting the supplier to deliver the materials as they will have a properly equipped vehicle to unload the timber. This not only saves time and effort, but also guarantees the safe arrival of the materials.

## WHERE TO PUT IT

Due to the weight of timber, find an area to store it that is easy to access; move it once, not two or three times! It should be close to the site and should not obstruct the access of wheelbarrows. Stack the timber with joists on top as you will need them first. Position it off the ground as otherwise water will soak in and make it much heavier to work with; it may even stain the surface. Place a cover over the timber in case of rain.

## LEAVE PLENTY OF TIME

Decks are easy to build, but time will pass quicker than you think. Allow twice as long as you predict to build the deck and don't rush it. Never work in dusk or dark conditions as power tools are not safe in this environment. If you can, get a friend to help as it will make the project much more enjoyable than struggling on with it on your own.

LEFT: *Any plants that encroach on to the decking will need to be trimmed away to allow maintenance of the deck. The plants' sap will also stain the timber if it comes into contact with the decking.*

LEFT: *Fix down weed block fabric to stop any weeds growing under the deck. This fabric prevents light reaching the soil and inhibits plant growth, but allows water through for drainage.*

LEFT: *It is best to protect the lawn from damage by covering it with a tarpaulin or sheet while you work. This also allows any dropped screws to be easily collected rather than lying in the grass waiting to be stepped on.*

LEFT: *It's a pain to have to cut the decking around obstacles. Consider the option of slightly moving services and fittings if it will make the pipe fit between beams, thereby avoiding having to work around them.*

# tools

Choosing the most appropriate tool for each job is essential in deck building. There is no point in using small, blunt or incorrect tools for a job as this will slow down the work, leave a poor finish to the materials and could actually be dangerous. Power saws, for example, should be able to cut through the largest timber you are going to use in one pass – not two or three. Utilize the right tools and everything will run smoothly.

## TOOL HIRE

It is better to hire more expensive tools such as a compound saw and larger masonary drills than purchase them for a single project. When you are hiring tools, especially power tools, make sure you receive a set of instructions or tuition from the hire shop staff as to the correct way to use the equipment.

Before leaving the hire shop check that all guards are in place and that all blades are sharp – there is nothing more dangerous than using blunt tools.

*Compound saw*

*Short spirit level*

*Circular saw*

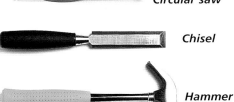

*Chisel*

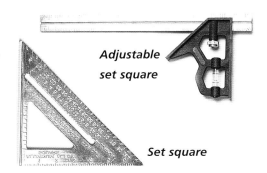

*Adjustable set square*

*Set square*

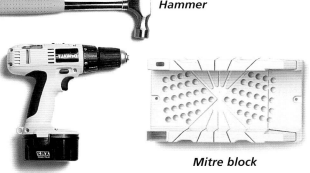

*Hammer*

*Mitre block*

*Cordless screwdriver/drill*

*Bolster chisel*   *Bolster hammer*

*Screwdriver*

*Mains drill*

*Screwdriver bit*

*Wood drill bit*

*Masonry drill bit*

*Saw*

*Long spirit level*

# BASIC TECHNIQUES

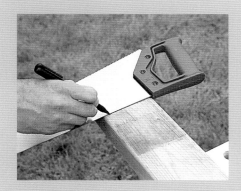

ABOVE: *Marking at 90°. Conveniently, the manufacturers of many hand saws now build 90° angles into the handles, making marking out very easy. Simply position the saw.*

ABOVE: *Sawing at 90°. With a sharp hand saw, start to cut at the edge furthest away from you and cut through. Do not let the offcut fall down as it will tear the timber.*

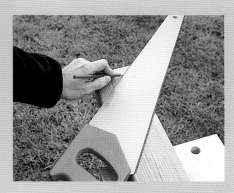

ABOVE: *Marking at 45°. As with the 90° cut, the saws also have 45° angles built into them. Mark as before, making sure the angle runs in the right direction.*

ABOVE: *Sawing at 45°. Using your thumb as a guide, start where the thinnest end will be and cut across as before. If the offcut tears there is less chance of it showing.*

ABOVE: *Cutting a concrete block. Wearing goggles, place a bolster on the block and use a club hammer to nick the two edges. Trace along the joining line until the block breaks itself.*

ABOVE: *Sealing cut ends. All cut timber should be painted with a preservative to prevent decay. Use the same solution as the timber has already been treated with.*

**Face mask**

**Pencil**

**Spanner**

**Long tape measure**

**Short tape measure**

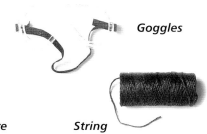

**Goggles**

**String**

# decking terms

All decks are built from the ground up with key elements connected to produce a strong, lasting structure. The following terms, used throughout the book, are explained below.

**1 Beams** are fixed to the top of posts and support the joists. The larger the beam, the greater distance between the posts, and the larger the posts.

**2 Footings** support the deck and restrict movement to natural timber expansion and shrinkage. Normally 30cm (12in) square and 15cm (6in) deep, they are situated on firm, undisturbed soil. Concrete building blocks can be used as an alternative.

**3 Joists** create the framework for the deck boards to be fixed to. The joists need to be fixed at 40cm (16in) centres to prevent the deck from having a bouncy feel to it. The thicker the deck boards the larger the spacing you can have between the joists.

Your decking supplier will be able to advise you on this. If in doubt use smaller spacings. Decking is the showpiece of the work. Your deck design and pattern will dictate the joist construction underneath. Deck boards should not be wider than 150mm (6in) as the wider the wood the more likely it is to cup, warp across the width, and collect water.

**4 Ledger boards** are joists that are bolted or fixed to the side of a house to create a fixing point for the deck. They should be fixed so that the top of the deck is below the door sill to stop rain water entering the house.

**5 Noggins** are small spacers used to keep the joists at a set distance. As larger decks can wobble, the noggins also make the deck more rigid.

**6 Posts** support the deck above the ground and must be of sufficient size to carry the weight of the deck and its load. The minimum size is a 100x100mm (4x4in) post.

## SAFETY

- *Don't skimp on support for wooden boarding – warping or collapse of the timbers could be dangerous. Ensure that all the timbers are properly nailed or screwed down*
- *Provide safety rails where there is a marked drop to the ground and install handrails for the safe use of steps. A raised edging board prevents chair legs slipping off the edge*
- *Block off the underneath of the deck – rodents damage wiring and burrowing animals undermine foundations*
- *Clearly define steps and changes in level, especially when shallow*
- *Ensure that the deck boards are laid perfectly level with no protrusions or wide gaps*
- *Check timber for rough bits and sand away splinters*
- *Use grooved planking for extra grip, especially on steps and wet or shady decks*
- *Use rot-resistant timber to prevent sudden collapse in years to come. Regularly apply preservative and check for degradation*
- *Use a high-pressure water jet to remove algal build-up*
- *Employ a qualified electrician if you are in any doubt about fitting external electrics*

# decking tiles

Decking tiles can be laid without a complex support structure. A simple system of sleepers or battens can be laid and the tiles screwed directly to them. Because decking tiles have no structural support, they must be laid on a flat, level site. They are not suited to clay soils which expand and contract as the decking moves around unless a heavier joist system is installed, in which case it would be better to use traditional deck boarding instead.

RIGHT: *Decking tiles are the fastest solution for covering an old patio as they can be laid directly on top.*

## HOW TO LAY DECKING TILES

*1. With the area excavated to the correct depth, cover the soil with weed block fabric. If the ground has poor drainage you will need to put down some gravel to improve the drainage situation. Lay out the joists and interlock them as per the manufacturer's instructions.*

*2. As the joists are laid the interlocking system should square-up the deck at the same time. It is important to make sure that all joints are flush as any proud ones will make the decking squares unstable. Once fully assembled, check the squares' angles and screw the joists together to secure the base.*

*3. With the base secured, the tiles can be fitted. Create the pattern by moving the tiles around until the desired effect is found. They will require four screws per tile to fix them down, one at each corner, positioned between the surface boards to hide them.*

# building a deck

If you have followed all the pointers on preparation on the last few pages, you should have everything ready to start building. Take your time and work it out carefully before you begin to avoid time-consuming and potentially costly mistakes later.

**1.** *Use a tape measure to mark off equal distances for the lag bolt holes. Check to make sure the joist and deck board will be below the doorstep to prevent rainwater from running in.*

**2.** *When choosing the positions of the bolt holes, avoid the mortar joints – the brickwork will provide a better fixing. Use a wood bit through the wood, then a masonry bit to penetrate the brick.*

**3.** *Hammer a rawl bolt through the timber and into the wall. Make sure the nut is on before you hammer it home otherwise the thread will be burred over and the nut will not fit.*

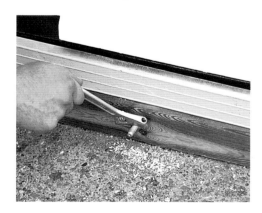

**4.** *Tighten the nut with an adjustable spanner until the nut starts to be drawn into the timber and the wood is held tight to the wall. Check the level again using a spirit level.*

**5.** *Fix the first joist to the ledger board. It is important to make sure that the top edges of each timber are level with each other.*

**6.** *The outer joists can be attached with screws, which should be long enough to go through the first timber and into the end of the adjacent timber by at least 2.5cm (1in).*

**7.** *With a builder's square or a large set square, line up the last joint and fix with a screw; then check that all the other corners are at 90°. If the deck is square the diagonal measurements will be equal.*

**8.** *Measure out and fix supporting joists at 40cm (16in) centres. Fix from each side by screwing in at an angle. If no edging is to be used, this method can be used to hide the screws from view.*

**9.** *Measure and cut two rows of noggins to stretch across the beams. Alternate their position so you can get the nails in. Use screws on the outside of the deck frame and nails on the area hidden by the deck boards. Place the noggins on the ground to provide extra support to the frame.*

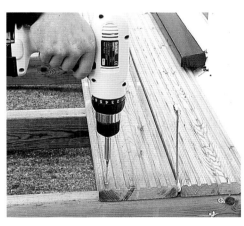

**10.** *Screw the first deck board into position. Make sure it is parallel to the first joist as this will set the pattern for the rest of the boards.*

**11.** *Use a spacer such as a spanner to set an even distance between the deck boards. This will allow room for the timber to expand when it is wet.*

**12.** *Once the ends of the deck boards have been fixed down, the rest of the deck can be screwed down. Use a string line to line all the screws up together.*

**13.** *(left) If the deck boards are warped, insert the spacer between the boards and use a chisel to lever the boards to the correct position. Then screw the board firmly in place.*

**14.** *(right) To finish the edge, screw down a length of board to use as a straight edge. Make sure you cut the boards flush with the joist.*

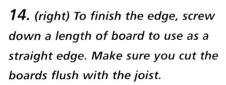

# creating angles

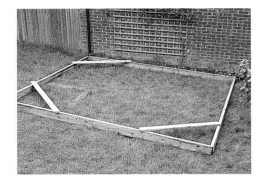

**1.** *Lay the frame timbers out in a rectangle of the overall size of the deck. Using a number of offcuts as markers, place one over each corner to create the shape required. Measure the sides to check they are even, if necessary.*

**2.** *When all sides are the correct length, mark each for cutting, taking care to measure the outside of the frame. Cut each to size and at a 45° angle. Place the timbers in position and check the lengths and angles once again.*

**3.** *Check diagonal measurements with a tape before assembly to check for square, because it is important that the sides are parallel. If they are not placed in a parallel position, the deck boards will not run square across the deck.*

**4.** *It is important to get the corner at a 90° angle so that the rest of the angles fit together correctly.*

**5.** *To create a 45° corner in the deck frame, cut one of the timbers at 45° and the other at 90° and screw them together.*

**6.** *Fix the first two joists into place across the frame – these will ensure that the frame remains rigid.*

**7.** *(left) Measure up and secure the remaining joists at 40cm (16in) intervals. To accommodate the angled sections of the outer frame, cut the joist ends at 45°.*

**8.** *(right) With acute angles, even though the timber is not flush with the post, coach bolts will easily take the weight.*

# diagonal boards

**1.** *(left) Diagonal boards need to be laid with the use of a square to ensure the angle is correct. Once you have the first board at the right angle, use spacers to position the next few boards, but check with the square from time to time.*

**2.** *(right) Overhang the boards with the largest overhangs at one end as this will give you offcuts of a useful length. Fix with two screws at each end and two over each joist to stop any cupping. Space evenly as before and fix in the middle of the boards.*

**3.** *As you work across the deck, cut short boards around obstacles such as manhole covers to make access easier.*

**4.** *Fix joists far enough apart for access to the manhole cover and cut the boards so the joins overlay the joists.*

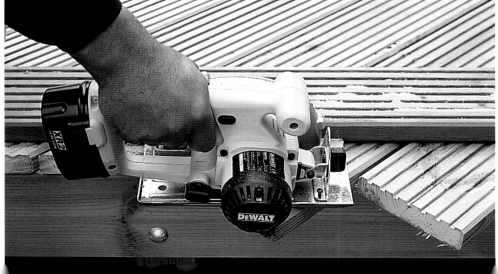

**5.** *(above) Saw off the overhanging boards with a circular saw. Use a hand saw in tight corners.*

**6.** *(left) Clamp a straight edge to the deck and run the saw along it to achieve a uniform overhang on straight sections. Cut the boards flush with the frame if you are adding an edging.*

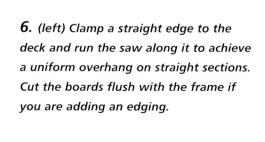

# problem solving

If the deck over runs on to the lawn, use a weed block fabric to stop the grass growing under the deck. Use large nails to fix it in place.

Most decks which are laid adjacent to a house will have to take a drain or two into consideration. There are two different ways to deal with drains, but decide first whether you will need access to the drain for cleaning or other maintenance.

**1.** Build a box around the drain to protect the grids and provide support for the deck boards above.

**2.** Alternatively, make a cut-out the width of a board so you don't need to install additional support for the boards.

## MANHOLE COVERS

**1.** Arrange the joists so they run either side of obstacles such as manhole covers. This will allow you to fix the boards in such a way that they can be removed to allow access to the manhole cover without too much upheaval involved.

**2.** With all the full length joists installed, the noggins can then be fixed between them. These will stop the deck expanding and warping the joists. Again, fix them so they form a framework around the manhole cover and will support the joins in the decking boards.

**3.** Cut each board so that the lengths butt-up together in the middle of each supporting timber and so will allow easy access to the drain. Space and fix each one down at the ends and, with a spirit level, match up the boards opposite.

## DEALING WITH DRAINPIPES

Drainpipes come in many different shapes and designs, but it is simple to accommodate them when adding the decking boards.

**1.** Use a hole saw to make a neat hole for the drainpipe to pass through the decking. It may be necessary to use extra pipe fittings to get the pipe to go through vertically – this saves trying to drill a hole at an angle to suit the pipe.

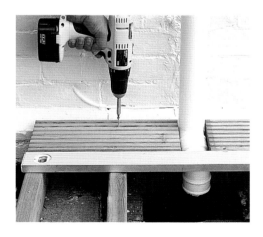

**2.** If the drainpipe runs horizontally as it passes though the deck boards, simply cut the boards either side to let it pass through. Use a spirit level to make sure the lengths either side line up.

# WALL OBSTRUCTIONS

**1.** When building a deck against the house wall, you have to take air bricks into consideration. To prevent obstruction and restricted air flow, cut away any timber that will cover the air bricks and add a second length of joist outside the first to carry the deck board.

**2.** Where there are plants or other obstructions in the way which mean you cannot add a second, outer piece of timber in front of the first, simply cut the timber around the air brick. Slide the timber carefully behind the plants to avoid damaging them and fix it to the wall.

**3.** When adding noggins to the support structure, start with any that are needed to bypass air bricks and plants. It is best to screw rather than nail them in place. Leave enough space for plants to grow.

**4.** Fix the deck boards onto the deck in the normal way. When you arrive at the air brick, leave a decent sized gap for air circulation. This will also allow sufficient space for the plant stem to grow thicker.

# raised-level decks

If the site where you want to position the deck is uneven, you will have to support the deck on vertical posts sunk into the ground. The tops of these posts can be aligned to make a level surface for the deck. Once the posts are installed, the deck joists are bolted directly to the posts. This is also a good solution where the site is sloping, and allows the deck to be raised on taller posts at one end and still be level on top. If the end of the deck is high above the ground, add a handrail for safety. You may also be able to incorporate a useful storage area under the deck.

## HINTS AND TIPS

ABOVE: *If you have a cutaway corner on the deck, place the posts further back to avoid having screws on the front joist and to leave space for the supporting joists.*

ABOVE: *The set-back post allows extra room for the joist to be fitted. Be careful to avoid having screws in the front joist. Before the deck is laid, paint cut surfaces with preservative.*

*1.* (above) Lay out the deck joists in position. Install the posts where needed and cut to the correct height using a long spirit level between posts as a guide.

*2.* (left) To install the posts, dig a hole and place a concrete block in the bottom. Stand the post on top. This helps to spread the weight. Use coach bolts to fix the joists to the posts.

**3.** The frame is now supported on strong posts and is perfectly level. Use a post for every join or angle, and add extra posts on long straights for added support. Remember that the tops of the posts must be below or flush with the tops of the joists so they don't obstruct the decking boards.

**4.** Measure out and fix all the supporting joists in position. Add noggins to the support structure, starting with any that are needed to bypass air bricks and plants. It is best to screw rather than nail these in place.

**5.** With the rest of the noggins added to the base, start laying the deck boards from the front edge of the deck. You can use a block to keep the edge flush with the front of the joist.

**6.** With the boards screwed at both ends, stretch string across the deck to align with the base timbers. Screw the rest of the boards to the joists, adjusting the gaps as you go.

**7.** Fix a straight edge down across the deck and use a circular saw to trim off the excess boards. Set the saw to a depth just a little more than the thickness of the board to give a cleaner cut.

## MAKING THE FRAME FIRST

Instead of sinking in the posts and bolting the frame, timber by timber, to them, it is also possible to make the complete frame first and then bolt it to the posts.

**LEFT:** *This garden slopes away from the house so the deck is raised at one end. A raised deck is cheaper and easier to construct than a raised patio.*

*1.* *(above) Measure up and lay out the frame timbers on a flat surface, using a spirit level as a guide. Fix them together to form the frame, then add the joists. Move the frame into position and support it temporarily in place with offcuts of wood.*

*2.* *(left) Install permanent posts at the corners of the deck. Mark off the correct height and cut off the excess timber at the top of the post.*

*3.* *Use a wood drill bit to make a hole for the coach bolt to go through. Repeat further down the post for security.*

*4.* *Hold the frame in position, line up the drill holes and bolt the frame securely to the posts with coach bolts. Check the level and square of the angle from time to time as you work.*

*5.* *Concrete the post in place, allow to dry and pack the soil back into the hole with a piece of timber for added weight. Paint all surfaces with preservative before fixing the decking boards down.*

*6.* *Install noggins between the joists to add strength. Always start laying the deck boards from the front edge and screw each end down. With a spacer in place, fix down the next board.*

# built-in extras

The built-in extras, such as edgings, steps and pergolas, are the finishing touches that make the deck complete. They should not be seen as an afterthought, but an integral part of the deck.

## edgings

Edging covers the ends of the boards to create a finished and professional look to the completed deck. Edging can also be used on the tread of steps as the smooth wood finish stands out more and makes the steps more visible. As well as the aesthetic reasons for the edge, edging also stops the ends of the decking boards splintering if people kick them. Some decking suppliers produce an edge moulding but a reversed decking board works equally as well. Edging can be used between stages of projects by offering a simple disguise for joist posts that need to be hidden.

**RIGHT:** *This freestanding deck has an edge all round which adds a finished look to the structure. It also stops animals and children crawling underneath.*

*The edging can be a specially made edge moulding or, as in this case, a decking board screwed on with the grooves facing in. This produces a strong edge which is easy to replace if damaged.*

## RAISED DECK EDGINGS

*1. Measure and cut a board to edge the deck. Treat the cut ends with preservative and screw in place.*

*2. Cut and fix another board of the same thickness as the joist to run between the posts at ground level.*

*3. Screw a pattern of vertical boards to the joist above and the board below to fill the gap.*

*4. Where the edging meets soil you can knock the bottoms of the edging boards into the ground.*

# building steps

**1.** *When measuring up for the steps, do not have the steps tight between the wall and fence shown here – the steps may expand, moving the fence as well.*

**2.** *With a tape, measure out the timber, allowing for some movement. Paint all exposed ends with preservative and screw together with framing screws.*

**3.** *With the base box completed, build a second box but reduce the depth by twice the width of the deck board that is to be used as the tread of the step.*

**4.** *Secure the two boxes together by using offcuts screwed to the inside of the boxes at the back and sides. As before, use framing screws for the fixings.*

**5.** *Paint any newly cut surfaces with preservative and allow them to dry. This is the last chance to get to this timber before construction. Measure and cut two treads for the lower step, butting the boards up close together.*

**6.** *With the two treads cut from the decking board, secure in place with two screws at each end to fasten down each one. Cut two more for the top step.*

**7.** *(left) Level off the base where the steps are to go; use a concrete paving slab if required. Place the steps on the level surface and check for level again. Attach to the main deck with screws.*

**8.** *(right) The finishing touch for the steps is the top treads. As before, screw down with two screws each end.*

# pergolas

Self-assembly pergolas are available from garden centres and mail-order suppliers and are perfect for adding on to a deck. Following the instructions, you should be able to put one together in just a few hours. The one featured on these pages has four uprights, two side beams, four cross beams and two trellis panels.

The wood is treated with a preservative stain that will protect it from rotting and will not harm plants growing on it. When you have unpacked the kit and are ready to begin assembling it, it is a good idea to have someone to help you and you will also need a hammer, nails, gloves and a stepladder. Wear gloves to prevent splinters and as protection against the preservative stain applied to the wood.

If you prefer to build a pergola from scratch, you can buy the wood and cut it to size at home. You will need to stain and preserve the wood as well. Naturally, this is a cheaper option than buying a pergola kit.

*1. Support two of the uprights and lower one of the un-notched side beams into the groove. Decide on the spacing of these uprights before securing them into the ground.*

*2. When you are happy with the overhang at each end of the side beam, secure it to the uprights with galvanized nails as shown. You may choose to use two nails at each end.*

*3. Once the two sides of the pergola are complete, join them together by dropping in one of the four cross beams. Put the end ones 'outside' the uprights for a stable structure.*

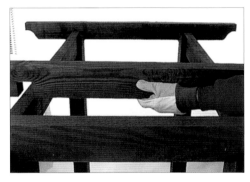

*4. With the far end cross beam also in place, space the other two out equally. The width of the pergola is set by the notches in these cross beams.*

*5. (left) Nail the cross beams to the top of the side beams. Then position and nail the first trellis panel in between the uprights. Raise the panel 15cm (6in) off the ground to protect it from moisture.*

*6. (right) With the second trellis panel in place opposite the first, the pergola is complete. This sequence has not included the vital task of fixing the uprights securely into the ground.*

# fixing on a handrail

**1.** Measure the position of the bolts on the posts; stay four times the diameter of the bolt from the edge of the timber. Pre-drill the holes for the coach screws.

**2.** Position the upright and secure the bottom coach screw into position with a spanner. Leave a small gap underneath the post to allow water to run away.

**3.** With a level check that the post is upright and secure in position with another coach screw. You might need a hand to hold the post upright.

**4.** (right) Fix more posts at equal distances across the bridge, no further apart than 1.5m (5ft), to support the rails. Fix a rail across all the posts using a level as you go. Remember it must be secure as people will lean against it.

**5.** Fix the handrail in place by screwing into the posts rather than the rail. The screws should be twice the thickness of the handrail, to secure it safely.

**6.** Find the centre of the rail and position the first batten, checking it is upright. Use a block of wood as a spacer and secure the tops of the other battens.

**7.** As with the top rail, use the same spacer to create even distances between the bottoms of the battens and fix them securely in place.

# adding a bridge

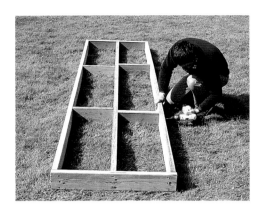

**1.** *Measure the length of the bridge by laying a joist across the stream from the deck to the other side. This will also give the position for the footings.*

**2.** *As you would with a deck, build a frame that is the width required for the bridge. Use a central joist to add strength to the frame.*

**3.** *With the frame complete, add noggins to prevent wobble – they will also increase the ridigity of the frame. A moving bridge is dangerous.*

**4.** *(right) With help, lift the frame into position and level both ways. Concrete two posts in place to support the bridge on the other side of the stream. Bolt the posts to the frame with two coach bolts per post. Check for level as you go. Drainage is not a problem as it is with a deck as the boards are so short that the water will drain away. As in other decks, use preservative on all cut surfaces.*

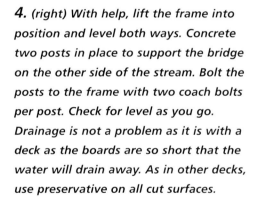

**5.** *With the other end secured to the posts fix the bridge to the deck by toenailing the frame to the surface, using long screws through the boards into the joists.*

**6.** *When fixing the first tread, use a small block to create an even overhang at the front of the bridge. Space the boards slightly apart to allow for movement.*

**7.** *Use self-drilling screws to stop the boards splitting. The last tread may have to be cut to fit. If its width is reduced too much swap it with the next tread in.*

# building a seat

This simple bench consists of two piers of brickwork, built without the need for any cut bricks, and a slatted seat that is screwed unobtrusively to the masonry and will complement your deck perfectly. You can build it directly on any firm decked surface. For a harmonious look, choose bricks that match those of your house if you plan to site the seat close by.

The seat can be left with a natural finish or can be stained or painted if you prefer a coloured finish. Apply two coats of preservative to the finished bench to protect the wood. The slats allow rainwater to drain away freely, but if you prefer a solid seat, simply close up the gaps between the slats and glue them together with waterproof wood adhesive before screwing the bench top to the supporting framework.

*1. Build up the piers, positioning two bricks side by side and a third at right angles to them in each course. Check that each face is truly vertical.*

*2. Decide on the width of the bench and build up the second pier in the same way. Use a spirit level on a timber straightedge to check that the two piers are precisely level with each other.*

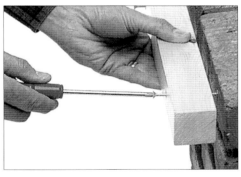

*3. Cut two support blocks from 5cm (2in) square timber, making them slightly longer than the depth of the piers. Fix one to the outside of each pier with screws and wallplugs.*

*4. Cut two seat edge slats to length and attach them to the ends of the seat support blocks. An overhang at either end will help to conceal the support blocks when the seat is complete.*

*5. Screw on the first seat slat so that it rests on top of the front edge slat. Use a spacer to position the remaining slats. Countersink all screw heads.*

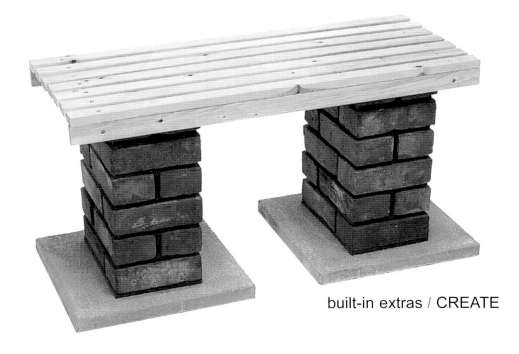

# deck finishes

Woodstain is a simple and effective way to finish your deck and there's now a multitude of tantalizing colours from which to choose. Modern woodstains are pleasant and safe to use and many are water-based, making brush cleaning a joy. They are usually combined with a wood preservative, serving two functions at once. Choose your colour carefully, however: it will take quite a bit of work to alter if you decide you want a change.

## STAINING THE DECK

There are two basic stains you can apply to the deck. The first is a semi-transparent or low-pigmented stain which will show the wood to its best effect but will require more frequent restaining. The second is a solid or heavy pigmented stain, which produces a deeper colour and is the best choice if wood defects need to be hidden. It is longer lasting and easier to apply, so this is a good choice for low-grade timber. Choose a water-based stain if possible and avoid products which will harm your plants.

## CHOOSING A COLOUR

The choice of colour will depend partly on personal preference and partly on the surroundings of the deck. While you may fancy a bright golden yellow, it will look terrible in a traditional cottage garden, so take your time to choose carefully.

Woodstains come in many different shades of brown as well as a wide choice of more exotic colours. If you leave the wood uncoloured it will eventually fade to a silvery grey, so if you want it to maintain its new wood look, you will need to stain it in a natural timber shade. However, many people choose a forest green, blue-green or soft blue-grey to complement their plants without being too vibrant. In the right setting, really strong colours such as bright blue, white or terracotta look fabulous.

**BELOW LEFT:** *This deck has been sealed with a clear preservative, allowing the natural colour of the wood to show.*

## HINTS AND TIPS

- *It is difficult to remove stain once it has been applied*
- *A strong colour may restrict your choice of plants and other garden features*
- *If the deck is in an exposed position, you will need to reapply stain more frequently*
- *Heavy wear will cause the stain to fade more quickly and it may become patchy*
- *Reapply stain as it fades: keep a note of the colour*

## WOODSTAIN VS PAINT

Unlike woodstain, paint will completely cover the underlying wood with a solid layer of colour, so it is good for use with cheap timber. Although painting takes longer, it is easy enough to apply and areas of deck which are difficult to reach can be painted before assembly. On the surface of the deck, you will have to make sure the finish is non-slip to avoid accidents. One of the main disadvantages of paint is that it really needs to be renewed every year as it will start to flake off.

Woodstain, on the other hand, will just fade slowly and gracefully. Heavy wear or excess damp can make painted surfaces shabby very quickly so choose woodstain if you use the deck a lot or it is in a particularly damp or shady position.

ABOVE: *Neutral tones will fit in with any garden scheme and you are unlikely to tire of them.*

TOP: *Strong colours are really eye-catching, especially if you colour co-ordinate the containers too.*

# HOW TO APPLY WOODSTAIN

ABOVE: *Choose a good quality, coloured preserving woodstain and apply it to dry wood using long, even strokes. Work the stain into the grain, giving it a thorough soaking. Aim to achieve an even coat and, if necessary, apply a second coat when the first has dried. Follow the manufacturer's instructions to avoid problems.*

ABOVE: *Apply a dark coloured woodstain or paint to the ends of beams and joists to disguise them and make them less of an eyesore. Work the stain or paint well into the grain of the wood. If you are using paint to cover the ends, make sure it is suitable for use on preservative-treated wood.*

# maintenance

As with any outdoor surface, there are routine tasks to be carried out on your deck to ensure that it stays looking smart. Most of the work is quick and easy provided you do it fairly regularly and tackle potential problems sooner rather than later. Remember that wood is a living material which will reward you with its beauty if you take the trouble to look after it well.

It pays to go over the deck with a fine-tooth comb at the start of the season, looking for any damage that might have occurred over winter such as loosened boards. Then give the deck a thorough clean. Begin the job

**BELOW:** *Sweep dirt along the grooves to stop it from falling between the deck boards. If debris has fallen underneath the deck, a powerful wet-and-dry vacuum can be used to extract it.*

by clearing off ornaments, pots and pieces of furniture to give you access to the whole deck. Then, using a stout yard broom, sweep away all the dead leaves and other litter, moss and soil, working carefully along the grooves to help prevent debris from falling between the planks.

ALGAE AND STAIN REMOVAL
Particularly in a shady spot, algae and moss may have built up due to

autumn and winter dampness and this should be removed using a stiff hand brush and a strong antifungal wash or garden disinfectant designed for the purpose. If the problem is severe and the deck has become slippery as a result, it may be necessary to cover the worst affected areas with galvanized chicken wire mesh, firmly tacked down to provide extra grip underfoot. Next to a building check the state of the guttering or overflow pipes – water may have been pouring directly onto the deck over winter.

If the deck has become dirty or badly stained, one way to rejuvenate it is to use a high-pressure water sprayer. You can hire these, but they are only suitable for decks that have not been painted with a surface treatment. The jet is very powerful and may lift off paint or varnish. Rust marks from furniture can be especially hard to shift and if the sprayer

**ABOVE:** *If the deck is laid when the timber is wet, the wood will shrink and the screw heads could then be raised above the surface during the drier months. Tighten the screws down.*

doesn't work, you may have to resort to using a chemical rust remover or a sander to lift off the top layer.

## STRUCTURAL WORK

Before the deck comes into regular use, check that the support structure is still sound and that there are no rotting timbers. In rural areas check that burrowing animals have not undermined the supports and block off their access if this has occurred.

Wood expands and contracts with changes in moisture levels and if the deck was laid when the timber was wet, when it dries out in summer, you may find that the screws have loosened. Check all screws and tighten up with a screwdriver if necessary.

If some of the deck has been badly damaged, remove the affected boards and replace or cut out the affected area and piece in with matching material.

## OTHER TASKS

If you did not cover the soil beneath the deck at the outset, then weed growth may be a problem. Weeds look unsightly sticking through the cracks but reaching their roots can be tricky in a restricted space. Spray leaves with a systemic weedkiller.

Surface treatments will need to be re-applied before they start to look worn and shabby. It's much easier to apply a quick coat to an existing treatment than prepare from scratch.

## HINTS AND TIPS

- *Once a week sweep the deck to remove all leaves and debris from the surface*
- *Once a month remove any weeds or plants growing between boards or out from under the deck*
- *In the autumn wash down the deck with a good algaecide/moss inhibitor*
- *Once a year wash down the deck and remove the furniture and ornaments. Repair the deck if necessary and re-finish if required*

ABOVE: *If the decking is damaged or splinters appear on it, cut the splinters off with a sharp utility knife and then sand down the wood with the grain until the surface is smooth again. Use a block to keep the sandpaper flat.*

ABOVE: *All outdoor timber will attract algae and mould. In the autumn, wash down the boards with an antifungal and mould and algae killer to help to reduce the growth which can be very slippery and dangerous in wet weather.*

ABOVE: *If the deck surface is damaged or stained, it should be relatively easy to replace the affected boards. Unscrew the board and either replace the whole length or, as here, cut the board and replace just a section of it.*

# plant

# choosing plants

While more or less anything goes in gardens today, certain styles of planting seem to work particularly well with decking. The crisp, clean lines of these solid wooden structures often confer a markedly 'architectural' feel which looks even more impressive combined with bold, sculpted flowers and foliage as well as ornamental grasses and bamboos.

You can plant directly on the deck using all manner of containers but for larger elements such as trees and vigorous climbers, it makes more sense to plant through the deck so that the root system has access to a much greater volume of soil. This really needs to be thought about at the construction stage since it is much more convenient to plant a large specimen first and build the deck around it. As well as the purely practical advantages, planting through specially shaped apertures in the deck can produce very stylish results, especially when bands of identical plants are used. If the deck is too far off the ground, consider using recessed planters flush with the floor level to produce a similar effect.

## USE YOUR IMAGINATION

A deck can be thought of as a raised viewing platform providing a different perspective on the garden and its plants. By surrounding it with lush plantings you could create the illusion of a floating raft surrounded by water regardless of whether the ground is naturally damp.

The trick is to be bold. Plant dramatic swathes of taller ornamental grasses and plants with grass-like leaves such as *Iris sibirica*, crocosmia and day lily (*Hemerocallis*). Contrast these with broad-leaved perennials including hostas and bergenias. You can also try out large ferns such as *Dryopteris filix-mas* and ferny-leaved

LEFT: *The herbs in this built-in container set close to the house are ideally placed for kitchen access. You could also grow a mixture of salad crops or strawberries.*

RIGHT: *Large ferns make wonderful specimens for shade. Grow them in pots or in borders surrounding the deck with other shade lovers like hostas, sedges and bamboos. Ferns also look good in an Oriental setting, perhaps with a mulch of rounded cobbles and pebbles.*

plants like the statuesque goat's beard (*Aruncus dioicus*). These plants all suggest moisture, yet they are perfectly happy growing on any good garden soil.

### DIVERSE PLANTS

A bog garden adjacent to your deck allows for even more luxuriant planting. Simply line a shallow depression with pond liner punctured a few times to allow excess water to drain away, then backfill with compost-enriched soil and give the whole area a thorough soaking.

You can then grow one of the most spectacular of all garden plants, *Gunnera manicata*, as well as the sculptural rheums and rodgersias, the royal fern (*Osmunda regalis*) and ferny-leaved astilbes and filipendulas.

In a sheltered city garden you could let your imagination run riot and give your deck a jungle feel. For a subtropical flavour you could use any of the above-mentioned foliage plants, choosing ones with scarlet, orange or white flowers. Then add other exotica including graceful clump-forming bamboos (forms of

ABOVE: *When planting on and around a deck it pays to be bold. Here a swathe of white marguerite daisies makes a classic statement.*

RIGHT: *A variegated phormium provides a strong vertical accent that contrasts well with the horizontal lines of decking and is impressive enough to stand alone.*

*Phyllostachys* and *Fargesia* are generally problem free), glossy-leaved *Fatsia japonica* and New Zealand flax (*Phormium*).

Hardy palms like *Trachycarpus fortunei* strengthen the illusion of gardening in a hot climate and certain small ornamental trees also have the right look. Try the sumach (*Rhus typhina*), the gold-leaved *Robinia pseudoacacia* 'Frisia' or the golden form of the Indian bean tree (*Catalpa bignonioides* 'Aurea').

## EASTERN INFLUENCES

Although a shady aspect is not ideal for decks because of slippery algae, a deck sheltered from strong sunlight could become the central focus of a restful Japanese-inspired planting. In Japan it is quite common for wooden verandas (a type of deck) to be surrounded by gravel and stepping stones.

To enhance the atmosphere you could introduce a bubbling water feature set into the deck surrounded by pebbles and cobbles and hang wind chimes from an overhead pergola. Plant the surrounds with mainly cool green foliage, varying the leaf texture and shading as much as possible. Shrubs including acid-loving red- or white-flowered camellias, rhododendrons and azaleas, as well as white or blue lace-cap hydrangeas, will provide the odd touch of colour, but the emphasis is on foliage – try combining plants like ferns, hostas, spotted laurel (*Aucuba japonica*), Japanese maples, bamboos, ornamental grasses and sedges.

## MEDITERRANEAN FEEL

In a hot, sunny spot, decking combined with gravel allows for a more Mediterranean style of planting with drought-resistant types such as many of the 'silverlings' like carpeting lamb's ears (*Stachys byzantina*), white daisy-flowered *Rhodanthemum hosmariense* and lacy artemisias. Use plenty of herbs and aromatic plants like catmints (*Nepeta*), lavenders, thymes, sages, bronze fennel and oregano to create soft drifts that will contrast pleasingly with the stronger lines of the decking.

Then introduce a few architectural plants including perennials like *Acanthus spinosus* and verbascum as well as yuccas, phormiums or astelias, the latter with their striking, metallic sword-shaped leaves. Pots of brightly coloured pelargoniums and succulents would provide the perfect colourful finishing touch.

**LEFT:** *Make a dramatic entrance by planting identical containers with architectural plants like* Fatsia japonica *or perhaps a pair of neatly clipped topiary spirals or elegant ball-headed standards. These square trellis planters are ideal for permanent plantings.*

**BELOW:** *For the greatest impact, plant seasonal flowers like this vibrant petunia as single specimens. Planting identical pots in a row is especially dramatic.*

# colour guide

The next few pages are designed to give you ideas of how best to combine colours in your deckside planting. Firstly, how to mix blues and purples in the most successful combinations.

You can create all kinds of different effects by combining certain shades or by restricting your choice of flower and foliage to a single colour way. If you are not sure which plants work well together, keeping colour schemes simple is a recipe for success. The end result can be dramatic, elegant or contemporary depending on what shades you decide to use in your planting arrangements.

## RICH AND VIBRANT

Certain deep velvety purples and the vivid purple-reds like cerise and magenta combine perfectly with purple-blues. These shades can be found in many summer flowers including the following plants.

- fuchsias
- pelargoniums
- *Heliotrope* 'Marine'
- *Impatiens* (busy Lizzie)
- petunias
- verbena

And in winter, use blooms of pansies and violas as well as those of primrose and polyanthus, especially the jewel-like Wanda hybrids. Put a real zing in the display by adding a hint of lemon yellow or orange.

## BLUES AND PURPLES

There are many shades of lilac- and lavender-blue or purple-flowered bedding and patio plants. But there are few true blues such as gentian or sky blue, apart from felicias, violas and pansies. Blues and purples complement yellows and lime greens and help to cool down hot colours.

**ABOVE: Impatiens** *(busy Lizzie)* **'Mosaic Lilac' offers subtle purple-pink tones which blend well with stronger hues, especially deeper blues.**

## HOT SPOTS

Finally, metallic bronze-purples create the illusion of heat and look wonderful against a red-brick wall. Try them in terracotta-coloured baskets and wall containers for a Mediterranean look. Good plants include basil 'Purple Ruffles' and *Heuchera* 'Palace Purple'.

## PASTELS

- *Ageratum*
- *Brachycome multifida* 'Blue Mist'
- *Campanula isophylla* 'Stella'
- *Convolvulus sabatius*
- *Fuchsia*, such as 'La Campanella'
- *Impatiens* 'Blue Pearl'
- *Laurentia* 'Blue Stars'
- *Lobelia erinus*, such as 'Lilac Cascade'
- *Nemesia caerulea* 'Elliot's Variety' and 'Joan Wilder'
- *Petunia*
- *Scaevola aemula* 'Blue Wonder'
- *Sutera cordata* 'Lilac Pearls'
- *Verbena*
- *Viola*

ABOVE: Lobelia *'Cascade' is a superb plant for hanging baskets, with a dramatic, tumbling habit and varied tones of purple, blue and white.*

ABOVE LEFT: Verbena *'Sissinghurst' has vivid pink blooms.*

LEFT: Viola x wittrockiana *'Impressions Blue Shades' produces blooms in cool water colours and is perfect for shade.*

## DEEP SHADES

- *Ageratum*
- *Fuchsia*
- *Heliotrope* 'Marine'
- *Impatiens* (busy Lizzie)
- *Lobelia erinus* (trailing and bush forms)
- *Petunia* (especially the trailing Surfinia group)
- *Verbena*, such as 'Homestead Purple' and 'Tapien Violet'
- *Viola*

BELOW: Brachycome *'Blue Mist'.*

BELOW LEFT: Ageratum *'Blue Danube' has rich blue tones and a soft texture.*

# pretty pastels

Pastel schemes have always been popular for baskets, containers and borders with so many soft pinks and lilac-blues to choose from, and in recent years plant breeders have tended towards more subtle and romantic colourings.

You will find many pastel mixtures among plants like pansies, impatiens and lobelia and bedding with beautifully shaded and edged petals.

Arrangements can be rather insipid unless lots of lush greenery, some white flowers and a few stronger colours are peppered in. Try deep purples, crimson and cerise pinks for contrast. One alternative is to mix pinks with soft apricot and peach, using silver and white or lime green as a neutral background. Another is to combine pale yellow, cream and silver with touches of lilac and lavender.

## AIR OF ELEGANCE

White and silver displays have an air of distinction and are easy to put together successfully. They work particularly well with white-painted woodwork and metalwork and look good surrounding buildings with classical proportions where they can be used to add elegance. To enhance the display still further, add just a touch of pink or salmon and lime green. For a shady spot, to add a note of purity, try white flowers with green and white variegated foliage and apricot-pink highlights.

ABOVE: *The delicate apricot-pink of this* Begonia x tuberhybrida *contrasts well with other pastels and stronger colours. Large-flowered doubles also provide* strong upright form for hanging baskets *and other such container displays.*

BELOW LEFT: *Pale pink verbena.*

## PALE PINKS

- *Begonia sempervirens*
- *Begonia* (tuberous-rooted)
- *Brachycome* 'Pink Mist'
- *Diascia*
- *Fuchsia*
- *Impatiens*
- *Pelargonium*
- *Petunia*
- *Verbena*

# SILVERS, GREYS AND WHITES

- *Argyranthemum*
- *Begonia* (tuberous-rooted)
- *Fuchsia*
- *Helichrysum petiolare*
- *Impatiens*
- *Lobularia* 'Snow Crystals'
- *Osteospermum*
- Pansies and violas
- *Pelargonium*
- *Petunia*
- *Plecostachys serpyllifolia*
- *Rhodanthemum hosmariense*
- *Santolina chamaecyparissus* (cotton lavender)
- *Senecio cineraria* 'Silver Dust' and 'Cirrus'
- *Sutera cordata* 'Snowflake'
- *Verbena*

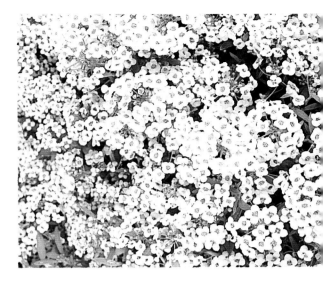

**ABOVE:** Lobularia *'Snow Crystals' (white alyssum) makes a delicate froth of white that works well filling in a pastel display in a hanging basket.*

**LEFT:** *Argyranthemum frutescens (marguerite) has bright white, yellow or pink daisy-like flowers.*

**BELOW LEFT:** Diascia *'Ruby Fields' produces tubular, salmon-pink flowers.*

**BELOW:** Cineraria *'Silver Dust' has elegant, lacy silver foliage.*

# bright colours

Yellows and creams add sunshine and combine effectively with many other colours. Don't forget variegated foliage and feel free to experiment with daring, contemporary schemes.

Citrus shades of lemon yellow, clear orange and lime green make a mouth-watering display. Avoid silver foliage and instead use plenty of greenery with yellow- or white-variegated foliage and orange-leaved coleus (*Solenostemon*). Blue stains and paints for woodwork and walls are very popular, and this refreshing colour scheme looks stunning against such a backdrop.

**RIGHT**: *This dark viola, with its brilliant yellow centre, will add dusky lowlights in a yellow or cream scheme.*

## LIME FOLIAGE

- *Fuchsia*, such as 'Golden Marinka'
- *Hedera helix* (English ivy)
- *Helichrysum petiolare* 'Limelight'
- *Lamium maculatum* 'Aureum'
- *Lysimachia nummularia* 'Aurea'
- *Pelargonium*
- *Solenostemon* (Coleus)
- *Tanacetum parthenium* 'Aureum' (golden feverfew)
- *Thymus*

## VARIEGATED FOLIAGE

- *Chlorophytum comosum* (spider plant)
- *Euonymus fortunei* cultivars
- *Felicia amelloides* 'Variegata'
- *Glechoma hederacea* 'Variegata'
- *Hedera helix* (English ivy)
- *Helichrysum petiolare*
- 'Variegata'
- *Lamium maculatum*, such as 'White Nancy'
- *Nasturtium* 'Alaska'
- *Plectranthus forsteri* 'Marginatus'
- *Salvia officinalis* 'Icterina'
- *Sedum lineare* 'Variegatum'

## CONTEMPORARY

Bright, but simple, combinations tend to have a modern look. Try lime green with a fizzy, day-glow pink or a combination of white flowers and white or yellow variegated foliage shot through with cerise or magenta. Pair up true blues with lemon yellows and lime foliage and combine deep velvet purples with scarlet and splashes of silver. An alternative approach is to go for a more subtle, minimalist feel. Try grey metallic containers with lavender, cream and silver planting or silvers, greys and palest purples with a contrast of purple-blacks and deep, blood red.

## YELLOWS/CREAMS

- *Asteriscus maritimus*
- *Begonia* (tuberous-rooted)
- *Bidens ferulifolia*
- *Brachycome* 'Lemon Mist'
- *Calceolaria* 'Sunshine'
- *Lysimachia congestiflora*
- *Lysimachia nummularia*
- Marigold
- *Mimulus*
- Nasturtium
- *Osteospermum* 'Buttermilk'
- Pansies and violas
- *Tagetes* 'Lemon Gem'

LEFT: Bidens ferulifolia *'Golden Eye'* has *starry blooms and attractive foliage.*

ABOVE: Asteriscus maritimus.

ABOVE RIGHT: Tagetes *'Naughty Marietta' has mahogany and gold flowers.*

TOP RIGHT: Tagetes *'Yellow Jacket'.*

## VIVID PURPLE-PINKS

- *Fuchsia*
- *Impatiens*
- *Lobelia*, such as 'Rosamund'
- *Pelargonium*
- *Petunia*
- Primroses (hybrid)
- *Portulaca*
- *Verbena*

# deckside beds

Choosing appropriate plants for a deckside garden is an amalgam of common sense and imagination. Because of the constraints of small spaces, often difficult planting conditions and the need to choose plants that offer the best value, it is important to make some practical choices. The element of imagination is equally important, as effective planting will bring the garden to life.

To get the most from a restricted space, it pays to have a clear planting theme in your mind's eye, to appreciate the limitations of the conditions – shade, sun, damp ground and so on – and then to try to unify the planting. But, to the uninitiated, what does this mean? For a start, it probably means having a balance of vertical interest – climbers, larger shrubs and even the odd tree – and horizontal interest in the form of smaller shrubs, perennials, bulbs and annuals. You do not need a wide variety of different plants to make your deckside borders look well planted, but their position in the border is crucial.

PLANT SIZE

Not everyone grasps that big plants can in fact do very well in small spaces. As a consequence, they tend to choose lots of smaller plants, which will not only give the garden a bitty, restless look, but which are much more labour intensive to maintain. Among the big, bold plants that would do well in a small space are evergreen shrubs, such as the broad-leaved *Fatsia japonica* and the yellow-splashed *Aucuba japonica* 'Crotonifolia', spiky cordylines and yuccas and the attractive *Choisya ternata*, with its whorl-like leaves and clouds of scented white flowers that appear in early summer.

It is important to ensure that the deckside garden has some kind of structural frame of planting, around which smaller groups of plants, including perennials and annuals, can be composed. Even if you have no more than a small raised bed, it is still worth including a couple of evergreen shrubs to provide a peg on which to hang the remainder of the planting scheme.

**RIGHT: Persicaria affinis** *is perfect for the deckside bed as it is evergreen and forms handsome cushions of foliage.*

**FAR RIGHT:** *Allow plants to overflow on to the deck to soften the edges, especially in an informal garden where the deck edges can appear too hard.*

## SEASONAL EFFECTS

It is well worth considering the seasonal element of the planting, and doing your best to make sure that the garden offers year-round interest. This is obviously harder to do in very small spaces, but even in a tiny border you can change the planting as the seasons progress, so that you always have something interesting to observe. It could house bright spring bulbs, followed by a selection of summer flowers and herbs, with late-summer annuals and chrysanthemums for autumn, and heathers, cyclamens and ivies in winter, for example.

## PLANTING UP THE BEDS

If you cannot afford to plant up the deck beds extensively all in one go, then concentrate your planting efforts on the bigger elements first, perhaps filling in the empty spaces with big annuals that you grow yourself from seed – tobacco plants are excellent space fillers and do well in partial shade as well as sun, unlike many of the annuals. In the first summer, take any cuttings you can and make sure you do this each year to increase your stock of shrubs. Quite a few perennials can be layered or divided to augment supplies.

## USING PLANTS

It is often best to pick several species from one genus that you know will work well in the environment than to go for a range of different plants. Planting gains its impact from making a bold statement, and grouping plants by type certainly increases the effect. For example, pelargoniums are great in most small spaces, not least because of the many different forms, which include trailing types for softening the edges of the deck, richly scented ivy-leaved ones that can be used in cooking, and brilliant-coloured flowering regal and zonal varieties, some of which can even be trained into architectural standards.
 Fuchsias are another good candidate for a good long season of interest, again with a wide range of flower types and colours. Like pelargoniums, some types can be trained to create standards, if you wish.

# DECORATIVE PLANT SUPPORTS

A little light support props up tall plants and those that fall forward or lean over the edge of the deck more than they should. Rustic supports made from woven or bent twigs not only do their job, but also make more of the plants. They are easy to make yourself from prunings.

**ABOVE:** *Bent hazel stems, wired or tacked together, make decorative low plant supports. They usually last two or three years if taken under cover in winter, but are cheap to buy and easily replaced when they are past their best.*

**LEFT:** *An even simpler support like this one can be pushed into a border temporarily at any time of year to hold up a plant. You cannot hide the support, but this does not matter as it becomes part of the display, adding a touch of rustic style to the deckside border.*

**ABOVE:** *Climbers, such as this golden hop (Humulus lupulus 'Aureus'), don't need a large bed to grow in, though make sure you culitvate the soil deeply.*

**LEFT:** *Mimulus make great deckside plants for a splash of summer colour.*

# feature plants

When planning deckside borders, you need to ensure that the eye is drawn to specific elements in them, rather than allowed to meander in an apparently random way. In larger gardens, designers normally create a series of compartments which help to focus attention on individual elements within the larger whole. In the area around a deck, this luxury is not really applicable, as the space will not normally allow it, although you can copy the concept by creating points of interest with garden ornaments or particular plants.

The plants that serve this kind of purpose best are those with strong eye-catching interest, simply because you need something reasonably large to notice it. Ideally, such a plant should look good most of the year, becoming a more or less permanent feature of the garden. You can, of course, use perennials or deciduous shrubs for the same purpose, but you will want to make sure that the deckscape still looks good without them in the winter months.

## EYE-CATCHING SHRUBS

Among the best shrubs to act as a focal point are those with distinctive foliage and a handsome form. A good subject is *Fatsia japonica*, an evergreen with large glossy divided leaves and attractive berries in winter. It forms a pretty large bush eventually, and can make a good end-of-border plant to screen the end of the garden

from the house. Another good candidate is the Mexican orange blossom, *Choisya ternata*, or winter-flowering *Mahonia* x *media* 'Charity'; both have the benefit of being scented, too. Equally good for the purpose of making a focal point would be large spiky cordylines or yuccas, perhaps in a

complementary container, or even the Abyssinian banana plant, *Ensete ventricosum*, again in a container, as you will need to overwinter it indoors. A large palm, such as *Trachycarpus fortunei* or the tree fern, *Dicksonia antarctica*, makes a good focal point for a deck.

LEFT: *Plants can act as focal points just because of their bright colour – this is* Canna indica *'Raspberry'.*

ABOVE: *Climbers can be striking focal points, such as this wisteria. It is only effective when it is in flower, however.*

## USING ARCHES

If you do not want the plant in a solo spot, then consider creating an arch, over which you can grow a few climbers or twining plants. This, again, will draw the eye, particularly in summer when plants are in flower, though of course you could, if you prefer, turn it into a permanent feature by planting evergreen climbers, such as ivies, over it.

Alternatively, use an arch or pergola as a support for some exotic-looking foliage climbers, such as big-leaved vines, the evergreen clematis *Clematis armandii* which is also scented, or the climbing hydrangea, *Hydrangea anomala petiolaris*, with its large flat corymbs of creamy flowers. In warmer areas, you could try *Campsis x tagliabuana* 'Madame Galen' with its wonderful burnt orange trumpet-shaped flowers.

## PERENNIALS

A small bed of large perennials can also provide a focal point. Try creating a bed with some show-stopping perennials that grow to 1.2m (4ft) or more – *Euphorbia characias wulfenii*, ligularias, rodgersias and the big hellebore, *Helleborus argutifolius*, are all good candidates for this kind of treatment, with perhaps smaller perennials edging the bed and sprawling over the paving – try the small campanulas, epimediums and geraniums for this purpose.

For a sunny spot, try clouds of *Crambe cordifolia*, with big blue-green leaves and starry white flowers, and some silver-leaved giants, such as the striking *Eryngium giganteum*. *Macleaya cordata* would combine well with *Crocosmia* 'Lucifer' in a slightly less sunny situation.

**RIGHT:** *A striking bowl of pink petunias acts a focal point on top of the pillar on this raised deck. It stands out from the otherwise cool white planting and white accessories.*

# HINTS AND TIPS

- Unless you are in a hurry to see the final effect, there is no need to pay extra for a large plant; small specimens establish themselves better than large ones and quickly catch up
- Plant feature plants a suitable distance from other plants in the garden to avoid overcrowding, shading or the risk of smothering smaller species
- Select a site where the full beauty of the plant can be appreciated from various parts of the deck. Position it so that it becomes part of several different views when seen from different directions in the garden

- Since a small area only has room to house a very few of the larger shrubs, be sure to choose only the most striking examples. Plants that provide the right effect for the style of the deck and that suit the site and growing conditions will always constitute the best value for money
- Choose only top-quality plants, well-furnished with evenly spaced stems and healthy foliage
- Species that provide interest in more than one season are especially valuable close to the deck; witch hazel for example has autumn foliage tints and flowers in winter and spring

LEFT: *Grasses can make great feature plants for the deckside garden. From left to right:* Carex 'Evergold' *(front),* Alopecurus pratensis *'Aureovariegatus',* Deschampsia flexuosa *'Tatra Gold',* Carex ornithopoda *'Variegata',* Koeleria glauca *and* Molinia caerulea *'Variegata'.*

# temporary planting

Despite all the work needed to grow, plant and look after bedding plants, they are more popular than ever, for beds and borders as well as containers and hanging baskets. Bedding plants are ideal for instant colour, as they are generally planted out just as they are starting to bloom. They also have a long flowering season and prolific blooming potential, so they can be relied on to keep a small area ablaze with colour for months on end, unlike other kinds of plants that come and go during the summer, leaving expanses of green.

## CHOOSING COLOURS

Nowadays, there is a move away from traditional delicate pastels and old formal favourites, such as *Begonia semperflorens* and ageratum, towards stronger, bolder colours, such as reds and orange. Subtropical-looking tender perennial plants, such as datura, canna and hedychium (ginger lily), are particularly popular. Named varieties of gazania and compact 'patio' dahlias are very much in demand, while species fuchsias and shrubby salvias in bright reds and blues are also very sought-after. Exotic-looking annual climbers, such as mutisia, *Mina lobata* and *Lablab purpureus* (hyacinth bean) are perfect for covering arches or trellis quickly and a decorative way of screening sheds or walls.

## HINTS AND TIPS

*Try the following plants for a continuous display of blooms all summer long:*
- *Argyranthemum*
- *Brachycome*
- *Fuchsia* (bush and trailing)
- Ivy-leaved pelargoniums
- *Lobelia*
- *Petunia*
- Zonal pelargoniums

**LEFT:** *Antirrhinums produce a stunning display over a long season. This is a seed mixture called 'Royal Carpet'.*

**BELOW LEFT:** *Deep pink tobacco plants (*Nicotiana*) are mixed with* Lobelia erinus *'Colour Parade', a bush lobelia.*

**BELOW:** Begonia semperflorens *'Venus' makes a neat pink carpet and will grow happily in sun or shade.*

**ABOVE:** *Gazanias love a hot sunny spot and are fairly drought-tolerant. Raise plants from seed or cuttings every year.*

**BELOW:** Eschscholzia *'Harlequin Hybrids' make a bright splash of colour. Simply sprinkle the seed into the border.*

## TREND-SETTING PLANTS

If you want to stay ahead of trends, look out for unusual half-hardy perennials with striking flowers, such as *Leonotis leonurus*, which has tiers of pompon-like orange flowers, and *Sutherlandia frutescens*, which has silvery foliage and scarlet pea flowers followed by big inflated green pods. Many of these plants can be spotted in the 'new varieties' pages of the mail order seed catalogues, making it relatively inexpensive to raise your own plants from seed or plantlets.

If you want to be first with the latest in new plants, it is worth cultivating the specialist nurseries known for their new introductions. Find them at plant shows and put your name on their mailing lists, then sit back and wait.

ABOVE: Verbena *'Raspberry Crush' is a reliable and attractive all-purpose plant for filling gaps in borders.*

LEFT: Sutherlandia frutescens *is easily raised from seed, although plants are sometimes available from nurseries specializing in tender perennials. It has curious inflated seed pods after the orange flowers are over.*

RIGHT: *Coleus has vivid foliage but needs some shelter to perform well. It comes in a range of vivid colour ways.*

## SCENTED PLANTS

- *Lathyrus odoratus* (sweet pea)
- *Malcomia maritima* (Virginia stock)
- *Matthiola bicornis* (night-scented stock)
- *Matthiola incana* (stock)
- *Nicotiana* 'Fragrant Cloud'
- *Zaluzianskya capensis* (night stock)

**RIGHT:** *Pelargoniums are fairly drought-tolerant plants which will keep flowering throughout the summer months as long as they are regularly deadheaded. Do not overfeed these plants as they will grow leafy instead of flowering well.*

## TENDER PERENNIALS

While seed-raised bedding plants can be replaced every season, it becomes expensive to treat choice tender (half-hardy) perennials in this way. If you want to maintain a size-able collection of these plants, a frost-free greenhouse is a very useful facility.

Take cuttings of half-hardy perennials in late summer, root them in small pots and keep them in a light frost-free place for the winter.

# permanent planting

There are a few basic rules for choosing plants for deckside beds. The first is to pick plants which will survive happily in the conditions you have on offer, whether it is a dry and sunny corner against a sheltered wall, or an area of damp soil in deep shade.

The next is to choose plants of the right size – check out the eventual size of the plant when you buy to make sure it won't soon swamp the others around it. Don't rule out large plants for small beds, though, as some variation in size will improve the planting scheme. Aim also for variation in foliage colour and shape to add interest.

As the deck will probably be close to the house and may be visible from the windows, aim for year-round interest and colour in your deckside beds, picking a variety of evergreen and structural plants to give you something to enjoy, even in winter.

## SHRUBS

Shrubs add a framework to beds and borders, providing height and structure to the scheme. Pick a selection of both deciduous and evergreen varieties for varied interest. The evergreen shrubs will create a backbone, while the decidous ones will add seasonal highlights and changes. Some widely available shrubs, such as hebe, helianthemum, potentilla and *Genista lydia*, are naturally compact and perfect for most beds. You can also get compact varieties of larger shrubs, such as berberis. The advantage is that they never outgrow their welcome so you do not need to keep cutting them back hard to fit.

## CONIFERS

Conifers encompass a fascinating selection of evergreen shapes, foliage textures and colours, providing a year-round framework for a deckside bed. Choose from prostrate, mat-forming plants, neat dome shapes, precise spires or cones in blue, green, lime or yellow.

BELOW: *Compact varieties of berberis are perfect for deckside beds. From left to right:* Berberis thunbergii *'Bonanza Gold'*, B.t. *'Bagatelle'*, B.t. *'Helmond Pillar'*, B.t. *'Aurea' and* B.t. *'Atropurpurea Nana'.*

BELOW LEFT: *Three compact conifers for a deckside bed. From left to right:* Picea glauca albertiana *'Conica'*, Picea mariana *'Nana' and* Picea glauca albertiana *'Alberta Globe'.*

## PERENNIALS

Perennials fill out the lower tiers of the garden. Since the individual plants are smaller than shrubs, these are the plants that offer the most opportunity for decorating the deck in seasonal colour. A well-planned border should include a changing selection of perennials for every season of the year, even winter. Those that have very long flowering seasons are useful for providing continuity, but do not overlook plants with shorter display seasons as you will look forward to their appearance every year; plants such as omphalodes for spring, peony for early summer and sedum for autumn.

Although the most popular perennials are grown for their flowers, plants such as hostas and ferns are in great demand as foliage plants, for creating backdrops for the flowers or for filling difficult shady spots where most perennials will not grow.

By choosing the right perennials for your beds, you can keep the deck full of colour and variety, and also complement the year-round framework of woody plants.

**ABOVE LEFT:** Primula japonica *is one of the candelabra primulas, so-called because of the way the flowers are arranged up the stem.*

**ABOVE RIGHT:** *Bearded irises have spectacular scented flowers in early summer.*

**RIGHT:** Euphorbia griffithi *'Fireglow' has tinted foliage and bright orange flowers.*

# plants for sun

There is a rich and varied selection of plants, many of them from the Mediterranean regions of Europe, that do best in dry sunny situations. These are ideal plants for a hot, sunny deck, or even a south- or west-facing balcony. Because they are so well adapted to drought conditions in their natural habitat, such plants are relatively low maintenance, requiring little attention and doing surprisingly well in fairly poor soil. Many of them have attractive silver leaves, and you can make this a theme of the planting if you wish, perhaps marrying them with some plants with variegated leaves.

## CHOOSING PLANTS FOR SUN
Among the best plants for dry sunny conditions are the wormwoods (*Artemisia*), of which there are many different forms and sizes. *Convoluvus cneorum* is a pretty slightly tender plant with very attractive blue-green foliage and white flowers with a prominent yellow eye. Pinks do particularly well in hot sun, and those with the strongest scent, such as 'Mrs Sinkins', are always popular. Potentillas also do well in sunny places, and there are many different forms to choose from, from quite large shrubs to little mat-forming ground-covering ones.

Rue (*Ruta graveolens*) is another good foliage plant – a herb in fact – with strongly aromatic divided blue-green foliage; 'Jackman's Blue' is one

of the most popular forms. *Santolina chamaecyparissus* is another aromatic herb with silvery foliage that makes a good border edging. You can clip it back each autumn to make a mini hedge. *Brachyglottis laxifolia* is another good silvery leaved shrub, but a bit bigger (about l.2m/4ft) and will make a good edging to a deck, sprawling attractively over the edges of the decking boards

Lavender, too, makes an excellent edging for a path or border, and can be clipped back to keep it to a more formal shape. Of the bigger shrubs,

buddlejas thrive in light soil and dry conditions, and the pretty *Buddleja alternifolia* 'Argentea' has attractive silvery leaves and lavender, scented flowers in early summer.

**ABOVE:** *Fuchsias are classic bedding plants that can be bought widely and inexpensively as rooted cuttings in spring. They revel in full sun.*

**RIGHT:** Hibiscus syriacus *'Woodbridge'. Hardy hibiscus thrives in a warm, sunny, sheltered spot with well-drained soil. Wind can damage buds and blooms.*

## PLANTS FOR GRAVEL BEDS

If you have gravel beds around your deck, you can plant a range of sun-loving small perennials, which will help to soften the look of the gravel. The same principle can be applied to the tops of walls, or crevices in a dry stone wall. Stone troughs and shallow containers also make ideal homes for these kinds of small sun-loving plants.

Among the best plants for this kind of situation are small saxifrages and sedums, which thrive in very dry poor soil. They have large fleshy leaves that retain moisture well, and make an attractive carpet of foliage, studded, when the time comes, with flowers on taller stems. For planting in the cracks of paving stones, try the little and aptly named daisy-gone-crazy, or *Erigeron karvinskianus*, with its array of pink fading to white daisy flowers. Also good for crevices and cracks are the little campanulas, which will seed themselves happily almost anywhere, as indeed does the larger *Alchemilla mollis*, with its velvety green-grey leaves and lime-green flowers. Another good candidate is baby's tears or helxine (*Soleirolia soleirolii*).

**ABOVE:** Dahlia *'Alva's Doris' has showy scarlet blooms. Dahlias make a stunning late summer display in a sunny border.*

## PLANTS FOR SUN

- *Achillea*
- *Agapanthus africanus*
- *Alstroemeria* hybrids
- *Anthemis punctata cupaniana*
- *Centaurea*
- *Crambe cordifolia*
- *Crocosmia*
- *Cynara cardunculus*
- *Euphorbia*
- *Gladiolus*
- *Kniphofia*
- *Lavandula*
- *Linum*
- *Papaver*
- *Penstemon*
- *Perovskia*
- *Phlomis*
- *Phygelius*
- *Salvia sclarea turkestanica*
- *Sisyrinchium striatum*
- *Verbascum*

## SHRUBS FOR SUN

Most shrubs do best in situations that provide direct sun for half the day or more, but a site with strong direct sun all day which also has hot, dry, poor soil is difficult to colonize. Few shrubs are happy in such conditions. But by choosing carefully from among the more drought-resistant shrubs, and taking some trouble to get new plants established, it is possible to garden in even the most difficult spot. If the soil is not too impoverished, buddleja, *Lavatera olbia* 'Rosea' and hardy hibiscus will fare well, adding extra colour later in the season when it is most needed.

And in poor dry soil in front of a wall, ceanothus or *Fremontodendron californicum* make good drought-resistant shrubs suitable for wall-training. Low spreading shrubs, such as cistus, senecio, santolina, *Genista lydia* and hebe, are ideal for covering dry banks or for the front of a border. Larger shrubs, including olearia, tamarix, *Romneya coulteri* with its huge white poppy flowers, Japanese bitter orange (*Poncirus trifoliata*) and brooms, including the Spanish broom *Spartium junceum*, make a taller back row for a border. It is always worth improving problem soil as much as possible, since this makes it possible to grow a much wider range of plants. By adding plenty of well-rotted organic matter and nutrients, plants such as hardy hibiscus, buddleja, clerodendron, helianthemum and others will all thrive in previously difficult places.

RIGHT: *A trio of shrubs for a sunny deckside bed. From left to right:* Salvia officinalis *'Tricolor',* Perovskia atriplicifolia *'Blue Spire' and* Cistus.

## VERSATILE HEBES

Hebes are pretty, bushy summer-flowering evergreen shrubs with characteristic bottlebrush-like flowers. They thrive in a sunny, sheltered spot in light, free-draining soil, flowering in summer. Some are scented.

BELOW: *Top row from left:* **Hebe corstophinensis** *'Cranleighensis',* **H.** *x* **franciscana** *'Variegata' and* **H. gracillima** *'Great Orme'. Bottom row:* **H. amplexicaulis** *'Amy' and* **H. matthewsii** *'Midsummer Beauty'.*

## COPING WITH POOR SOIL

First improve the soil by digging in as much well-rotted organic matter (such as garden compost or animal manure) as possible. On sandy or gravelly soils this quickly breaks down and disappears, but it will last long enough to help hold water while new plants get established. You can assist poor dry soils further by digging in water-retaining gel crystals, which last virtually forever. A 2.5–5cm (1–2in) layer of gravel, granite chippings or even cobblestones works as a good mulch on these soils (water condenses underneath the stones overnight, thus helping plants survive), and only needs topping up every few years. The secret of planting in these conditions is to plant in autumn, when the soil is moist and winter rains will help new plants to become established. Water plants in dry spells the following summer. If planting in spring is inevitable, you must water new plants regularly throughout their first season. Avoid planting in summer entirely.

# plants for shade

Although there are only a very few plants that will cope with deep shade – most notably ivies – most areas have at least some light, and there is a much wider variety that will cope with these partially shaded conditions. Some prefer the shade to be dry and others cope better in damp soil, but provided you take the time and trouble to find out which plants will thrive, you can create wonderful gardens in shady conditions.

If you want privacy on your deck, and plant trees or large shrubs to provide it, the areas beneath their canopy are already earmarked for shade-loving small shrubs and perennials. Indeed, it is well worth your while, even in a tiny border, having at least one large shrub or small tree, just so that you can vary the habitat provided, and increase the range of plants you can grow.

## DRY SHADE

In a small garden, you are unlikely to get too much damp shade, unless you live in a part of the country with very high rainfall. The shade cast by buildings in cities, let alone any trees, is more than likely to create dry soil conditions as well, so it is these drier shady conditions that you will, in the main, have to contend with. Bear in mind that the area under the canopy of a tree receives relatively little rain, so this shade will be drier than most.

Fortunately, there are some very attractive plants at your disposal, although you may need to rethink some of your gardening concepts. Brightly coloured displays of hot coloured annuals will not be for you. In their place, you can grow some singularly beautiful foliage plants and a few flowering ones that cope with these conditions, although their flowers tend to be in paler shades – whites and pale blues in the main. A green and white scheme – the result of this kind of planting – looks extremely good in most gardens, and is very restful and relaxing to the eye. Once you have got used to the concept, you will find your eye is more attuned to noticing form and texture – both virtues of shade-loving plants.

## CHOOSING PLANTS

The ubiquitous hosta is probably the king of all shade-loving plants and should definitely be a major player in any shade planting scheme. Other larger shade-loving plants you could try to include *Acanthus mollis*, big-leaved bergenias, stately foxgloves (*Digitalis*), hellebores, and Solomon's seal (*Polygonatum*).

Low-growing plants for shade include bugle (*Ajuga*), little anemones and cyclamens, the dead-nettles (*Lamium maculatum*), and the rather invasive evergreen *Vinca minor*, which has pretty blue flowers. Other good candidates are epimediums, with little heart-shaped leaves, and *Tiarella cordifolia*, with its spires of white flowers.

## PLANTS FOR SHADE

- *Acanthus mollis*
- *Aconitum*
- *Alchemilla mollis*
- *Asplenium scolopendrium*
- *Corydalis lutea*
- *Digitalis purpurea*
- *Dryopteris filix-mas*
- *Epimedium grandiflorum*
- *Euphorbia*
- *Geranium macrorrhizum*
- *G. phaeum*
- *Hedera helix*
- *Helleborus argutifolius*
- *Hemerocallis*
- *Hepatica*
- *Impatiens* New Guinea hybrids (annual)
- *Polypodium vulgare*
- *Polystichum setiferum*
- *Pulmonaria longiifolia*
- *Rodgersia*
- *Symphytum ibericum*

ABOVE LEFT: **Erythronium dens-canis** *is an endearing bulb which will clump up in a shady spot and form a carpet of speckled foliage. The small, nodding purple-pink flowers appear in spring.*

RIGHT: *Foliage predominates in most shady spots. Here, hostas, ferns and grasses create an interesting scheme with variation in shape, form and texture. The white edges of the hosta leaves add a bright splash while the cobbles provide further texture and help to suppress weeds.*

## PLANTS FOR SHADY WALLS

To clothe shady walls, ivies are the obvious choice, although the yellow-splashed or silver-variegated types will revert to all-green leaf colouring if deprived of sunlight. Other good candidates are creepers and vines; *Clematis montana* and *C. alpina* will both cope with a north-facing, shady wall. *Euonymus fortunei* can be grown as a wall shrub against a shady wall, as can the handsome *Garrya elliptica*. *Cotoneaster horizontalis*, *Crinodendron hookerianum*, *Humulus lupulus* 'Aureus' and *Lathyrus latifolius*, the everlasting pea, will all cope with partial shade, and *Passiflora caerulea*, normally supposed to like sun, can also do quite well in an alleyway, although it will not grow as large or flower as freely here as in full sun.

At the foot of the wall, the shadiest part, ferns are ideal candidates, and look particularly good when planted in a ribbon formation alongside the wall. *Helleborus argutifolius*, the big evergreen hellebore with green flowers, copes well with partial shade, as do several of the euphorbias. Another good bet for this kind of situation is the big *Geranium phaeum*, a large evergreen with handsomely divided leaves.

## WOODLAND PLANTS

For a more woodland-style shade garden, consider growing some of the plants that do well in these conditions. Pulmonarias are among the most appealing shade-loving plants,

## SHRUBS FOR SHADE

- *Aucuba japonica*
- *Choisya ternata*
- *Elaeagnus pungens*
- x *Fatshedera lizei*
- *Fatsia japonica*
- *Hydrangea quercifolia*
- *Ligustrum japonicum*
- *Mahonia* x *media* 'Charity'
- *Rhododendron*
- *Skimmia japonica*
- *Taxus baccata*

ABOVE: *Hydrangeas are great subjects for a shady spot and come in shades of white, pink and blue. The colour may depend on the acidity of your soil.*

RIGHT: Rodgersia aesculifolia *is a bold perennial with large, sculptural leaves. The foliage is slightly shiny and reflects available light.*

and their attractively mottled leaves and pinkish-purple bell-like flowers look particularly good when they are planted in large drifts. The hardy cyclamens, again with pretty white- or silver-splashed leaves, are another good candidate for a shady spot under trees, as are the sweet-scented lily-of-the-valley which have waxy white bell flowers. In the right conditions, both will rapidly spread to provide excellent ground cover.

There are a number of clump-forming plants that do well in woodland conditions, including the attractive bronze-leaved hepatica with spires of blue flowers, and Japanese anemones, with white or pink flowers. The feathery-leaved corydalis is another good plant for dry shade.

It is always worth growing a few bulbs in a semi-woodland area; snowdrops and winter aconites in particular, thrive in partially shaded conditions. Both will do well in grass around the bole of a tree. Some species of narcissus, which are more delicate than big blowsy daffodils, will also do well in light shade, and, of course, bluebells thrive in peaty soil and partial shade. A good combination would be a couple of big evergreen *Helleborus argutifolius* underplanted with bluebells.

## GROUND COVER

- *Ajuga reptans*
- *Bergenia*
- *Epimedium*
- *Euonymus*
- Ferns (various)
- *Hedera helix*
- *Lamium maculatum*
- *Pachysandra terminalis*
- *Soleirolia*
- *Tellima grandiflora*
- *Tiarella cordifolia*
- *Tolmeia menziesii*
- *Vinca minor*

# containers

You can grow almost anything in a pot provided it's big enough. Choosing the right plants is very important but the pots you select will also have an effect on the overall picture. One of the advantages of growing in containers is flexibility. Using pot liners allows you to mix and match seasonal colour and you can move displays around if you feel like a change.

Dressing your deck is always more successful when you go with one particular style. Consider the scale of the decked area and select your pots accordingly. Small pots scattered over a wide expanse of boarding will seem lost and insignificant. The structure should be strong enough to take the weight of one or two large contain-

ers and these will help to visually 'anchor' your collections of smaller pots and other planters.

Make use of seasonal flowers including annuals, tender perennials and bulbs and when going for a bold display or a more contemporary look, use just one variety per pot rather than a mixture. Pots can

be heavy to move around so use a plastic pot as a 'liner' and replace these inner sleeves with a fresh display when the original begins to look a bit tired. Wicker baskets painted with yacht varnish to prolong their life make attractive outer covers.

A backdrop of potted evergreens, flowering and foliage shrubs and well-behaved perennials will give continuity of display and give the deck a 'garden' feel. For long-term planting use a well-drained potting compost based on loam and containing a slow-release fertilizer.

For extra height, use small ornamental trees or for a more formal look, shrubs trained as ball-headed standards. Alternatively grow a few climbers over cane wigwams, metal spirals or obelisks.

**LEFT**: *Interesting effects can be created using recessed planters, flush with the deck or by slotting containers into specially shaped apertures.*

**ABOVE**: *Hydrangeas make surprisingly good pot specimens but need plenty of moisture and a little shade to really flower prolifically.*

## CHOOSING POTS

- *Terracotta* Ranging from classical to contemporary, even rustic. Weathers over time and can be painted with specialist products. Avoid pots with cracks or flaking and buy guaranteed frost-proof. In cold climates wrap planted pots that can't be moved under cover with layers of insulating material

- *Glazed ceramic* These come in all shades. Enhance the Oriental flavour of pots glazed blue or jade green by surrounding with 'streams' of differently graded cobbles and pebbles. Or for urban chic, try coloured glass beads

- *Plastic* More expensive examples make quite convincing stone or terracotta look-alikes. Applying artist's acrylic paints can help to 'age' the pots. Perfect where weight is an issue

- *Metallic* Lightweight containers. Try a row of identical containers planted with grasses or soft-coloured herbs for a more muted display

- *Wood* Leave natural and treat with preservative (plastic inner liners help lengthen their life further) or paint an appropriate colour. Can be contemporary or rustic

# foliage plants

One of the greatest contenders for a container is the hosta (or plantain lily as it used to be commonly known). There are many different forms, but one of the large varieties, with huge, thickly ribbed bluish-green waxy leaves, makes a wonderful rosette shape in a container – a very handsome sight even when out of flower. In flower it produces a tall, white spire of lily-like blooms. Hostas planted in beds are prey to slug damage, but planting them in containers helps to reduce this problem, particularly if you set the container on a bed of sharp grit. Several forms planted together make an excellent display from May until the autumn.

There are plenty of other foliage plants to choose from for containers. One worthwhile solution is to pick a fairly small or slow-growing evergreen, plant it in the centre of the container, and change the planting around it from season to season. A clipped box ball in the centre of a medium-sized pot can play host to snowdrops or small white tulips in spring and bright white osteospermums ('Whirlygig' is particularly striking) in summer, followed by button chrysanthemums or cyclamens in autumn. A few ivy plants to trail over the side helps to break the formality of the pot.

Even trees can be grown in large pots, and one of the best performers in this respect is the Japanese maple (*Acer palmatum*) with its delicate, hand-shaped filigree leaves. Some of them turn brilliant colours in autumn, and although expensive, are well worth including in a small garden. Be warned, however, that some are sensitive to wind chill and may become scorched or even not survive in an exposed position unless given additional shelter.

## HINTS AND TIPS

- **DO** group containers of different shapes and sizes to create more impact
- **DO** use pots of the same colour or material to provide a linking theme
- **DO** use baskets and wall pots to soften walls and vertical structures
- **DO** use specific styles of container to emphasise a particular theme
- **DO** include at least one large pot in a group of small pots to anchor the display
- **DO** use liners so that you can swap the pot with a fresh display when it's over
- **DON'T** mix plants with different requirements in the same pot. Some will inevitably suffer and spoil the rest of the container display
- **DON'T** only use seasonal flowers. Include some evergreen shrubs and trailers as framework planting within pot groupings
- **DON'T** leave spent flowers on show – deadhead regularly to keep it neat

FAR LEFT: *The delicate foliage of Japanese maples contrasts beautifully with broad-leaved evergreens. Provide shelter from strong sunlight and wind and keep them well watered.*

# flowering plants

In spring you can create massed displays of bulbs, ideally with some kind of orchestrated colour theme, be it a single colour or a twinned theme, such as yellow and blue, for example. If you plant a good number of tulips or hyacinths together in a pot, they look far more impressive than scattered among other bulbs.

In summer you can create a mini border effect by putting containers of larger annuals and perennials behind the smaller ones. Big tobacco plants, lilies, or alliums, with perhaps achillea or cosmos, could form the back row, while smaller plants – daisies, helianthemums, pelargoniums and so on – form the front rank. Again, it helps to have some kind of colour scheme, but it could be either softly toning – blues, pinks, whites and silvers, perhaps – or a strong strident contrast of hot colours such as yellows, pinks and reds, depending on the style of the garden and the situation, as well as your preference.

If you want to grow climbers, you will need to ensure that they have a large enough pot in which to spread their roots, but most climbers can be successfully grown in a pot about 45cm (18in) in diameter. The plants will, of course, need to be watered regularly and fed during the growing season, as the container will limit their ability to take up food and water through the normal processes, and it will be up to you to supply it all for them.

ABOVE: *Wooden containers blend well with decking and don't have to be rustic. This one is planted with pieris.*

LEFT: *A standard bay tree planted in a galvanized container and set against a sunny white-washed wall gives the deck a very modern feel.*

RIGHT: *The clean lines of today's galvanized, zinc or aluminium containers make them a must for contemporary gardens. Miniature bamboo is used here to stylish effect.*

# bedding plants

Bedding and patio plants are the category in which most summer container plants can be found. In recent years there's been a huge increase in the range of material available. Some of the new arrivals represent a significant improvement whilst others are more like novelty items – fun to experiment with, but don't risk basing your whole display on them!

### GETTING AN EARLY START

Half-hardy annuals and tender perennials in the form of seedlings, plugs or young plants are available from late winter to mid-spring. But you will need a warm, light spot to grow them on until they are ready to move outdoors, and that could mean up to four months, depending on time of purchase. If you have the facilities, this is the cheapest way to plant a container, short of raising your own from seeds and cuttings. Prick out seedlings and pot on plantlets as soon as you get them home. Alternatively, plant up your container straightaway (plug plants make planting up the sides of baskets very simple), and grow on in a heated greenhouse or conservatory.

### INSTANT DISPLAYS

From mid-spring to mid-summer, bedding and patio plants are available in a very wide range of sizes, from small plants in modular trays to individually potted plants including larger specimens. You will have more

choice at the start of the season and plants also tend to be in better condition when they first arrive. Varieties sold as single colour strains are useful for co-ordinating arrangements and F1 hybrids, although more expensive, tend to ensure greater consistency and performance over other kinds. Starter kits that include a range of container plants in a single pack are useful if you are just starting out or if you only want a small quantity. If you have nowhere to keep plants or newly planted containers under cover while there is still a risk of frost, then it's best to plant later using more mature material for an instant display.

### BUYING TIPS

● Choose good, bushy plants, well-clothed in leaves that have not yet started to flower, or with plenty of flower buds and just one or two open.

● Unless they are variegated, plants should be a healthy green with no yellowing. Red, brown or purple tinting may indicate chilling or nutrient deficiency. Spots and yellow streaking on foliage indicate disease or viral infection.

● Avoid plants that have been cut back or have had old flowers trimmed off – they have probably been hanging around for some time.

● Avoid seedlings and plants that are pale and drawn. They will have been weakened through growing in poor light levels.

● Don't buy plants that are displayed in exposed conditions outdoors during cold periods in spring. They may look all right but could later show signs of chilling injury.

BELOW: *Marguerite daisies are prolific flowerers and they look fresh and contemporary in blue glazed pots.*

- Avoid plants with wilted shoots and dry soil. Erratic watering may have damaged their root systems.
- Avoid pot-bound plants where a mass of roots fills the pot and protrudes through the drainage holes in the bottom. Equally, be suspicious of compost with very few roots visible – it could be a sign of vine weevil or some other root problem, such as overwatering.
- Check plants thoroughly for signs of pests and diseases before purchase. The white discarded skins of aphids are easier to spot than the living insects. Under glass, whitefly could also have taken hold – you will notice these as tiny white triangular insects that fly up when foliage is disturbed. Fuchsias are a favourite. Do not buy from places infested with whitefly, as the pest is difficult to eradicate, even with chemical sprays.
- If you are unsure, ask the staff

## BUYING MAIL ORDER

*- There are several advantages to buying seedlings, rooted cuttings, plugs and young plants by post. However, be sure to get your order in early*

*- Buying mail order allows you to try out new varieties before they are available in garden centres*

*- It also means you can make an early start if young plants and seedlings are not available locally*

*- You could save money by using*

*rooted cuttings as opposed to larger pot grown plants*

*- Cut out the problem of plants that are difficult to germinate, such as begonia and impatiens, by buying germinated seedlings or plug plants*

*- The main disadvantage of mail order is that plants can suffer with delays or damage in transit*

*- Be prepared to deal with plants immediately they arrive*

when it will be safe to move the plants outdoors permanently in your area. Also note that in autumn and winter, plants such as primroses are sometimes displayed outdoors but may only be suitable for very sheltered positions and for indoor use.

# self-watering containers

Self-watering containers, such as the trough shown below, have a reservoir in the base. These containers can keep plants watered for up to a week before the reservoir needs refilling, even in summer. The generous size and plastic construction both help to

conserve moisture. The hole at the top of the moulding in the reservoir allows water to overflow just before it reaches the main potting compost. Compost in the indentation below the main pot acts like a wick to draw up water from the reservoir.

### WALL POTS AND BASKETS

If attractively planted, wall pots and hanging baskets can transform a high-walled deck or basement garden, and there is nothing to stop you using shade-loving plants, if the situation demands it. Ferns and ferny leaved plants, such as corydalis, work well in these kinds of settings. So do the delicate trailing plants like verbenas and diascia, *Tradescantia* and nasturtiums, although these will all still benefit from being placed in a much sunnier situation. Pansies are good candidates for hanging baskets, as are begonias and lobelia, and of course trailing helichrysum and nepeta. You will get a more attractive effect if you limit the planting to three or four different plants in one container, and opt for a limited colour palette rather than the archetypal blaze of colour usually associated with hanging baskets.

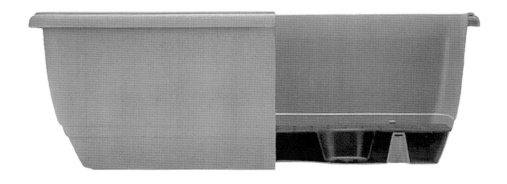

# making a windowbox

Wooden windowboxes are versatile and easy to build in any shape or size. The aim is to make a wooden surround that will enclose a standard plastic trough. Tongue-and-groove cladding is an ideal material to make the sides of the box; simply use as many planks as necessary to give the height you want. Be sure to use the heavier weight structural cladding; the one used here has a detailed profile that gives the box more style.

By using a plastic liner, the interior of the box is not in direct contact with the compost and is less liable to rot. Also, it is very easy to change the display by replacing the trough with another one planted up in a different way. The plastic trough shown here is 60cm (24in) long which is convenient for most locations.

**1.** *Measure and mark the pieces of cladding that will form the end panels of the box. For a snug fit, make these 17cm (6¾ in) wide.*

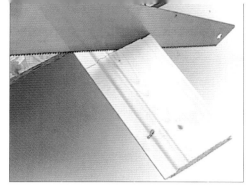

**2.** *Saw the end panels to length and sand the cut edges for a smooth finish. Each end panel will consist of two pieces of cladding.*

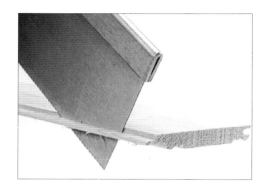

**3.** *Using a tenon saw, cut off the thinnest part of the tongue on the piece of cladding chosen to form the top of each end panel.*

**4.** *Squeeze some woodworking adhesive in the groove of the top piece of cladding and carefully push the two pieces together.*

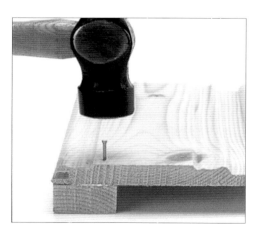

**5.** *Using panel pins or fine nails, attach the bottom edge of the end panel to a batten cut to the same width. Use adhesive to create a firmer bond.*

**6.** *Nail and glue battens along each side edge of the end panels. Punch the nail heads below the surface. Wipe off any excess adhesive with a damp cloth.*

**7.** *Cut long pieces of cladding and assemble them in pairs to make up the side panels. These should measure 63cm (25in).*

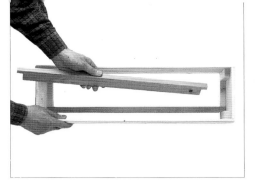

**8.** *Add adhesive and attach the side panels to the end panels with nails, creating a bottomless box that will fit around the trough.*

**9.** *Cut two pieces of roofing lathe to fit inside the box. Saw and remove a notch at each end so that they will rest on the battens.*

**10.** *Push the support rails down on to the end battens. Screw them in place or leave them loose for removal when cleaning the box.*

**11.** *Drop the trough inside the wooden windowbox so that it rests on the two rails. Drill holes in the plastic base of the trough to let water drain out. Plant up the trough like any other container and place inside the wooden box.*

BELOW: *Here, the bright yellow daffodils echo the cheerful colour of the windowbox. The centres of the colourful primroses pick up on it, too.*

## STAINING THE WINDOWBOX

Some years ago, the only options for staining wood were varying shades of brown. Today the range of stains and preservative paints is quite staggering. And what is more important, many are water-based, making them more pleasant to apply and safer to use with plants. Coordinate your plant displays carefully with the colour of the container.

BELOW: *Translucent, water-based wood stains such as these are available in a range of bright colours. They allow the grain of the wood to show through.*

# decorating containers

Decorative paint effects, such as stencilling, have been fashionable indoors for some time. Now they are moving outdoors; painted flowerpots are the latest patio accessories. But there is no need to spend a fortune because you can paint your own. Use stencils, handpainted patterns or colour washes to make new pots look much more expensive than they really are, or to give old pots a new look. You can also make new terracotta pots look weathered by dabbing shades of green, grey and yellow on to a colour-washed pot with a sponge, to simulate moss and lichen growth. After painting, add a coat of varnish to make the colours weatherproof.

Painting is also an effective way of overcoming the grey drabness of cement and concrete containers. You can buy paints formulated for concrete surfaces or use those sold for masonry. The range of colours available is very wide, although generally speaking the more natural earth shades will suit your containers better than other colours. Follow the manufacturer's instructions when using these paints – some require protective gloves, for example.

You need not limit yourself to conventional pots. Wicker baskets, cane picnic hampers and woven log baskets all make good containers, first lined with plastic and treated to protect them from the elements.

## STENCILLING WITH MASONRY PAINTS

Masonry paint is ideal for decorating terracotta containers. Since it is designed to protect brickwork and house walls, it forms a weatherproof finish. The only drawback is that the colours are usually in the pastel range, but you can create brighter shades by adding colourizers.

**ABOVE:** *A simple stencilled flower motif is a popular choice for a pot. Ensure that the stencil does not move while you work.*

*1. Attach the stencil securely to the pot with tape and apply the leaf colour by dabbing carefully with a stubby bristled stencil brush.*

*2. The first colour dries quickly and then you can add the petal colour. Make this by adding blue colourizer to basic white paint.*

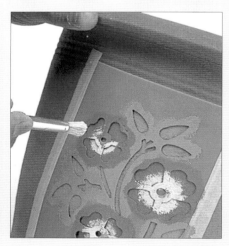

*3. To create a central ring in each flower, simply dab in some white paint. When dry, add a yellow blob in the centre of each flower.*

## USING PAINT

You can now buy small pots of paint in earth tones or brighter shades specifically designed for painting terracotta and cement containers. Start with a clean dry pot and apply the paint according to the manufacturer's instructions. Plain painted pots can be used to enhance a colour scheme and a soft Mediterranean- or vivid Moroccan-blue contrasts well with orange, red, yellow or white and silver plantings. Ordinary artist's acrylic paints can also be used, though they might not last as long. Cover with a clear acrylic varnish, as extra protection, and line terracotta with plastic to prevent moisture seeping in and lifting the paint. Being plastic-based, acrylic paints will also bond to plastic containers. When painting plastic, thoroughly scrub with detergent to remove any traces of grease, which will prevent the paint from sticking and, on glossy surfaces, give the paint something to key onto by rubbing over with sandpaper. Textured masonry paints in neutral colours can be used on large plastic pots to great effect and these look well in a modern setting. For brighter shades use tubes of masonry paint colourizers. This paint also bonds easily to concrete and terracotta.

*RIGHT: Attach the stencil with small pieces of masking tape. Use a stencil brush to pick up the paint (for this gothic design we have used gold), and then remove excess paint on paper. Apply in light circular movements, running over the edges of the stencil.*

*BELOW: Clockwise from top left: a seaside theme with stencilled shells, a weathered finish achieved by brushing with a mixture of acrylics, a stencilled gothic design in gold on a brown background, and red gloss applied in two coats over a universal primer.*

# GILDING A CONTAINER

Painting and gilding can transform a humble cast cement planter into something quite special. The patterns on this cement casting are ideal for picking out in gilding. For the base coat, choose from the huge range of pastel-toned masonry paints on offer.

*1. Start by applying a coat of exterior wall paint all over – here lovat green. Make sure the paint reaches all the crevices.*

*2. Lightly brushing with gold paint emphasizes the intricate detail of this wall planter. Filled with suitable plants, it could grace the walls of a stylish deck area.*

*3. Fill the painted wall planter with compact plants such as primula, pansies and trailing ivy. Attach it securely to the wall.*

## PAINTING WICKER BASKETS

New or secondhand wicker baskets need treating to protect them from rotting when left outdoors in all weathers. Since their natural colour soon fades in the sun, stain or paint them in natural or bright colours, depending on your planting scheme. Line them before planting.

ABOVE: *Wicker baskets with loop handles are available in many styles and sizes. Treated with water-based wood stain, they make charming planters, ideal in a country garden.*

RIGHT: *An informal mixture of pink and red flowers gives this well-filled basket its air of country charm. They include drooping fuchsias, flaring petunia trumpets and snapdragons.*

## COLOR-WASHING POTS

Terra cotta can look raw and orange when new. You can "age" the surface quickly, using a diluted color-wash of artist's acrylic. As the water is absorbed into the terra cotta, an uneven and natural-looking covering of white pigment remains. This is how to create a pink finish.

RIGHT: *Using diluted white artist's paint, roughly apply a wash to a dry container. Mix your colors together, here ultramarine and crimson, with some more white paint. Apply the paint to the dry container in rough, downward strokes to create darker and lighter "weathered" streaks. Remember to apply the darker colors cautiously.*

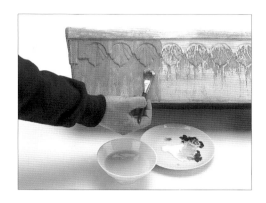

LEFT: *This pastel display is perfect for a shady spot. It contains a variegated ivy and pink and white sultan snapweeds to complement the pink trough.*

BELOW: *Color-washing works with many different colors. Here a yellow trough is perfectly enhanced by the daisy flowers of* Osteospermum *'African Summer,' little purple* Brachycome multifida, *and the variegated foliage of* Thymus x citriodorus *'Aureus' and* Salvia officinalis *'Icterina.'*

# terra-cotta containers

Most garden centers sell a wonderful range of terra-cotta containers. Some are simple but elegant clay pots, while others are much more ornate, often with detailed moldings. The color can vary, too, ranging from almost powdery white to deep, smoky brown. This is partly to do with the way the clay is fired. Always check whether pots are frostproof or only frost-resistant, as this will affect the way you have to treat them.

## TERRA COTTA ON THE DECK

A collection of simple terra-cotta pots on and around the deck evokes a sunny Mediterranean feeling. This impression is amplified by using certain kinds of plants, for example, spiky specimens and those with succulent leaves or brightly colored flowers. Ornamental grasses, sedges, and various grasslike plants are all the rage now, because gardeners have begun to realize the potential of these wonderful plants. Tufted grasses like the deschampsias, and ones with blue foliage—perhaps, for example, *Helictotrichon sempervirens* and *Festuca glauca*—look great when teamed with terra cotta.

Also try plants with colorful flowers, such as shocking tulips for spring, and lavender, oleander, and bright red geraniums (Pelargonium) for a sunny feel in summer.

**BELOW:** *Spring daffodils and anemones enjoy the well-drained conditions that terra cotta offers.*

## WINTER CARE

- *Before buying, check whether your pots are frostproof or not.*
- *Treat vulnerable pots with a terra-cotta sealant to repel moisture and frost damage.*
- *In very cold climates, protect pots with a thick wrapping of straw and plastic, or use several layers of bubble wrap around the pots.*

## WATERING TIPS

Because they are porous, terra-cotta pots tend to dry out very quickly. This makes them well suited to plants that like dry conditions, such as those from Mediterranean regions. With other plants, however, you may need to make special provisions to keep the compost moist. Either stand the pot in a saucer or treat the terra cotta with a sealant so that the compost inside retains moisture.

LEFT: *Terra cotta blends well with red and pink tones, here skimmia, primulas, and trailing ivy.*

BELOW: *Terra cotta has a natural affinity with herbs, creating a Mediterranean feel to the display.*

# planting a narrow-necked urn

Terra-cotta containers come in many shapes and sizes, but among the most elegant are the Mediterranean-style urns. The problem with these urns is that they use up a lot of compost and make repotting hard.

RIGHT: *To avoid filling the whole urn with potting compost, wedge a hanging basket snugly into the neck of the pot. Simply lodge it into position and plant it up. It can be easily lifted out when the plants need to be replaced or when they need fresh compost.*

BELOW RIGHT: *Some containers have a strong character of their own. Here, ivy accentuates the shape of the urn without competing for attention.*

LEFT: *A shady basket with ivy,* Dicentra *'Pearl Drops,'* Hosta *'August Moon,' and* Lamium maculatum *'Pink Pewter.'*

RIGHT: *An all-white scheme with alyssum, petunias, and ivy for a sunny, contemporary deck.*

FAR RIGHT: *A bold and colorful spring basket display with narcissus, primulas, anemones, and ivy, all attractively packed in with sphagnum moss.*

# hanging baskets

Hanging baskets let you use what is otherwise a hostile environment—the wall of a house is like a sheer cliff face with no toeholds! But fix in a few screws, hooks, and brackets, and you can transform bare bricks into luxuriant hanging gardens.

Generally speaking, the display is only temporary, so you can change the plants from season to season and have great fun experimenting with different schemes. Hanging baskets can be used to draw the eye toward an attractive feature, such as a decorative window, and there are a number of ways to make such vertical displays even more eye-catching. Hang an identical basket on either side of a doorway and right away you have doubled the effect. And, with several baskets hanging in a line, it is possible to create a continuous and dramatic ribbon of color.

## PLANTING A BASKET

There are all kinds of hanging basket liners, but none so attractive as living sphagnum moss. Being soft, green, and moisture retentive, it lets plants be tucked in through the sides of the basket, plugging any gaps in an attractive way. It is a good idea to soak the moss in a bucket of water before you begin and lightly squeeze the excess before use. The secret to success with moss is not to skimp on it, otherwise the potting compost will leak and the vulnerable rootballs will tend to dry out.

Obviously, the smaller the rootball of the plant, the easier it is to manipulate it through the wires of the hanging basket, but you can squeeze larger rootballs into an oval to fit them through more easily. Alternatively, use a piece of stiff paper to roll the shoots up so that the plant can be fed from the inside of the basket out. With pots of bedding ivy, simply split the compost apart with your fingers and plant the rooted cuttings individually.

*1. Stand the basket on a bucket for stability. Cut a circle from an old potting compost bag and place it black-side down in the basket. Fill the plastic circle with potting compost.*

*3. Cover the basket sides with the sweetly scented white alyssum, feeding the rootballs through the gaps so that they rest horizontally on the soil.*

**2.** *The plastic acts as a reservoir for the plants, trapping water and preventing soil from washing through. Tuck lots of sphagnum moss under the edges of the plastic for camouflage.*

**4.** *Pack moss around the necks of the plants to keep them from drying out. Add a sultan snapweed, a pot of lotus, petunias, ivy, and a white pelargonium.*

# HANGING A BASKET

Hanging baskets are traditionally suspended by a doorway, where the shape and style of the display can be best appreciated. However, there are plenty of other options. Hang them from the end of arbor poles or suspend a collection of baskets from brackets to decorate a large, plain wall. Wall planters are more often used in the latter situation, but being smaller, they are better suited to more intimate spots, where they add fine detail.

**1.** *Put the bracket against the wall and mark the position of the screw holes. Using a hammer-action drill and the correct masonry bit, drill the top hole in the wall. Push a wall anchor into the hole, making sure that it fits tightly.*

**2.** *Fix the top screw loosely so that you can check the position of the second hole. Make any necessary adjustments.*

**3.** *Drill and plug the second hole and screw the bracket firmly in place against the wall. Use matching round-headed screws.*

# spring displays

Even though it may be too cold to sit outside in the spring, the deck is still visible from indoors and a colorful display is welcome after a long winter. Good plants for spring containers are bulbs—daffodils, hyacinths, tulips—and polyanthus, wallflowers, stocks, and bellis daisies. When planting in containers in the spring, choose plants that are still in tight bud to give them time to adjust to the conditions before the flowers open. Add a few evergreens, such as ivies and conifers, to set off the flowers.

# terra-cotta wall pots

This spring display is a rich blend of jewel-colored primulas (*Primula* 'Wanda') and deep pink hyacinths, beautifully enhanced by a terra-cotta wall basket with classical-style relief.

*1. (right) Line the pot with black plastic to retain moisture, and make a hole in the plastic in line with the drainage hole. Half-fill the pot with potting compost.*

*2. (right) Firm the compost lightly, then remove the hyacinths from their pots. Place the hyacinths against the back of the terra-cotta wall pot, leaving space for the primulas in front. You may need to shake some of the compost from around the roots to create more room.*

*3. Fill the remaining space in the pot with the primulas. Don't worry if the hyacinths look a bit awkward at first—the primulas will soon cover up the bulbs. Squeeze the primula rootballs into an oval shape so you can fit in as many as possible. Water regularly and deadhead as the flowers fade.*

# alpine sink display

The traditional container for alpines was an old-fashioned "butler's" sink, but you can adapt modern sinks by covering them with hypertufa. This is a mix of equal parts by volume of cement, gritty sand, and moss peat with water to mix into a paste. Use wire wool to rough up the surface of the sink and cover with tile adhesive to help the hypertufa to bond.

All containers must have drainage holes in the bottom. Most alpines will thrive in a free-draining compost with some organic matter to hold moisture. Moisture-loving plants, such as tiny alpine primulas, *Dodecatheon* and *Ramonda*, are happy in a mixture of equal parts soil- and peat-based potting mix. Be sure to group plants that will happily share similar conditions. Most alpines will thrive in a situation where they get direct sun for at least half the day, although very drought-tolerant, sun-loving kinds, such as sedums and sempervivums, need a very sunny spot. Water sink gardens in dry weather, and feed plants occasionally with weak tomato feed.

**1.** *Cover the drainage holes with crocks. These prevent soil from running out but let excess water drain away freely. Almost fill the sink with equal parts of lime-free gritty sand, soil-based compost, and coir, coarse peat, or sterilized leaf mulch.*

**2.** *Decide on the arrangement, starting from the center. Tip each plant out of its pot and use a small trowel to scoop out a hole. Nestle plants into the corners so the sink has a well-filled but natural look. Make sure a few plants trail over to soften the sides.*

**3.** *Choose a few small pieces of stone and tuck them in among the plants as you work. These add contours, trap condensation in hot weather, and help to keep plant roots cool. When all the plants and rocks are in place, spread a layer of gravel or granite chippings over the whole surface as a stone mulch.*

**4.** *The sink garden looks good right away, but will improve as plants blend together and spill over the sides. Water well and raise up on bricks for extra drainage—a vital consideration.*

# spring manger basket

A large, manger-style basket can create an impressive wall feature to brighten up a bare expanse of brickwork. It could also be used under a window, like a window box. Though not very wide, there is room along the length for a good selection of colorful spring plants.

*1. (left) Line the back and base of the basket with black plastic and the front with moist sphagnum moss, tucking it under the plastic. Pour some compost into the basket and plant some violas through the gaps between the bars into the compost behind.*

*2. (right) Plant three pots of tulips into the compost behind the violas, breaking up the rootballs so the tulips form more of a line at the back, rather than three tight clumps. Fill the spaces between the tulips with more compost.*

*3. (left) Add some yellow polyanthus (here 'Crescendo Primrose') and some pink bellis daisies, planting them between the tulips and the violas. Fill any gaps with more compost, then tuck in more moss along the front of the basket to cover the compost. Once the tulips fade, replace them with more pot-grown spring bulbs.*

# metal bucket display

Metal pails make fun containers, especially for children's gardens, and are easily converted to hanging baskets with a length of silver-colored chain. Because of their size, dwarf bulbs are particularly suited to hanging baskets, especially dwarf narcissi, grape hyacinths, scillas, and *Anemone blanda*, all of which flower over a relatively long period of time. Once flowering has finished, continue to feed and water, maintaining the foliage to let the bulbs build up reserves and flower again the following spring.

*1.* *(left) Choose a variety of spring bulbs—these are* Narcissus 'Tête à Tête,' Muscari armeniacum *(grape hyacinth),* and Chionodoxa luciliae. *Put a layer of gravel or small bits of polystyrene into the buckets to provide a drainage layer.*

*2.* *Add a little soil to the buckets. Use a gritty, free-draining potting mixture, as there are no drainage holes in the bottoms of the buckets. If it helps, remove the bucket handles to make planting a little easier.*

*3.* *Remove some of the compost from around the roots of the daffodils. Plant them into one of the buckets. Split up a clump of muscari by gently teasing the roots apart, and plant around the daffodils. Fill the gaps with compost.*

*4.* *In the other bucket, plant a clump of muscari in the middle. Make an outer ring of pale chionodoxa. Cover exposed roots or bulbs with potting compost and water to settle it in. Keep the compost just moist; do not overwater.*

# spring primula basket

In this display, a fresh scheme of yellow and white spring flowers and foliage contrasts with a dark green basket. The basket is a self-watering model to cut down on maintenance. As it has solid sides, all the planting has to go in the top, so choose at least one plant with long trails to soften the edges. Hang the basket in a lightly shaded, sheltered spot.

*1. Self-watering baskets have to be assembled when new. Follow the directions carefully. Despite their name, they do need some attention: Check water levels regularly and refill the reservoir when necessary.*

*2. Add a layer of moist compost to the basket. Try the largest plant for size, and add more compost if the top of its rootball does not come to within an inch of the basket rim.*

*3. Plant two drumstick primulas in the basket, nestling them down into the compost. Next fill the gaps left on one side of the basket with one or two variegated euonymus plants. Add more potting compost as you go.*

*4. Next add two yellow primroses, one on each side of the basket's watering tube. Leave space around the rim of the basket for some trails of ivy.*

*5. Split apart a couple of pots of variegated ivy by gently teasing the roots apart. Plant them around the edges of the basket and fill the gaps around their roots with more compost and firm well. Water thoroughly.*

# woodland tub

This recycled fiber pot has been planted with dainty woodland plants for an endearing spring display that will flower year after year. As these are all woodland plants, this tub is perfect for a shady deck and brings the spirit of the countryside to your back door.

*1. Choose a large fiber pot and cover **each of the drainage holes with rocks to** keep the compost from seeping out. Next fill the pot to within a few inches of its rim with a soil-based compost.*

*2. Choose a selection of woodland plants, and, leaving them in their pots for the time being, arrange them together in the container while you decide on a pleasing arrangement.*

*3. Plant the foliage plant first—here a hardy fern—then add the flowering primulas. Knock each one carefully out of its pot and plant it without breaking up the rootball.*

*4. Tuck in a few edging plants, such as ivies and violets, around the edges of the pot to soften the look. Fill any gaps between plants with more compost and firm lightly. Water well and keep moist.*

# summer displays

In summer, bedding plants, summer-flowering bulbs, patio roses, dwarf shrubs, herbs, and perennials all contribute to a riot of color on the deck. You can choose a traditional mixture of colors or, for a more sophisticated effect, a scheme based on just one or two colors. Use color with care—decide whether you prefer a strongly contrasting effect or a subtly harmonizing one. In the summer months, containers will need more care than at other times of year. Feed tubs once a week to prolong the flower power and water regularly in dry weather.

# Mediterranean summer tub

This sunny terra-cotta pot contains a range of plants redolent of the Mediterranean—osteospermums in white, red, and pink, purple basil, fragrant bay, cockscomb (*Celosia*), and silver-leaved ozothamnus.

**1.** *Select a sufficient number of drought-resistant plants for the tub. Fill the tub with a soil-based compost to within six inches of the pot rim. Start by putting the tallest plant at the back.*

**2.** *Knock each plant out of its pot, carefully supporting the stem as you go. Gently tease out any large roots coiled around the rootball, but avoid breaking it up. Plant the other osteospermums in front of the first one.*

**3.** *Complete the display by planting the smaller plants around the edges of the tub, with the bay tree in the middle. Add more compost, firm, and water well.*

# bright wall planter

This terra cotta–colored wall pot contains a selection of bright bedding plants in vivid but carefully matched colors. It is unusual to combine an orange-red container with deep pink flowers, but the overall effect is one of rich tones and strong hues, perfect for standing out on a wall behind the deck. The deep-pink double petunia in the center is 'Purple Pirouette'; it is enhanced by sultan snapweed 'Accent Lilac.' The ivy-leaved pelargoniums, 'Butterfly' and 'Summer Showers,' provide both foliage and flowers.

Keep the planter well watered; wall-mounted containers dry out even quicker than hanging baskets, so check twice daily in hot weather.

*1. This type of wall pot is designed for use indoors or out; for outdoor use, first make holes in the base for drainage. Tap through the weak points marked on the base using the tip of a screwdriver.*

*2. Half-fill the basket with a peat-substitute compost that will retain moisture in a small, densely planted container. Start to plant the basket, using the darker flowers in the center and the paler flowers at the edges.*

*3. Knock the plants out of their pots and plant the rootballs as closely together as possible to the same depth as they were in their pots. The denser the planting, the better it will look—if you have a tiny gap, try one more plant.*

*4. Fill any gaps between plants with more compost, firming it gently between the rootballs. Water the finished container very well. Tease out the trailing stems of the ivy-leaved pelargoniums over the front of the planter to soften the edges. Hang it in a warm, sheltered, sunny spot.*

# variegated viola basket

In a border, you can enhance the beauty of individual flowering plants with a suitable backdrop of foliage. Here the same principle has been applied to highlight a mass of purple viola blooms. The velvety violas need to be surrounded by lighter foliage to do them justice, so here they are combined with the cream-edged leaves of fuchsia 'Sharpitor' at the back of the basket, variegated ground ivy (*Glechoma hederacea* 'Variegata'), and a cream-edged trailing ivy, *Hedera helix* 'Mini Adam.' The fuchsia is hardy, so plant it out in the garden when the display is over.

**1.** *Line the base of the basket with a circle of black plastic cut from an old compost bag. Camouflage the plastic by packing sphagnum moss under it.*

**2.** *The lining will trap moisture and act like a reservoir to keep the compost from drying. Fill the basket with compost and pack more moss around the edges.*

**3.** *Separate a pot of rooted ivy cuttings by gently teasing the roots apart. Plant some of the cuttings between the wires of the basket down the sides, pushing the roots through into the compost.*

**4.** *Pack moss around the ivy cuttings to keep them moist. Soak the remaining plants before adding them to the basket. Add the fuchsia at the back and violas in front.*

**5.** *Add the ground ivy and trailing ivy plants around the edges of the basket. Add the remaining violas and fill the gaps between the rootballs with more compost. Water the basket well.*

# country-style wicker basket

Wicker baskets lend themselves to informal displays of country garden flowers, such as penstemon, achillea, lythrum, astilbe, and phygelius in varying shades of pink and red. For best results, choose plants that are about one and a half times the height of the basket.

**1.** *Loosely line a wicker basket with black plastic and make a few holes in the bottom. Place a few inches of clean gravel in the bottom, then partially fill with soil-based potting compost.*

**2.** *Put the tallest plants—here lythrum—in the center back of the display to create a graduated effect. Use a mixture of flower shapes for contrast, vital in a display with restricted colors.*

**3.** *When all the plants are happily arranged, fill the gaps between the rootballs with compost and firm well. Roll the plastic liner over to make a firm edge and tuck it inside the basket rim.*

**4.** *Water the basket well. Next add a chipped bark mulch, which will look decorative, team well with the basket, and help to keep the plants' roots cool and moist.*

# hanging ball

When properly planted, a normal hanging basket will eventually grow into a generous, well-filled shape. To make a perfect sphere, you need a special container and neat plants. You can make your own ball of bloom using two 10-in. hanging baskets and twenty sultan snapweed plants. This container uses twice as much compost as a normal hanging basket, so is much slower to dry out, and the layer of moss all around creates better insulation to keep the plant roots cool. These are both important factors when growing sultan snapweed, as they prefer cooler, moister conditions than most other container plants.

The ball could hang in partial shade or in a spot that receives a few hours of sunlight a day. Morning and evening sun is best, as sultan snapweeds scorch easily in bright light.

This display is much heavier than a normal basket, so check that brackets and supporting chains are strong and firmly fixed. This container makes a dramatic centerpiece to a deck. Team it with pyramidal or pillar topiary shapes surrounded by a colorful carpet of plants for a formal look. For a more country-garden effect on the deck, team it with a selection of informal containers filled with flowers.

*1. Prepare two identical moss-lined wire baskets. Plant a row of sultan snapweed as close as possible to the base of each. Use buckets for support.*

*2. Tuck moss around each plant and fill the baskets to the brim with compost; firm well. Plant another row of sultan snapweed at the top of one basket.*

*3. Water the baskets thoroughly and top up the compost again if necessary. Place a piece of wood or cardboard over the basket planted with just one row of plants, and hold it down firmly in place.*

*4. Invert this basket over the second basket and check that the plants are randomly arranged. Make sure the baskets are perfectly aligned, one over the other, then gently pull out the card.*

*5. Use plastic-coated wire to secure the two baskets together at several points around the rim. Green wire shows up least. Twist the ends together firmly with pliers. Hang up the basket securely.*

# instant cottage garden

Create an instant cottage garden on your deck with these terracotta tubs overflowing with old-fashioned bedding plants, including dwarf sunflowers, sweet alyssum, snapdragons (antirrhinums), nicotiana, pelargoniums and simple white daisies.

*1. Choose plenty of different annuals and a pair of simple matching terracotta pots, one larger than the other. Cover the drainage holes with crocks, then part-fill the pots with compost.*

*2. Plant the biggest and boldest plant (the sunflower) towards the centre back of the larger pot to act as a focal point. Next position some slightly shorter plants, here red snapdragons, around it.*

*3. Choose something striking as the centrepiece of the smaller pot, but allow the centrepiece of the larger pot to dominate the display. Here we have used a red pelargonium in the small pot.*

*4. Add more flowers to fill the pots, working from the back towards the front, with the smallest at the front. Fill the gaps between the roots with more compost and firm lightly. Water well.*

# pink and green windowbox

Green is a colour which is guaranteed to go with any plants, so it is the perfect shade for a windowbox. This subtle sea-green box is enhanced with soft pink osteospermums and dusky silver foliage to lift the whole display. See pages 124–5 for details of how to make the simple windowbox.

*1. Three osteospermums in varying shades of pink, plus six silver-leaved Senecio cineraria plants complement this silvery green windowbox perfectly and will be enough to fill it.*

*2. Drill some holes in the bottom of the plastic windowbox liner to aid drainage, then slip it into the wooden box. Half-fill the liner with potting compost and firm it down gently.*

*3. Remove the osteospermums from their pots and arrange in the box. Plant the darkest ostespermum in the centre of the display. This will attract the eye and dominate the scheme.*

*4. Tuck the silver cinerarias in at either end of the windowbox. Angle them outwards slightly so they grow over the edges of the box. Top up the compost between the plants, firm and water.*

# fiery annuals

Large plastic tubs make excellent and economical homes for temporary displays of seasonal colour, especially those in hot colours to complement the terracotta colour of the tub. Whatever plants you choose, make sure you have a large centrepiece – this tub features a striking black-eyed susan (*Thunbergia alata*) supported on a cane. It will soon grow to the top of the cane and flower all summer. Here it is accompanied by African marigolds, French marigolds, red salvia 'Vanguard', colourful coleus, ornamental cabbage and *Argyranthemum* 'Jamaica Primrose'.

*1.* Gather together a selection of plants for a bright scheme of red, orange and yellow. Fill the tub with soilless potting compost and insert a cane into the compost to support the climber.

*2.* Plant the centrepiece first – here the climbing black-eyed susan. Plant it close to the base of the cane, then tie the top growth loosely to the cane to encourage it to grow upwards.

*3.* Group other plants of the same type close together and plant contrasting plants next to each other to create some excitement. Add more compost between the plants as necessary.

*4.* A foliage plant, such as this fiery coleus, makes a good foil for a group of flowers. Plant the cabbage close to the edge where it will form a huge rosette. Firm the compost and water well.

# autumn displays

Decks can easily lose their impact in autumn as summer annuals come to the end. To maintain the display, raise or buy a late crop of annuals for midsummer planting. By late summer, they will be in bloom and ready to replace other spent plants in your containers. Alternatively, winter-flowering pansies, dwarf dahlias and bedding asters are available in garden centres already in bloom, so replant summer containers for an autumn display. There are also countless very attractive autumn-interest perennials which team up nicely for some interesting effects.

# pansies in simple pots

With such an array of plants available, it is tempting to pack as many different plants as possible into a pot. However, this very simple display of pansies carefully matched to a pretty pot has an understated elegance.

*1. (left) Cover the drainage hole with a small crock. This frost-resistant, ceramic pot is painted with an Oriental-style design. The purple pansies will pick up on the blue in the pot and enhance it.*

*2. Loosely fill the pot with potting compost and firm lightly. Top up again to within 5cm (2in) of the pot rim. Pack in as many plants as possible. A pot this size will take four pansy plants.*

*3. Carefully push each plant out of the pack through the hole in the base. Remove any dead leaves or flowers. You may need to squeeze the rootballs gently in order to fit them into the pot.*

*4. When all the plants are in place, fill any gaps between the rootballs with potting compost, leaving about 1.5cm (½in) between the top of the compost and the pot rim for watering.*

# campanula basket

This pretty wicker basket has a rustic look, so the planting style has been chosen to be soft and relaxed, just like a cottage garden border. Here, *Campanula carpatica* 'Blue Clips' is teamed with gold-leaved trailing ivy for a late summer and autumn display. Hang the basket from a rustic pergola or stand it on a table, but choose a spot where you can really appreciate the flowers close-to.

*1. (left) Line the basket with black plastic to protect the wicker and prevent the compost drying out too quickly. To make trimming easier, put some gravel in the base to keep the plastic in place.*

*2. Add more gravel or small pieces of broken polystyrene to create a drainage layer. Part-fill the basket with soilless compost and firm lightly.*

*3. Plant the ivies around the edges of the basket, arranging the longest trails so they create a rim of greenery that spills over the basket's dipped edge.*

*4. Fill the centre of the basket with the campanulas. Try not to hide the handle as this is part of the display. Fill in any gaps with compost, then water lightly.*

# stately pink urn

Paint effects can transform inexpensive plastic urns into containers that earn their place as focal points on the deck – this one has been painted to look like real stone. When planting up an urn like this, choose a simple but striking planting scheme. This one uses a limited colour palette of deep pink winter-flowering heather and berried gaultheria, lighter pink *Sedum spectabile*, pink ornamental cabbages and variegated ivy with cream markings. Since plastic containers are lightweight, it is essential to weight the base of the urn down well with gravel or crocks. This will prevent the container falling over.

**1.** *Put a good layer of crocks or gravel in the base to weight it down and aid drainage. Part-fill with compost and begin planting from the back with the tallest plants, here sedums and heathers.*

**2.** *As this is only a temporary seasonal display, use a mixture of whatever plants look good together and are the right size. Next position the gaultheria towards the centre of the urn.*

**3.** *Angle the ornamental cabbages towards the outside of the urn for added impact. Tuck trailing ivy around the front edge to soften the urn. Top up with more compost and water well.*

# autumn shrubs

This handsome pottery strawberry tower has been filled with a selection of autumn-interest shrubs for a rich combination of colours. The dark foliage of *Leucothoe* 'Carinella' has been teamed with the pink berries of gaultheria and a range of autumn-flowering heathers – all cultivars of *Calluna vulgaris* and *Erica vagans*.

*1.* Cover the drainage hole with a crock, then part-fill the pot with compost to just below the bottom planting pockets. Use ericaceous compost as the heathers need acid conditions. Firm the compost lightly.

*2.* Buy heathers in small pots so that the rootballs will fit into the planting pockets. Tip out the plants and push them into the holes. If the rootballs are congested, tease out a few of the roots.

*3.* (left) Add more compost to cover the roots and bring the level up to the next pockets. Plant the remaining heathers.

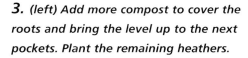

*4.* Plant the top of the pot next. It is vital to fill up the container with plants because plants put in at the end of the growing season will not grow much more but need to make an impact.

*5.* Add two or three ivy plants round the rim, pulling the trails through the pot handles and round between the heathers in the side pockets for an instantly mature effect. Water well.

# winter displays

Small evergreen shrubs with variegated, silver or aromatic foliage, such as euonymus, santolina and rosemary, together with ivies, make the backbone of most winter displays in tubs, windowboxes and hanging baskets. Add long-lasting berries of skimmia and flowers of winter jasmine. Use young plants bought from garden centres and give them a season's use in containers before planting them in the garden. For flowers, add winter heathers or pansies.

*1. Line the back and base of the basket with black plastic and the front and sides with sphagnum moss. Use a thick, tightly packed layer of moss to act as insulation.*

*4. When planting the cyclamen, tilt them slightly forwards so that the foliage hangs over the edge of the basket. Fill in with more compost and water lightly.*

# winter cherry wall basket

The festive winter cherry (*Solanum pseudocapsicum*) arrives in the shops in late autumn and makes an ideal subject for a basket next to the back door for the holiday period. Here,

*2. Add compost to the base of the basket to just below the level of moss. Break up pots of rooted ivy cuttings and plant through the bars into the compost.*

pure white cyclamen and white variegated ivy provide a foil for the red berries. For a richer combination, try deep red cyclamen and dark green ivy. Although these plants are thought of as houseplants, they will survive outdoors in a sheltered spot in town, especially if they can be protected from rain and frost.

*3. Pack moss around the neck of each ivy and build up the moss lining to the top of the basket. Plant two winter cherries at the back of the basket.*

# wirework ivy chicken

An endearing chicken-shaped basket is planted with moss and small-leaved trailing ivy to make a display which looks good all year. A chain has been attached to the basket so it can be hung from a pergola. Keep the compost moist and the ivy trimmed to maintain the shape.

*1. (left) This wire basket is actually an egg holder but it makes a great hanging basket. You will need about three ivy plants, depending on the size. Choose an ivy with small, neat leaves.*

*2. (right) Stuff the head of the basket with moist sphagnum moss. Next line the body of the basket with more moss, creating a thick outer layer and leaving the centre hollow for planting.*

*3. Fill the middle of the basket with a moisture-retentive potting compost. Work it into the interior space and firm it down gently.*

*4. Divide up the pots of ivy, separating out the individual cuttings. Plant them in the top of the basket, arranging them in a circle to ensure even coverage.*

*5. Cut lengths of florists' wire and bend them in half. Cover the body with ivy by pinning the trails into the moss at intervals. Water the basket and keep moist.*

# festive tub

Festive holly and ivy foliage form the basis of this winter display, backed up by traditional berries and evergreen foliage, with ornamental cabbage which makes a long-lasting alternative to winter flowers. If you cannot find a standard-trained holly, you could remove all but one of the stems of a poorly shaped bush to convert it into an instant standard. Alternatively, use a bush holly with fewer plants around it. Two identical tubs could be used either side of a doorway for a grand entrance.

*1. (left) This display uses holly 'Golden King', golden heather* Erica arborea *'Albert's Gold',* Gaultheria procumbens *with its red berries, pink* Calluna vulgaris *'Alexandra', ivy and ornamental cabbage.*

*2. (right) Cover the drainage hole with a crock, then part-fill the pot with a soil-based compost.*

*3. Stand the holly in the centre of the tub and plant the golden heather at the base to soften the upright line of the trunk. Firm in gently.*

*4. Plant gaultheria and pink heather at the front and the taller cabbages at the back. Add the ivy at the side. Add more compost, firm gently then water in.*

# evergreens for shade

Many types of evergreen plants are suitable for shady spots, and have the added advantage of year-round colour. This half barrel contains an evergreen fern (*Asplenium scolopendrium*), the thick rounded leaves of elephant's ears (*Bergenia cordifolia* 'Purpurea') and *Gaultheria procumbens*, grown for its red berries.

**1.** *Choose a roomy half barrel and loosely fit a large black bag into the bottom, leaving the surplus rolled up around the top. Almost fill the barrel with compost.*

**2.** *Trim away the excess plastic with scissors, leaving a 5cm (2in) overlap. Roll the edge of the liner over and tuck it between the compost and the tub.*

**3.** *Begin by planting the biggest, most striking plant near the back of the barrel. This fern is the hardy hart's tongue fern (Asplenium).*

**4.** *Plant the bergenia to one side of the fern and the gaultheria on the other to hide the compost and fill the tub. Top up the compost and water well.*

# wicker wall pots

These baskets are ideal containers for a simple but effective display. For maximum impact, team two similar baskets together and plant them so that although each one is different, they both have something in common to hold the display together – in this case charming winter pansies.

*1. (left) Line the baskets with bubble plastic for insulation – this should prevent the compost freezing in cold weather. Begin filling the baskets with compost and firm gently.*

*2. When the liner is well bedded down, trim the top, leaving an overlap of 2.5cm (1in). Roll the edge of the plastic and tuck it down inside the basket.*

*3. Plant the largest plant first, placing it centrally at the back of the basket. Slightly mound up the soil underneath to make it stand out better.*

*4. Tuck smaller plants in round the sides, packing in as many as possible for a full display. Fill any gaps with more compost and water in the plants.*

# glazed pink heather pot

Larger, low-level containers, such as tubs and troughs, allow for more expansive displays based around heathers. Try combining them with miniature conifers, evergreen shrubs and grasses or alpines. Here a simple conifer forms the centrepiece of a pink heather pot.

*1. (left) Cover the drainage holes with crocks or pebbles to prevent the compost washing out the bottom of the tub. This glazed tub will hold moisture better and need less frequent watering than plain terracotta pots.*

*2. (left) Fill the container with potting compost up to about a third. You don't need to use ericaceous compost as winter-flowering heathers do not require acid conditions.*

*3. (left) Position the conifer centrally in the tub so that the top of the rootball is about 2.5cm (1in) below the rim. This conifer is Chameacyparis thyoides 'Purple Heather'.*

*4. (right) Space the heathers evenly around the conifer, squeezing the rootballs slightly to make them fit in the tub. These heathers are Erica carnea 'Rosalie', E.c. 'March Seedling' and E. darleyensis 'Darley Dale'. Fill the spaces between the rootballs with more compost until the container is loosely filled to just below the rim. Water well.*

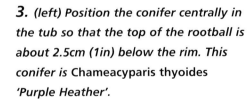

# edible displays

Edible plants can be surprisingly decorative as well as useful, so consider growing some in containers on the deck. Pots of evergreen and flowering herbs are good close to gangways and steps, where they will release their fragrance as you brush past them. Group favourite culinary herbs where they are convenient for the kitchen – suspended in a herbal hanging basket, perhaps. Save valuable deck space for plants that need sun and heat, such as tomatoes, peppers and aubergines; citrus plants, such as oranges and lemons, need this position too. In a small garden, use tubs and troughs to turn your deck into a productive vegetable garden. A wall or fence, covered with netting or trellis, is the perfect way to support a thriving crop of beans, peas or trailing courgettes. Use a large container to keep yourself conveniently supplied with a selection of salad leaves conveniently near the house. By growing them without the use of any chemicals, and picking within an hour of eating, you will enjoy the flavour of homegrown produce far better than anything you could buy.

RIGHT: *A strawberry planter allows lots of plants to be grown in a small space and makes protecting the fruit easier.*

FAR RIGHT: *Citrus fruit, such as this calamondin orange, can be stood out on a sunny deck in the summer months.*

RIGHT: *Most herbs are perfect for containers and will survive happily for many years. This pot contains two types of thyme, tricolor sage, dwarf lavender and houseleek.*

LEFT: *Here three terracotta pots have been placed one inside the other to show off the colours, shapes and textures of the mints growing in them.*

# salad leaves

Nowadays, many kinds of edible leaves are popular as garnishes and ingredients for green salads; planted together, they make a decorative and useful container display. The best 'ingredients' for a container salad garden are those that can be picked little and often: sorrel, purslane, rocket, land cress, salad burnet and cut-and-come-again lettuce, such as 'Salad Bowl'. Planted in spring, the same plants can be picked over lightly for most of the summer. If the container is large enough, add a few hearting salads, such as Chinese cabbage, Cos and normal lettuce and radicchio-type chicory. Where available, choose miniature varieties, as they take up less room and are faster-maturing. As soon as a plant forms a heart big enough to use, cut it, remove any remaining foliage, pull the root out carefully and put in a new plant. This way you can obtain a regular succession of salads from a relatively small space.

*1. Loosely fill a wooden planter (with drainage holes) with rich potting compost. Choose a selection of plants with a floppy or low, semi-trailing habit for the edges and corners.*

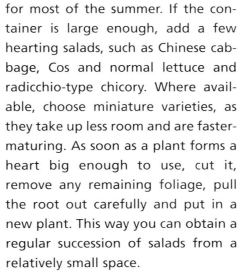

*2. Place the plants as close to the edge as possible to make full use of the space. The low plants allow light to reach all parts of the container. Add an edible-flowered plant, such as nasturtium, in the centre.*

*3. French sorrel is a leaf salad, with large, lemon-flavoured leaves. This perennial plant can be cut little and often over several years, but it will die down in winter to reappear the following spring. Chinese cabbages grow quickly and are safer from slugs and snails in a raised container, but make sure that the potting mixture does not dry out, otherwise they are likely to run to seed. The plants form chunky hearts.*

*5. Although the tub will soon look crowded, plants around the edge will spread out over the sides, while plants such as sorrel and purslane will be picked regularly.*

*4. Put in all the remaining plants 15cm (6in) apart. Water well after planting, and check daily, as the compost will start drying out fast when the tub fills with roots, and in hot weather. Begin liquid feeding after four weeks.*

# tomato hanging basket

Several kinds of edible plant make attractive hanging baskets, especially when teamed with complementary ornamental flowers. Tomatoes are a good example and are here teamed up with French marigolds. The marigolds attract beneficial insects that help prevent pests attacking the tomatoes, so you should not need to spray the plants, which is ideal for organic gardeners.

*1. Line a large hanging basket with a thick coco-fibre liner for insulation and an inner lining made from black plastic to hold moisture.*

*2. Loosely fill the basket with potting compost and firm the mix down gently. The weight of the compost will settle the liner into all the curves.*

*3. Trim the edges of the liner. Space three trailing tomato plants evenly around the basket. Fill the spaces between them with French marigolds.*

*4. Water the basket well. Use diluted liquid tomato feed to encourage heavy fruiting and avoid excess leafy growth.*

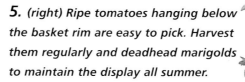

*5. (right) Ripe tomatoes hanging below the basket rim are easy to pick. Harvest them regularly and deadhead marigolds to maintain the display all summer.*

LEFT: *As the fruits mature on this bush variety, they provide attractive colours, ranging from pale green to bright red. The fruits on each truss usually ripen at different times, which avoids having a glut to eat up and means the fresh crop is spread over a longer period.*

# strawberry tower

Strawberries make excellent subjects for tubs, and high-rise containers are a good space-saving way of growing them. Strawberry plants are neat and compact, and also highly decorative.

Prevent slugs and snails spoiling the fruit by smearing crop protection jelly around the base of containers. A strawberry container can be started in autumn or spring. Strawberry runners are available in autumn and should be planted straight away so that the roots do not dry out. Small pot-grown plants are also sold in spring; plant as early as possible.

ABOVE: *As the fruits develop, protect them from birds with a net supported on a frame. Tuck the netting around the plant and hold it down with bricks. Pick the fruit daily. By early summer, the plants will have filled the container with fruit cascading down over the tiers.*

*1. Make a support to stabilize the tower of pots by screwing a length of wooden pole to a flat base and sit the biggest pot over it. Part-fill the pot with any good-quality potting compost.*

*2. Put six strawberry plants around the edge of the pot, spreading the roots out and firming lightly.*

*3. Set the second pot in place. This should be smaller to allow room for the first tier of plants to grow. Firm and level the pot and part-fill with compost.*

*4. Plant four strawberry plants around the edge, but not directly above those in the lower pot, so the fruits hang down evenly around the edges.*

*5. (left) Fit the smallest pot in place, put two plants in the top and fill to the brim with compost; firm well. Top up the other tiers if you need to. Water well.*

*6. (right) Pour gravel into the saucer for extra stability. Feed weekly with half-strength liquid tomato fertilizer.*

# container care

Above all else, the secret of successful containers lies in regular watering. Check containers daily in warm weather by testing them with a finger tip or water meter, and water whenever the potting compost starts to dry out. Keep as evenly moist as possible for optimum growth. In a hot summer, well-filled containers in full bloom may need watering twice a day. Mornings and evenings are the best times to water; during the middle of the day the water can simply evaporate before the plants have had a chance to take it up.

### HOW TO WATER

Use a watering can or a slow-running hosepipe to water. Apply enough water to each container so that it permeates right to the bottom of the pot. If you merely wet the surface layer each time, the plants will produce very shallow roots and will be even more prone to drying out.

Avoid overwatering, however. If you allow the water to pour out the bottom of the container it will take with it all the nutrients in the compost and deprive the plants.

Take particular care with containers which do not have drainage holes, or pots that are standing in saucers, as there is nowhere for the excess water to run. Very few plants can survive in sodden compost as there is no oxygen for their roots. Water only when the surface of the compost feels completely dry.

### REWETTING DRIED COMPOST

Potting compost which has dried out completely, especially a peat-based product, is difficult to rewet because the compost shrinks, letting water trickle down the insides of the pot rather than being absorbed. This is often a problem in hanging baskets as they dry out quickly, but it can be a problem in all containers in hot or windy weather.

The quickest solution is to stand dried-out pots in a deep container of water, such as a bucket, for several hours until the compost is completely rehydrated. Do not leave them overnight as roots can drown.

If containers are too large, make a shallow depression in the centre of the compost and fill it with water. It will soak in slowly. Top it up several times so that the moisture permeates the compost which will start to swell. Do not be tempted to feed plants which have dried out badly until they have completely recovered.

## PLASTIC LINERS

**ABOVE:** *A plastic liner will help reduce the amount of watering necessary by retaining moisture in the tub. Black bin bags are perfect for the job – simply line the tub loosely, make a few holes in the bottom and fill up the tub with compost. Cut off the excess plastic, roll down the top and tuck it down between the compost and the tub so it is not visible.*

**BELOW:** *These drought-resistant plants don't need much watering. They are Sedum lineare 'Variegatum', echeveria, Sedum spathulifolium 'Cape Blanco' and Sedum spurium 'Purple Carpet'.*

ABOVE: *A hose is a great boon if you have lots of containers on the deck or if they are spread out. Set the hose so the flow is gentle or you will wash the compost away from the plant roots.*

ABOVE: *A watering can is well suited to smaller containers, or for those who only have a few containers to water. Fit a rose to the spout of the watering can for very small or delicate plants.*

# WATER-RETAINING GEL CRYSTALS

Water-retaining gel crystals can absorb great quantities of water so they are mixed with potting compost where they will slowly release their water and reduce the need for frequent watering. They are specially valuable in hanging baskets and small containers liable to drying out.

*1. Mix the crystals with water as directed on the packet. Leave them to absorb the water and stir the mixture thoroughly to make a thick gel. A stick or old chopstick will be perfect for stirring.*

*2. As they absorb the water, the crystals will swell up to many times their original size. When the gel has absorbed as much water as it can, add it to your potting compost in a suitable dish or tray for stirring.*

*3. Stir the gel thoroughly into the potting compost. Once it is combined, use the compost in the normal way for potting up containers and hanging baskets which are prone to drying out quickly. The gel will last a whole season, swelling when you water and slowly releasing its moisture into the compost as it dries out.*

# WATERING HANGING BASKETS

Hanging baskets need more regular watering than other other containers because they contain a higher density of plants in a small amount of compost and do not have solid sides to prevent evaporation. They are also far more exposed to the elements and can dry out on all sides.

**1.** *Water baskets at least once a day, twice in particularly warm weather. You will find that baskets in a windy site are far more prone to drying out. A regular watering can is fine for baskets which are quite low down, or if you have something to stand on.*

ABOVE: *Automatic irrigation systems are ideal for containers and deliver water via drip nozzles. Systems like this can be connected to an outdoor tap via a pre-set water computer.*

**2.** *An empty plastic bottle is also a useful aid to watering, especially if you have just one or two baskets. It is lighter and easier to direct than a full watering can. A slow but steady stream of water has the best chance of soaking into the compost rather than running off.*

BELOW: *Larger containers, such as half barrels, require less frequent watering and feeding than smaller pots due to the larger volume of compost.*

**3.** *Long-handled attachments can be bought to fit onto the end of a hosepipe to make watering baskets much easier. The attachments have an on/off button on the handle so you only need to squirt once the nozzle is in position. These are invaluable if you have a lot of high baskets to tend to.*

## FEEDING PLANTS

A good brand of potting compost will provide all the food a plant needs to start with, but after a time all the nutrients will be used up. From then on, regular liquid feeding is necessary. This restores nutrients to optimum levels, essential for the plant to grow and flower or fruit well. But even regular liquid feeding is not enough to keep the balance of trace elements in the compost exactly right, and potting composts lose their open texture in time. So plants that are grown in the same pots for a long time need completely fresh compost every few years. Either repot them into a container one size larger, or put them back into new compost in the same pot after shaking off the old compost.

**ABOVE**: *Keep all powdered feeds in a closed container, as they take up moisture from the air. Keep the feeding program simple as you are more likely to maintain it.*

**ABOVE**: *Liquid feeds are very popular. Do not make the feed too strong or you will burn the plant roots. It is better to feed your plants at half-strength twice a week than to overdo it.*

## REACHING HIGH BASKETS

*1. Easy-to-operate pulley systems can make feeding and watering hanging baskets much simpler. They clip onto the hanging hook or bracket and give access to the baskets for essential maintenance.*

*2. Reach up to the base of the hanging basket and pull it down firmly until it is the right height for you to tend to the plants. When you have finished, nudge the basket up to release the locking mechanism and push the basket back into place.*

# enjoy

# furniture

Garden furniture can be purely functional, like a wooden picnic table. But there are some beautiful designs around today that add greatly to the garden scene because they have such a pleasing form. Shop around to find chairs and tables that are both practical and capable of enhancing the view from the house, selecting furniture that fits into your overall scheme.

There is, today, no shortage of good garden furniture from which to choose. Manufacturers have created some excellent ranges of outdoor furniture from a variety of natural materials, much of it now imported relatively cheaply from the Far East.

Wood is one of the most durable and most sympathetic materials, and there is a wide range of furniture types from which to choose, from classic reproductions to modern designs. Since the furniture has to stay out in all weathers, it pays to buy the best you can afford, as it will undoubtedly last better and longer. For this purpose you need a good-quality hardwood, such as teak, which will cope well with all weather conditions. Cheaper softwoods need an annual coat of preservative to prevent them rotting.

Painted metal garden furniture can also look good – the idiom borrowed from the French with their classic dark green circular fretwork tables and round-seated café chairs with bent backs, which look good in most small gardens especially urban ones. Beware opting for white, however, as it gets grimy very quickly.

LEFT: *This table and chair set combining wooden slats with a metal frame, gives a light, airy feel to the furniture making it an ideal choice for a small deck.*

Dark green or slate-blue are better options. There is also a wide range of cast-iron furniture, some in quite ornate designs. Because it is very heavy, it has the virtue that it does not collapse or fall over easily, but it is difficult to move around the garden, which can be problem if you want to use more than one area for sitting out.

If you do not see what you want in the shops, there is nothing to stop you designing and making your own simple furniture. Plain benches or tables, for example, are relatively easy to construct, or you could use a hewn log or railway sleepers to make a simple bench. If you are furnishing the garden on a budget, then hunt out bargains in junk shops and unify any disparity in design by painting them in matching, or toning, colours. Even plastic furniture can be painted, and you can transform an old white plastic chair into something perfectly acceptable if the basic shape is attractive. Interesting industrial relics can make attractive patio furniture – the base of an old sewing machine can be topped with a piece of marble to serve as a small table, for example.

PRACTICAL CONSIDERATIONS
Chairs and tables can be expensive but there are designs to suit any budget and taste and you can always substitute cheaper furniture elements while you save up for what you really want. Consider practicality, comfort, style, longevity, maintenance and price. Also think about

whether or not you intend to leave chairs and tables out through the winter. If not, how you will store them? Waterproof covers are available for protecting furniture sets out of season but these are unsightly and could spoil the view from the house. Always check that wooden furniture comes from a sustainable source, especially when dealing with tropical hardwoods. It is especially important to avoid mahogany, as this is an endangered species.

RIGHT: *A basic wooden picnic table creates an informal atmosphere and is ideal for family dining but takes up quite a large space.*

BELOW: *This hi-tech aluminium set would fit into any corner. Combine with metal planters and architectural foliage for a contemporary look but don't forget some cushions – metal can be rather cold to the touch!*

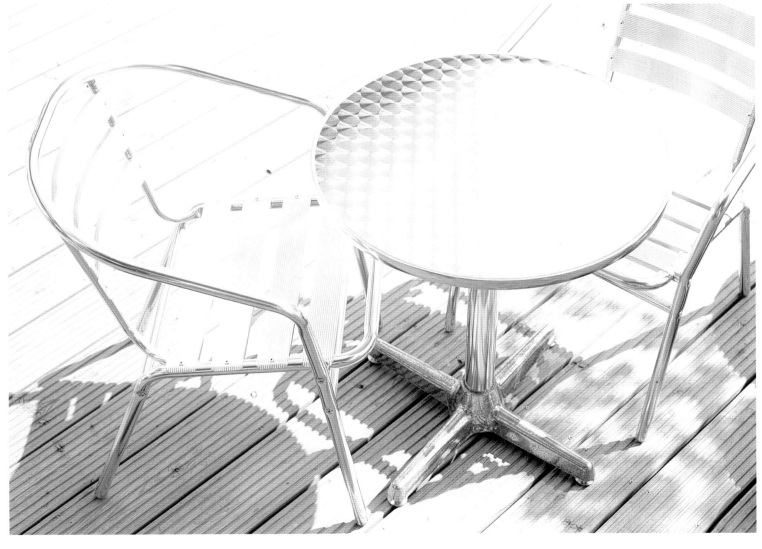

## VERSATILE WOOD

Having permanent seating on the deck is an enticement to sit out when the weather is fine. Wood is ideal for this because it dries off quite quickly after a shower and is warm and comfortable to sit on without the need for cushions. Wooden furniture is an obvious partner for decking. If your deck has been coloured, you can paint it to match or to contrast and if natural, most wood types will blend together with ease.

Treat softwood furniture with a preservative to prolong its life – some treatments combine colour with water-repellent agents and chemicals to deter rot. The more expensive hardwoods, including tropical types like iroko, have a much denser grain and are naturally more resistant to fungal attack. Use the recommended furniture oil to soak in, nourish and waterproof the wood. You can also use clear yacht varnish but this needs frequent application.

LEFT: *Hardwood furniture can be the most expensive type to buy but, with its up-market looks and excellent durability, it is a good investment. It tends to blend in well with decking.*

ABOVE RIGHT: *The Italian styling of this smart table and chair set adds a note of distinction. Cushion pads would make the seating more comfortable and an umbrella would give welcome shade on a hot day. Sets like this will last almost indefinitely but would benefit from indoor storage in winter.*

### STYLISH METAL

Some furniture designs combine wooden slats with a metal framework – you can often buy quite reasonably priced fold-away bistro style sets that are easy to store when not in use. Be aware, however, that unless the metal is galvanized or the framework is made from aluminium, stainless steel or chrome, it will rust.

Victorian cast iron bench seat ends or their reproductions are usually painted and some metal furniture is lacquered or coated with plastic to help prevent rust. But as soon as the paint or protective surface is damaged, rusting occurs, leaving unsightly stains on the deck. All-metal sets can be stylish but cushions are essential for comfort – metal is very cold!

### OTHER MATERIALS

Wood and canvas furniture such as director's chairs are often stylish. They are light and easy to move around but must be kept out of the rain. A waterproof locker built into the deck will allow quick access and is also perfect for storing cushions. Striped canvas chairs are fun and are usually cheap to buy.

## HOW BIG?

If you are planning to eat out of doors, it is worth remembering that you need a reasonable amount of space to do so. For a table and chairs for four people, you will need an area at least 1.5m (5ft) across, to allow you room to pull back the chairs from the table. A good solution if you want to eat out of doors on a small deck is to buy a bench, a table and a couple of folding chairs for guests. The slatted French café chairs are ideal for this purpose, as they fold up very small and are easily stackable in a shed or other store.

It is important in small spaces, such as decked balconies, verandahs or roof terraces, to pick furniture that fits well into the available space. Folding furniture certainly comes into its own here, as do benches that fit snugly against a wall, for example. If you are at all handy at carpentry, why not make a small table that is hinged to the back wall of the balcony or terrace, so that you can fold it down when not in use.

BELOW: *Outdoor furniture as beautiful as this reproduction steamer chair provides a strong incentive to sit out on the deck and enjoy the garden.*

## LOUNGING FURNITURE

On most decks there is not a great deal of available space for serious relaxation. However, a few good, carefully-chosen chairs that enable you to put your feet up while enjoying the vista you have created are a great bonus to a more relaxed lifestyle, plus a boon when friends come round.

Among the most attractive lounging chairs are the steamer chairs first developed for luxury cruises and now sold in many department stores. They have the architectural lines of a standard upright chair with the addition of an elongated leg rest. In natural hardwood, such as teak, and furnished with attractive boxed cushions in natural fabrics, such as linen and sailcloth, they make a worthy addition to any outdoor room.

The good old-fashioned deckchair is an excellent standby for the small garden. It folds up to take up minimum space and if the fabric used for

**ABOVE:** *Bright, stripy deckchairs help to create a relaxed seaside atmosphere on this simple deck. You could carry the motif further with a heavy rope surround, pebbles and silver- or grey-leaved plants in containers.*

it is of good quality, it will last very well. There is a wide range of suitable furnishing fabrics, some bright and others more subdued, and you can easily revamp old deck chairs with any strong sailcloth or canvas.

## CHOOSING FURNITURE

Do not be tempted to economize on the furniture or furnishings for your deck, especially if you are likely to spend a fair amount of time out there relaxing. They will have to last a long time, and the sturdier and better made they are, the better they will withstand the ravages of the outdoor environment. Ideally, choose all-weather furniture that you can leave out all year round, as most houses and apartments have little storage room to spare.

## FURNITURE CARE

The furniture should be scrubbed in the spring with a stiff scrubbing brush and some detergent, and then rinsed off with clean water before leaving it to dry naturally. A pot scourer will remove any stubborn lichen stains, but take care not to rub so hard that you damage the wood.

## VERY SMALL DECKS

If your deck is just too small to accommodate a full-sized table and chairs or a selection of loungers, then

**ABOVE:** *Simple director's chairs make a cosy corner for enjoying a cup of coffee.*

consider placing a simple, small garden bench at a suitable point where you can sit and enjoy some particular delight – whether it is a large container of wonderfully scented summer lilies, or nestling beneath the canopy of an attractive small tree or climber. Benches vary in size and scale, and a tiny iron bench will fit snugly against a wall on even the narrowest of decks.

# decorating a canvas chair

It is easy to customize a simple canvas chair with your own design to make a special feature for your deck. This one has been decorated with a stamp made from soft sponge and a leaf. The leaves should be as fresh as possible with prominent veins to create a good pattern. Be careful when applying the paint to the leaf stamp, and avoid pools of paint which will distort the pattern. It is a good idea to practise on a scrap of paper before you begin work on the chair to avoid costly mistakes. Use special fabric paints to create a permanent hard-wearing design. Washing-up sponges can be used to apply the paint.

*1. Paint the top of a large leaf with PVA glue and press it onto the soft side of a sponge. Once dry, cut the sponge from round the leaf. Repeat with a small leaf.*

*2. Cut a large and a small rectangle of sponge. Brush paint onto the soft sides. Lay the canvas on a hard surface and use the sponges to create a pattern.*

*3. When the red paint is dry, apply green paint to the leaves and make a leaf print on each rectangle. Leave them to dry, then iron to set the paint.*

# creating shade

In most climates, it is simply too hot to sit in direct sun at certain times of the year, especially if you are enjoying a meal al fresco. Shade is a requisite part of any deck and there are several ways you can achieve it. In changeable climates, consider temporary shade in the form of umbrellas, awnings or deciduous plants so you can still enjoy the sun when it is cooler.

### PERGOLAS

Pergolas are the obvious choice for providing shade over a deck, but many of them are fairly sparse wooden frames and actually cast little shade. They can, however, be clothed in a range of climbing plants which will soften their looks into the bargain (see pages 178–9). They can also be covered with a cloth or reed canopy to make a solid ceiling, which can be taken away when not in use.

### AWNINGS AND CANOPIES

On a deck, you can use the space much as you would a room in the house, with soft furnishings adding colour and interest, as well as providing protection from the elements. Awnings and canopies can be used to create much-needed shade, as well as privacy and seclusion, particularly if you have a ground-floor flat and garden, and the garden is overlooked by other tenants occupying the floors above you.

To create shade over a large area, you could support sailcloth strips on posts with stout string ties. You will,

however, need some rapid means of removing these or lowering them to a vertical position in the event of rain, otherwise they will fill up with rain water and tear loose from their moorings under the weight. You could also use very lightweight muslin, rather like mosquito netting, to create a light and airy summer awning, or a range of hand-dyed cottons in earthy colours – saffrons, terracottas and burnt oranges.

### CANVAS UMBRELLAS

If you don't want to erect an awning, then you can opt instead for one of the large new umbrellas. Among the most attractive are the large, natural umbrellas in bleached or green canvas-weave cotton with wooden supports. They are sturdy, long-lasting and look particularly good with a decked patio surface and attractive well-built teak furniture. Bring the umbrella indoors at the end of the summer season and scrub it well before drying it and folding it away.

ABOVE: *A beautiful wooden pergola is covered with a solid roof to create the ultimate in shaded dining areas. This creates a very elegant effect.*

LEFT: *A basic canvas umbrella is perfect for temporary shade – it can be moved around where it is needed and packed away when you want to enjoy the sunshine instead.*

REED SCREENS

Reed screens are another possibility for overhead shade. They are relatively light and very easy to fix in position to timber supporting struts and posts. They can also be used to cover a pergola to make it more effective. You can, if you wish, grow flowering or foliage climbers and creepers over them. In normal climatic conditions, they will last for around five years, but as they are relatively inexpensive, it is not a great problem to replace them when they wear.

MORE AMBITIOUS PROJECTS

If you do not want the full cost of a conservatory, you can make yourself a lean-to shelter on your deck with open sides and a roof of clear PVC. Beware that in a city this is inclined to get dirty, and if it is not to look gimcrack, you do need to give it a good annual scrubbing down. If the posts are painted a deep green, and you grow some interesting climbing plants up them, you can turn this into a surprisingly effective loggia for the spring and summer months.

# plants for pergolas

There is a wide choice of suitable plants to create shade over a pergola, some offering much denser cover than others. Ivies are great value as they are fairly quick growing – you will get a couple of metres in two or three years out of some of the swifter varieties – and so are the creepers, some of which you might find a little too enthusiastic, however. *Parthenocissus* can put on many feet in one season, but it is a deciduous plant, unlike ivy, so it will provide a screen only during the summer.

In southern Europe, no small outdoor space is complete without a vine, its large leaves giving wonderful dappled overhead shade in summer. Even in colder countries, vines can be used for the same purpose, although ornamental as opposed to fruiting vines might be more appropriate. *Vitis coignetiae* performs well in most conditions and has handsome large leaves that turn a wonderful ruby red in autumn. Combine your chosen vine with a scented climber, such as a jasmine, honeysuckle or rose, and perhaps another for flower power, such as one of the large-flowered clematis. They should all ramble happily together.

Another good screening plant is Dutchman's pipe (*Aristolochia macrophylla*), which has vine-like leaves and can be trained along poles or wires to form an attractive ribbon of

## CLIMBERS FOR PERGOLAS

- *Abutilon megapotamicum*
- *Akebia quinata*
- *Aristolochia macrophylla*
- *Campsis* x *tagliabuana*
- *Clematis armandii*
- *C. macropetala*
- *C. montana*
- *C. tangutica*
- *Eccremocarpus scaber*
- *Hedera* (ivy)
- *Humulus lupulus* 'Aureus'
- *Hydrangea anomala petiolaris*
- *Ipomoea tricolor*
- *Jasminum officinale*
- *Lathyrus latifolius*
- *Lonicera periclymenum*
- *L.* x *tellmanniana*
- *Passiflora caerulea*
- *Rosa*
- *Solanum crispum* 'Glasnevin'
- *Trachelospermum jasminoides*
- *Tropaeolum speciosum*
- *Vitis vinifera* 'Purpurea'
- *Wisteria sinensis*

foliage at the top of a fence, for example. Equally good is the golden hop (*Humulus lupulus* 'Aureus').

There is nothing to stop you using flowering climbers for screening purposes, and roses can make the best screens against cats, their thorny branches forming an impenetrable thicket, while offering the bonus of a once- (or twice- if you pick a remontant rose) a-year glorious display of flowers, most with delicious scent as well. 'New Dawn' seems universally popular and does well in most situations, its pale pink flowers blending well with most colour schemes. Another tough and vigorous rose is the richly scented, bright pink 'Albertine', or you could try one of the really big varieties, such as *Rosa filipes* 'Kiftsgate' if you have enough space for it to stretch itself – it will climb to 9m (30ft) or more, covering itself in clouds of white flowers in the summer months.

### TREES AND SHRUBS

You don't have to have a pergola to benefit from the shade potential of plants. Any small trees or large shrubs can be grown around the deck to cast shade across it at certain times of the day. Study the path of the sun carefully to establish the best posi-

**LEFT**: *Large-flowered clematis put on a spectacular show in summer.*

**RIGHT**: *Leafy climbers, such as this wisteria, will clothe pergola uprights as well as the horizontals overhead.*

tions. If the deck is large, then plant one or more small trees through a hole in the deck into the ground beneath. The dappled shade from trees is very attractive and comfortable to sit in. Apple trees cast espcially nice shade. If you can't plant trees through the deck, consider a large container to house them.

Tall bamboos are an excellent choice for casting shade and grow up to about 3m (10ft) in height, but you may be best advised to plant them in containers. Bamboos spread fast and your whole garden may well turn into a bamboo thicket unless you control their spread. If you do grow them in containers, you need to root prune them every couple of years. One solution is to grow them in a plastic container within a larger terracotta one. Every couple of years, you can dismantle the plastic container, trim out the roots (up to one-third) and then replant the bamboo into a similar-sized pot.

# water features

The sight and sound of moving water literally brings the garden to life. And even a still pool generates a special atmosphere with the changing reflections and all the bird and insect life it attracts. Decks offer wonderful opportunities for creating stylish and innovative water features that range from simple self-contained fountains to pools, rills and cascades.

## HINTS AND TIPS

● **DO** introduce the sights and sounds of running water close to the house and around sitting areas

● **DO** keep maintenance to a minimum by using self-contained water features

● **DO** make cobble springs and other features where the reservoir is hidden away so that children can enjoy water in safety

● **DON'T** forget to use armoured cable for electrical connections to water features plus waterproof connectors. Always fit an RCD or circuit breaker

● **DON'T** allow any depth of water where young children have access

● **DON'T** site moving water features with a fountain in a windy spot. The pump may be damaged if it dries out

## BUBBLE FOUNTAINS

Ready-made kits to construct water features take very little time or skill to install provided you have a convenient electricity supply, though buying the various elements individually may be cheaper and allow greater flexibility of design. Fountains with a hidden reservoir have several advantages. They are child-safe; they don't need cleaning out like conventional ponds; and there is very little labour involved in their construction. When planning the location of your water feature, try to avoid exposed areas where the wind might blow the fountain jet out of position. Left unchecked, this could quickly empty the reservoir and there is always the chance that it might damage the pump.

## WALL FOUNTAINS

A wall mask or waterspout creates the illusion of a natural spring, where water flows constantly into a small pool below. Some self-contained units simply hang on the wall and there is no plumbing or pipe work to worry about. The disadvantage with this solution is that the reservoir is often very small and could dry out. This in turn could damage the tiny submersible pump if you are not careful and do not keep a close eye on the situation. You can create your own water reservoir that is completely child safe, using an underground tank covered with wire mesh and camouflaged with pebbles. However, if you do not want to dig a hole, use a wooden barrel to act as a pool instead. With the submersible pump in the reservoir, the plastic tubing that feeds the mask or spout needs to be camouflaged. Either chip a channel for it on the surface of the wall, afterwards covering it with mortar and then camouflaging it with plants such as ivy, or alternatively drill through the wall at the base and pass the tube through and up the other side.

## RAISED POOLS

A lovely way to create a tranquil corner is to build a raised pool that incorporates a bench seat. This brings the water and its plants and wildlife up to a height where they can easily be appreciated and allows you to sit on the edge and dangle your fingers in the water. Raised pools can be made using railway sleepers or other heavy pieces of sawn timber that simply stack on top of one another and are bolted together. Use a butyl liner and tuck the edges in underneath the top layer, using an industrial

ABOVE: *The composition of this self-contained fountain and the two polished spheres is superbly balanced.*

ABOVE RIGHT: *Gleaming pebbles splashed by a bell fountain make an eye-catching feature. The reservoir and pump are under the deck, covered with wire mesh.*

RIGHT: *Some bubble fountains are like modern sculptures. This one has its own reservoir so just needs plugging in.*

staple gun to hold it in place. A relatively inexpensive alternative is to use breeze blocks rendered with cement and painted with masonry paint to match other elements in the garden. Camouflage the top with timber seating, paving slabs or heavy terracotta tiles. Textured building blocks are more expensive and you can of course build raised pools from brick, but this really is a job for a professional. The advantage is that the pool could be made to fit in with other features in the garden and you could even create a pool on two levels using interlocking rectangles.

## WATER SAFETY

If you are in any doubt, hire a qualified electrician to install electrical water features such as pumps and lighting outside on the deck. Use waterproof fittings and connect them to a residual current device (RCD) or circuit breaker. Remember to avoid having any depth of water exposed where young children are around – use a covered reservoir feature.

# small formal pools

Pools with a regular geometric outline suit decks better than informal pools. The simplicity of a flat sheet of water works well in relatively spacious surroundings, but you can also mirror the shape of the pool with appropriately shaped flower borders or formal clipped hedging around it. Finish off with a dainty fountain spray or gushing spring feature that not only looks and sounds good but also helps to keep the water oxygenated and healthy.

You can often buy rigid preformed liners for this kind of pool. Simply excavate out the hole, bed the liner in position and camouflage the edge under the decking boards. You can also use butyl rubber liner, but for a square or rectangular pool, the corners require careful folding to take up the excess. A pool with vertical sides and no shelving is unsuitable for wildlife, but ornamental fish and water lilies will be perfectly happy given sufficient depth.

When building a pool set into the deck, you may be able to avoid any excavations – just use a black, preformed liner, properly supported, and overlap the planks slightly to hide the edges. A raised pool with a wooden seat going all the way around it is another attractive option, providing a lovely area for socializing with a few friends or contemplating on your own. Square or rectangular-shaped pools look good with the rectilinear layout of most decks, but a circle or semi-circle at the base of a wall mask fountain can also be very striking.

## PREPARING THE WATER

The water in your feature will keep clean and clear once you have established some submerged aquatics as oxygenators. A pump connected to a filter will also help to prevent a shallow pool from becoming stagnant. Leave the bottom of the pool clear to create maximum reflection.

Choose your water plants carefully as many are overly vigorous and could rapidly swamp a small pool. Luckily, you can buy miniature water lilies that will flower in something as small as a wooden half-barrel. Be aware that fish need a depth of at least 90cm (3ft) in part of the pool as protection from winter cold. Have the quality and pH of the water tested by your aquatic centre before introducing fish. If any part of wooden decking comes into contact with the water, ensure that it has not been treated with harmful preservatives that could pollute.

When a deck is split between different levels you have the option of building a series of pools linked by gentle cascades. However, it is vital that you check what power and type of pump you require with your supplier; otherwise you might be disappointed at the speed and volume of water output.

# a potted fountain

Set up a potted fountain with care. Make sure that the pot and stones are all perfectly clean, as any dirt and grit will soon clog the pump. The submersible pump must be covered by water at all times. Adjust the jet so that the water trickles back into the pot and is continuously recycled – if too high, much of the water will go over the sides of the container. If the container empties, the pump runs dry and will be damaged.

Top up the water at least once a week, since evaporation will gradually lower the water level. A small bubble fountain like this only needs the smallest type of submersible pump; choose a low-voltage one, and plug it into an RCD. Then enjoy the sound of gently gurgling water.

*1. Use a tiny pump that will work in a small quantity of water. Attach clear plastic tubing to the nozzle and sit the pump in the pot. Drill a hole under the pot rim and thread the wire through.*

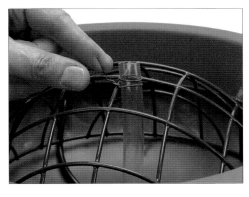

*2. Find a hanging basket frame the right size to sit inside the pot, covering the pump. Remove the chains and fit it firmly in place so it will not slip when weighted down with pebbles.*

*3. (left) Wire the tip of the nozzle to the framework of the basket to hold it securely. There is no need to fit a spray head, as the nozzle alone will produce a clean natural-shaped jet of water.*

LEFT: *Decking associates well with water of any kind. Here it is used to create a platform over an informal stream.*

*4. (left) Part-fill the container with water, covering the pump completely, with 5cm (2in) to spare. This ensures that the pump will remain covered with water when the fountain is working. Hide the pump and the hanging basket pump cover completely under a layer of smooth clean pebbles; choose a size of pebble that is in proportion to the size of the container.*

*5. (right) When the pump is switched on, a simple fountain effect trickles water over the pebbles. Adjust the pump valve to make the fountain jet a suitable height.*

# wildlife and water

Water is like a magnet for wildlife. It attracts all manner of insects, amphibians, birds and small mammals and in so doing brings the deck to life. But to attract wildlife, there are certain requirements.

In order for birds to drink and bathe safely there must be shallow water or a partially submerged stone for them to land on, and the area must be open so that they can keep an eye out for predators. Amphibians like frogs and toads also prefer a gently shelving access so that they can get in and out easily. This is important when tadpoles turn into adults and need to leave the water. At this point they are vulnerable and their access should lead into an area of long grass or a bog garden. Mammals like hedgehogs sometimes fall into ponds and can drown if there is no gently shelving access. Consider making a simple wooden ramp covered with galvanized wire mesh.

The health of the water is paramount, and it is important to site a wildlife pool in a sunny spot away from deciduous trees. If fallen leaves are not removed, they can rot, producing toxins. Establish oxygenators as soon as possible and build up marginal plantings to provide cover for aquatic animals and egg-laying sites for dragonflies and damselflies. Water lily pads will help to shade the water, helping to minimize algae.

## FOUNTAIN BARREL

If you don't have space for a wildlife pond, even a small barrel feature will attract wildlife in the form of birds, butterflies and damsel flies.

*1. Since the wooden barrel is not waterproof, line it with a large piece of pond liner. Push the liner firmly down inside. Trim off some of the excess but leave plenty around the edge. Stand the pump on a hard brick for stability and to raise it up to the right level. This small mains-powered model is ideally suited to such a feature.*

*2. Add cobbles in between the bricks to stabilize the bricks and stop the pump moving around. Now add the large stones – rounded boulders make an attractive contrast with small pebbles. Add water until it reaches the base of the boulders. This will leave enough room to add the plants and final stones.*

*3. Add the plants, potted in plastic mesh baskets. Plan the planting in advance. A low-growing water forget-me-not towards the front works well. Add cobbles and pebbles to make the feature look more like a natural stream. Neaten the edge of the liner. Fit a bell fountain head to the pump outlet and switch it on.*

## FURTHER STEPS

Although it will make the water pretty murky at first, it is a good idea to fill the base of the wildlife pond with garden soil before filling it with the hose. This will provide the plants and animals with essential nutrients. Animals will soon start to visit your pool, but you can get a good head start by 'seeding' the water from an established pond that already has a thriving aquatic community. Several weeks after the pond has been set up, add a couple of buckets of water and some sediment from the other pond. Avoid adding tap water to top up your pond, since the chemicals might upset the pond water chemistry and dissolved nitrates can cause algal blooms to occur.

## HINTS AND TIPS

● *DO ensure that the pool is well planted with lush vegetation to attract insects*
● *DO allow the water to release dissolved chemicals like chlorine, before you introduce plant life*
● *DON'T be tempted to introduce ornamental fish to a wildlife pond. They have voracious appetites!*
● *DON'T keep topping the pond up with tap water. It can upset the delicate balance*
● *DON'T allow floating aquatics to choke the pond*

## CONTAINER WILDLIFE POND

Marginal pond plants make fascinating container subjects and this water feature will attract wildlife to your deck. Any container that holds water is suitable, but a wide half barrel is best as it has a large water surface. Once planted up, keep the barrel topped up with water. In hot weather it can lose 2.5cm (1in) of water each week due to evaporation.

*1. Drape the pond liner loosely inside the tub and put 2.5–5cm (1–2in) of gravel into the bottom. Half-fill with water. Trim away the excess pond liner, then turn the edges under, smoothing out the creases. Use waterproof tape to secure the liner to the tub rim.*

*2. Begin adding plants; choose flowering and foliage marginal plants which contrast well in shape. Leave them in the net-sided pond pots that they are growing in when you buy them.*

*3. Three plants are enough, as they will soon grow. Top up with water to the rim of the container and check that the tape holds the edge of the liner firmly. Add a floating plant, such as fairy moss.*

# home comforts

A deck becomes more than just part of the garden when it is transformed by a few home comforts, such as lighting, heating, relaxing sounds and delicious scents. Be creative and enjoy!

## lighting

If you are going to spend time and energy creating a lovely deck, it is well worthwhile expending a little more time and money lighting it. Lighting the deck has many benefits, not all immediately obvious. In any garden it is a boon for security. Very few burglars will walk through a lit garden, and it also gives you and your neighbours a good view from indoors. Lighting will also make steps and changes in level safer in the dark. Lighting the garden will also mean that you can enjoy the grandeur of your garden at night as

well as in the daytime. Just a couple of judiciously placed lights can give your garden some of the dramatic appeal of a stage set. Trees and shrubs take on wonderful outlines, the contrasts in light and shade enhancing their qualities enormously. If you want to use the garden for entertaining, then lights are a must. Make sure the seating area is well, but subtly lit, the lights facing away from the area, not glaring on to it.

A little planning at the design and construction stage of your deck will not only make installation easier but also ensure that unsightly wiring is hidden away. Avoid reliance on powerful halogen security lights.

The range of outdoor light fittings available direct to the amateur from shops is fairly limited but mail order companies offer a wide choice.

### CHOOSING LIGHTING
Lighting schemes do not have to be elaborate or expensive. A simple lighting system might incorporate two or three all-weather lights, fixed

**LEFT:** *Modern downlighters are available mains-powered, as low-voltage lighting sets or as independent solar-powered units.*

to spikes secured in the ground and angled to create a spot of light wherever it seems most suitable or convenient. One light, for example, could be a downlighter on to the seating area, and two more could be fixed at further points in the garden to focus on specific features – a water feature, perhaps, or a particularly attractive shrub or tree.

If you are using the deck for entertaining, then make sure you also install any necessary lights for safety of access as well – for example, lighting the way along a path or down steps. The aim is to sit bathed in a subtle light, not the full glare of a floodlit football pitch, so direct the light upwards or downwards as required, away from any seating.

If you have an attractive water feature, you can light it using waterproof underwater lights, which can enhance its appeal greatly. If you can afford to, make sure some of the lights are on separate circuits so that you can switch different lights on or off, as required.

Outdoor lights are generally available in the three following types: tungsten lights which create a warm, golden glow; discharge sodium or mercury lights which give a diffused slightly greenish tinged glow; and low-voltage halogen lights which give a very white light.

Uplighters at ground level can be angled to focus on a particular plant or the branches of a tree and strong architectural plants can really be made to look dramatic at night.

Avoid flooding the whole garden with a security light – the effect is far from atmospheric and the light tends to cast huge, unattractive shadows around the garden. A pretty form of electric lighting are the tiny white fairy lights designed for outdoor use. Weave them through the climbers of an archway or pergola for a magical night time atmosphere.

**ABOVE:** *The flickering light of candles and lanterns adds a touch of magic to a deck at night. Place around sitting areas or gently illuminate a dining table.*

**LEFT:** *This elegant Japanese-style lantern operates via solar-powered batteries so there are no wires to conceal and you can move the light wherever you need it.*

## SIMPLE EFFECTS

You do not need to spend a lot of money on lighting effects in the garden. For example, ordinary clay plant pots make great candleholders and are relatively inexpensive, although quite stylish. Set them part-buried in the ground around a deck or barbecue area and just replace the candles as necessary. You can also make hanging candle lanterns of your own, using ordinary glass jam jars with plaited string round the neck to create a fixing. Chunky citronella candles not only look good, they also help to keep away insects at night. The same goes for incense sticks. On fine, still nights, use floating candles on the pond for special celebrations or float some in large, shallow bowls of water on the deck.

### NAKED FLAMES

If you want to create an air of luxury, consider outdoor candleholders and candelabras made of elaborate wirework or wrought iron and use heavy church candles in them, positioning them around the garden where they will illuminate shapely plants. Candle lanterns, candelabras and flares now come in a wealth of designs and are perfect for warm summer nights when eating outdoors. Choose from opulent, high-tech or rustic to create a style to suit your deck. Flares that stick in the borders around the deck are fun at barbecues and parties, as are candle lanterns hung from the trees or a pergola.

Metal lanterns with a galvanized finish will not rust and look charming in most situations. Set them amongst the plants, floating on your pool, hanging from the pergola or at the centre of the table. But don't leave naked flames unattended!

### MAINS ELECTRICITY

The effect of black mini-spot uplighters and downlighters is quite subtle and they are particularly useful for highlighting decorative trellis, ornaments, water features and plants. Dress trellis panels and climber-covered pergolas with tiny white fairy lights – lovely for creating a romantic atmosphere for an outdoor dining area. Another soft lighting technique uses recessed lights that are flush with the deck and safe to walk over. Their metal finishes offer a contemporary feel.

Ideal around doorways, there are several designs of wall light including those that match the period detailing of your house. You can connect these to an infra-red sensor so that the lights come on automatically when it gets dark. Use long-life bulbs where possible and, for safety's sake, connect to a residual current device (RCD) or circuit breaker.

## LOW-VOLTAGE LIGHTING

Low-voltage lights running off a transformer are easy for the amateur to install. The range is fairly limited – you normally buy a set of four or eight identical lights, such as spotlights on spikes to push into the ground or pots, globe lamps on a stem, or lights set into a column.

Some come with sensors which switch them on automatically at night. Solar-powered lights have come on in leaps and bounds and better brands now function quite reliably even in dull weather thanks to advances in rechargeable battery technology. They are similar in design to those that run off a transformer but have the advantage of being wireless, so can operate far away from an electricity supply.

**ABOVE:** *Mains electric lamps can provide unobtrusive low-level lighting for decks.*

**FAR LEFT:** *Deck lights can be very stylish indeed, like this metal pillar light with a rust-effect finish. Mail order catalogues from specialist firms are the best place to look for unusual designs.*

**LEFT:** *Exterior wall lights come in a range of styles from traditional to modern like this contemporary glass lamp.*

## HINTS AND TIPS

- *If you have any doubt whatsoever about wiring up lights for your deck, seek a qualified electrician. The dangers of electricity are all the greater when you are installing lights and switches for outdoor use.*

# heating a deck

Most people revel in the simple pleasure of eating outside, but are frustrated by the weather – rarely is it really warm enough, especially after dark. A heater is the answer; position it close to the dinner table and enjoy a comfortable evening under the stars, even if there is a slight chill in the air. Heaters are becoming more available and affordable and will greatly increase the amount of use you can get out of your deck space. Gas models are the most popular – simply replace the bottle when it is empty.

# hot tubs

Perhaps the ultimate in luxury and relaxation is to have a hot tub built on your deck. There are many models available to suit any style of deck and it doesn't have to be an eye sore. Imagine lying back with a cool drink,

the warm, comforting water swirling around you. There are many specialist companies who will plan, supply and install hot tubs at fairly reasonable prices.

Consider its location carefully before you have one built. A sheltered spot is preferable – while the water is warm you won't want to be sitting in a chilly breeze. Privacy is also an issue; make sure you choose an area of the deck which is not overlooked by the neighbours. The electricity and water supply may also affect where you should site your hot tub as services can be expensive to install. Don't forget that you need to cover the hot tub when not in use.

**ABOVE**: *If your deck is large enough to take one, a hot tub can be one of life's little luxuries. This one is set in a smart wooden surround to match the decking boards and makes an attractive feature.*

**LEFT**: *A heater could greatly increase the amount of use you get out of your deck. There are many stylish models on sale.*

# child safety

The deck is often the area of the garden which is closest to the house or the open kitchen door, so it should offer a comfortable place for youg children to play in safety. Decks are well suited as play areas as they provide a warm and dry surface, perfect for games and exploring. However, as with any area of the garden, there are hazards which should be avoided.

The deck itself can be a cause of injury, so plan it with children in mind. Make sure raised decks are enclosed to prevent falls, and consider gates for steps and access points. Laying the deck boards close together will prevent fingers getting stuck, and smooth boards, well sanded down before fitting, will avoid painful splinters. One of the biggest risks is from water, so choose child-friendly features, such as bubble fountains, container bog gardens or any other water feature without standing water.

Take care which plants you choose for deckside beds and containers – avoid sharp or spiky plants and those which are poisonous.

**ABOVE RIGHT:** *Container water features such as this fountain provide interest for both adults and children without posing any threat of drowning.*

**BELOW:** *A sturdy screen looks good and makes this raised deck much safer for younger members of the family.*

## HINTS AND TIPS

- *Fit a handrail or balustrade round raised decks to avoid children falling off the edge*
- *Make sure the deck boards are smooth and well sanded to avoid splinters*
- *Space underneath a raised deck should be enclosed to stop children crawling under*
- *Water features should not have any depth of standing water – have a bubble fountain with a hidden reservoir*
- *Consider having a lockable gate across the stairs on raised decks*
- *Make sure electric lights are properly and safely installed*
- *Don't leave children alone with lit candles or heaters*
- *Avoid very spiky plants, such as yucca and agave*
- *Be sure not to plant containers with poisonous plants; check when you buy them*

# delicious scents

Without question, if there is one attribute that no deck should be without, it has to be scent. Although so subtle as to pass unremarked occasionally, scent adds a magic ingredient to any garden, and is valuable in a city garden as an antidote to the less attractive smells of pollutants of one sort or another.

Many plants are scented, and their fragrance is by no means restricted to the flowers. In some plants the leaves are deliciously scented or aromatic – sage (*Salvia*), thyme (*Thymus*) and mint (*Mentha*) among them. Herbs are among the best plants for scent and if you have a sunny corner of the deck, it is well worth growing a small selection. Herbs are not only useful, but highly decorative too – good all-purpose plants for any garden.

ROSES AND SCENTED CLIMBERS
If you ask anyone to name a scented plant that they can think of, roses are going to come high on the list. Indeed, there are so many different scented roses, all exquisite, that it is hard to know which to choose. It helps, therefore, to have some idea of the different kinds of rose. Entire books have been written on rose classification, but for the average novice gardener, it is sufficient to group them into climbers, bush roses and little patio roses, and to say that there are old roses, which have been grown for centuries, and more modern versions (of which the patio rose

is one). The aim of modern breeding has been to get the best of all possible worlds – great scent, good looks, good habits – but despite all the efforts, some of the very old roses are still hard to beat. Everyone has particular favourites, but on a deck, you cannot go too far wrong if you concentrate on climbing roses, as they will give you the maximum amount of flower power and take up the minimum amount of space.

There are many other good scented climbing plants, not least among them the honeysuckles (although beware – not all species and varieties are scented). *Lonicera periclymenum* 'Serotina' is deciduous but is also highly scented. Jasmine has a powerful scent; the summer-flowering, white-flowered *Jasminum officinale*, in particular, can literally fill the garden with heady scent.

## SCENTED FLOWERS

- *Convallaria majalis*
- *Dianthus* 'Mrs Sinkins'
- *Erysimum cheirii*
- *Freesia*
- *Hyacinthus*
- *Iris unguicularis*
- *Lathyrus odoratus*
- *Lilium* 'Regale'
- *Malcolmia*
- *Matthiola*
- *Narcissus*
- *Nicotiana*
- *Pelargonium* (scented leaves)
- *Thymus* (scented leaves)

BELOW: *Stocks (*Matthiola incana*) are among the most highly scented and beautiful bedding plants.*

## SCENTED SHRUBS AND TREES

It can be a great delight to have a winter-scented shrub in the garden. *Chimonanthus praecox*, or wintersweet as it is commonly known, has spicy scented flowers in pale yellow that appear on the bare branches in winter. *Hamamelis mollis*, the Chinese witch hazel, also has sweetly scented little yellow flowers on bare branches. *H. m.* 'Pallida' has dense clusters of paler yellow flowers flushed with red. Other good shrubs for winter scent are the pretty pinkish-mauve flowered daphnes, such as *Daphne bholua*, and Christmas box (*Sarcococca*), with its small shiny green leaves and little white highly scented flowers.

Other good scented shrubs, for other seasons of the year, are mock orange blossom (*Philadelphus*), which has clouds of highly fragrant white flowers; lilac (with white or mauve flowers, which are wonderful for cutting for the house); and the scented flowers of some of the viburnums, in particular *Viburnum* x *burkwoodii*. As a star performer in a small space, grow the little magnolia, *M. stellata*. It has singularly beautiful starry white flowers in spring that are also highly fragrant. 'Royal Star' has bigger white flowers, and 'Rosea', pink-flushed ones. If you have acid soil, you can grow some of the scented azaleas, among them the strongly fragrant *Rhododendron luteum*, which has rich yellow flowers in late spring and the added attraction of autumn-tinted leaves as well.

For trees, some forms of ornamental cherry are scented, among them the Japanese cherry, *Prunus* 'Amanogawa', which is ideal for small gardens, and has semi-double scented pink flowers. The bird cherry, *P. padus*, has almond-scented white flowers in spring, as do *P.* 'Shirotae' and *P.* x *yedoensis*.

## OTHER SCENTED PLANTS

There is also a wide range of scented perennials, bulbs and annuals to choose from. Among the most strongly scented are those in the carnation family, including pinks such as the old-fashioned 'Mrs Sinkins', stocks (*Matthiola*), tobacco plants (*Nicotiana*) and bulbs, such as narcissus and freesias. No small garden should be without a short row of wallflowers, as there is nothing to beat their perfume on a sunny day in

**RIGHT: *Freesias are among the most scented of flowers and come in rich shades of red, purple, yellow and blue.***

late spring before other bedding plants have come into flower. Sweet peas are also deliciously scented, and ideal for cutting for the house. Grow them up a wigwam to save space, choosing a mixture of old-fashioned shades. Make sure the ones you choose have been bred for scent. Lilies are also among the most scented flowers, with a particularly rich, heady fragrance.

## SCENTED SHRUBS AND CLIMBERS

- *Brugmansia* (syn *Datura*)
- *Buddleja davidii*
- *Chimonanthus praecox*
- *Daphne bholua*
- *D. odora*
- *Elaeagnus pungens*
- *Hamamelis mollis*
- *Jasminum officinale*
- *Lavandula*
- *Magnolia grandiflora*
- *Myrtus communis*
- *Philadelphus* 'Beauclerk'
- *Rosa*
- *Salvia*
- *Santolina rosmarinifolia*
- *Sarcococca*
- *Syringa*
- *Viburnum* x *bodnantense* 'Dawn'

# soothing sounds

Gardens abound in sounds, ranging from rustling leaves to the repetitive but reassuring gurgle of water tumbling from a fountain. Many of these sounds are pleasurable and help us relax and enjoy our time outside, so why not make sure your deck can offer these soothing noises. The repetitious but lovely sound of water splashing from a fountain or trickling between stones is always soothing and comforting, especially in hot weather when it helps to create the impression that the temperature is lower than it actually is.

## RUSTLING PLANTS

Many small trees and shrubs, especially deciduous ones, make a light rustling noise when they are caught in a gentle breeze. Poplars, aspens and birches are especially good and can be grown in deckside borders or large containers.

Perhaps the best rustling plants, however, are ornamental grasses which quiver and rustle in the slightest breeze. The amur silver grass (*Miscanthus sacchariflorus*) is herbaceous and grows up to 3m (12ft) in a season, creating a superb screen for

RIGHT: *Grasses make wonderful rustling noises in a light breeze. From left to right:* Acorus gramineus *'Ogon',* Briza media, Ophiopogon planiscapus *'Nigrescens' and* Pleioblastus variegtaus.

privacy and shelter. The dead stems and leaves remain throughout the winter. There are several smaller forms, including 'Aureus', with striped golden leaves and 'Variegatus' with white-striped leaves. The herbaceous grass *Miscanthus sinensis* 'Purpureus' grows to about 1.5m (5ft) high and has purplish-tinged stems. Zebra grass, *Miscanthus sinensis* 'Zebrinus' grows up to 1.2m (4ft) high and has arching, yellow and green cross-banded leaves.

Bamboos, also members of the grass family, are also excellent for creating rustling noises. They are generally hardy and ideal for screening around the deck, or planting in containers. *Phyllostaohys nigra*, the black bamboo, develops beautiful tall black canes with bright green leaves. The canes are rather like polished mahogany. *Pleioblastus*

*variegatus* is smaller at 1.2m (4ft) high and forms a thicket of stripy white foliage, perfect for a container.

## WIND CHIMES

The gentle, repetitive yet unpredictable sounds of a wind chime are known throughout many countries where they are used to create light background sounds, ideal for reducing stress. Choose metal for a gentle tinkling or bamboo for a softer sound.

## WATER

The gentle splish-splash of a fountain or water spout is one of the most soothing sounds and there are various ways of achieving it. If you have a pond, either raised or at ground level on the deck, install a fountain in the middle. Various spray patterns can be created, ranging from those that form single or multiple columns of water to ones with a bell, tulip or

hemispherical outline of water, and each has its own sound. Most pond pumps can be adjusted to change the flow of water passing through them, and hence the height and sound of the fountain.

Due to their smaller size, bubble water features are more suitable for most decks. These come in a wide range of designs. Ask to see them working before you buy to try out the sound. Those which gurgle are especially enjoyable. The other alternative is a wall-mounted spout or fountain, where water pours from a hole in the wall into a pond below.

These features can produce a loud pouring noise, but the sound can be made more gentle by placing pebbles under the stream of water.

ABOVE: *Small-scale water features can be smart as well as functional.*

ABOVE RIGHT: *Wind chimes are a good way of drawing attention to a taller plant in a low background. This bamboo version makes a low, hollow sound.*

RIGHT: *Pebbles drilled and threaded on wire can make a knocking sound when the wind blows.*

# entertaining in style

Entertaining out of doors brings a relaxed informality to the proceedings by day, but turns any occasion into something quite magical after dark. Your deck can become the setting for a whole host of social events, from long relaxed barbecue lunches to elegant candlelit dinners. Rather like a stage, the deck can be dressed to create the perfect atmosphere for your guests.

Before you plan any social occasion, work out how much space you've got and how many people you can realistically accommodate. This will depend on the event – if it is a full-blown dinner then everyone will need to be seated in comfort at a table, if it is drinks and nibbles then guests can stand. Informal barbecues and buffets come somewhere in between and floor cushions and loungers are perfectly acceptable here as people tend to move around. The next major consideration is whether you need lighting or heating for your event if it is an evening occasion, or some way of shading the deck if it is a warm summer day.

## BRUNCH

Brunch is a fun and informal meal, perfect for serving on the deck. You won't need to seat everyone at a table – some people can sit on cushions, others on benches or loungers. Supply plenty of paper napkins and let them all help themselves from a buffet table. Serve plenty of coffee and fruit juice, and perhaps a jug of Bloody Mary. Barbecues are great for cooking brunch – chunky steak sand-

**LEFT:** *This beautifully decorated tea table makes the food look even more tempting. A deck is the perfect setting.*

wiches, sausages and burgers are all welcome. Or go for more traditional eggs, pastries, pancakes or kedgeree.

## LAZY LUNCHES

What could be nicer on a warm day than a long, lazy lunch on the deck at the weekend with friends? In Mediterranean countries, no garden is complete without a long table with benches either side, big enough to seat the whole family, plus all the neighbours. Serve up summery, lazy food which takes little time to prepare but a long time to savour – cool salads containing cold meat or fish, simple barbecues, homemade pizzas, paella or shellfish, with ice cream and summer berries for dessert.

## AFTERNOON TEA

Afternoon tea can be a dainty affair with delicate little cakes served on pretty plates at the table, or a more substantial meal with plenty of starchy savouries and cakes. The latter could be served like a picnic on a table cloth on the deck with soft cushions for guests to sit on.

For a special occasion, use dainty china and decorate the table with summer flowers.

Whatever type of tea you are serving, make sure there is plenty of tea and sandwiches, two essential items.

LEFT: *Table linen can really set the scene and make a simple meal into a special occasion. Here, a lacy blue and white set really reinforces the summer theme, perfect for lunch or tea.*

ABOVE RIGHT: *A serene and attractive setting for breakfast, lunch or dinner. Crisp white table linen and cushions add a simple elegance, while the wicker furniture makes a natural contrast. The plants in matching white containers create a light screen around the dining area to separate it from the surrounding deck, while a pergola casts light shade.*

RIGHT: *Lunch or tea can be served picnic-style on the deck. Lay it all out on a cloth and provide cushions for guests.*

197

## STARLIT DINNERS

Because of the need for lighting, either by candles or subtle electric lights, eating outside after dark brings a thrilling quality to the event. It is fun to make an effort getting the ambience just right, and guests will really appreciate the finer touches. Just because you are eating on the deck doesn't mean the evening is informal. Decorate the table with scented flowers, get out the finest table linen and silver cutlery and hang lanterns in surrounding trees to complete the effect.

## DRINKS ON THE DECK

A deck is the ideal place to host a drinks party on a balmy summer evening. And because you won't have to seat everyone at the table, numbers are less limited than any other type of party. Serve jugs of exotic punches and cocktails to enhance the outdoor theme, or stick to the summer classic – Champagne. Play gentle background music and serve trays of substantial nibbles – perhaps dainty kebab sticks straight from the barbecue.

**LEFT:** *A beautiful deck, decorated with flowers and colourful cushions. The parasol will provide comfortable shade.*

**BELOW:** *A range of elegant glasses and luxurious table linen will make a candlelit dinner highly memorable.*

**BELOW RIGHT:** *Soft pink scented roses and floating candles make a simple table centrepiece for dinner on the deck.*

## HINTS AND TIPS

- *Make sure there is plenty of space for guests before you invite them*
- *Tailor your event to the number of guests you can realistically seat at the table*
- *Set the scene with table decorations, flowers and music if appropriate – it is the finishing touches which really define the occasion*
- *Use electric lights or candles to create night time effects*
- *Consider heating or shading the deck, depending on the weather*
- *Be creative with the furniture – loungers, fold-away chairs or floor cushions are all useful fall-backs*
- *Tailor the food to the location – pick dishes which seem right for outdoor eating*
- *Be relaxed and informal as befits entertaining al fresco!*

# making guests comfortable

Dinners with friends can last for many hours, and it is up to you, as host, to make sure your guests are as comfortable as possible throughout. If it is a sit-down affrair, start by working out how many decent chairs you've got before you invite people. Makeshift seating isn't always comfortable enough for a long meal.

Provide cushions, too, if the chairs are hard – some wood and metal seats can be a bit unyielding.

Table size is also a big factor. Guests won't relax if they are wedged in together with no space to move their elbows. You need to be able to move around to be really comfortable.

Temperature should also be taken into consideration. If the weather is likely to be hot and you are serving lunch, then provide some form of shade in the form of a parasol or awning, even if it is just a temporary measure. If it is a cool evening, then buy, borrow or hire a heater – they really are very effective.

Make sure the lighting is not too harsh or shining in people's eyes. Security lighting is no good for creating a comfortable brightness in which to sit as it tends to dazzle and distract. Provide subtle ambient light instead in the form of electric lights, candles or garden flares.

## USING FABRIC

Fabric can be a wonderful source of colour on the deck and there are a myriad ways to employ it to jazz up the appearance of a dull deck, while adding comfort into the bargain. The most obvious application is for colourful cushions – for seats and as floor cushions – and tablecloths and napkins. Parasols and awnings are also an option. These kinds of colourful additions work particularly well in shady gardens, which have very little natural colour of their own and benefit enormously from the addition of some imported brightness.

These fabric accessories can be removed when not in use and stored indoors to keep them clean and dry.

## THE RIGHT WELCOME

Don't forget comfort is not only physical. Try to put guests at their ease as soon as they step through the door. Be ready for them and relaxed when they arrive so you can offer them a drink straight away rather than racing around in a panic and making them feel guilty. Simply having made a special effort with table decorations, candles or the food will make them feel they are really wanted, which will help them relax.

RIGHT: *Colourful cushions provide both comfort and colour for the deck. Try to match the cushion fabrics to the table cloth and napkins.*

BELOW: *A closely slatted pergola creates dappled shade, while director's chairs make comfortable temporary seating.*

BELOW LEFT: *Floor cushions provide the only place to sit on this deck. Light muslin curtains hanging from an overhead pergola create soft shade.*

201

# setting the scene

Whatever the occasion, entertaining on the deck can be fun and as much a feast for the eye as the palate. Good food, drink and company is obviously most important, but presentation is also vital to set the scene and define the event. This should apply to everything, from the atmosphere created by the lighting, to the crockery on which the food is served and the way the table is set. You don't have to own starched cloths, cut glass and bone china to lay a decorative table – the most important requirements are enthusiam and ingenuity. Indeed, table settings created on a budget often look more inventive and unusual than those with a conventional approach.

### CENTREPIECES

Every table needs a focal point and it is, more often than not, in the centre of the table. The usual choice is a flower arrangement or a bowl of fruit, but it can be fun to dream up something a little more exotic. The important thing to remember is that although the centrepiece should be large enough to make a statement, it should never take over the table, leaving little room for anything else and forcing your guests to peer over it to talk to one another.

**ABOVE:** *Candlelight creates a wonderful ambience for any occasion. Use lanterns and jars around the deck but make sure they cannot be knocked over.*

**LEFT:** *Beautiful coloured glasses can be teamed with richly coloured table linen and gold cutlery for a sumptuous effect.*

### TABLECLOTHS

A tablecloth will really set the style of your table. Use heavy damask or linen for formal meals, and simple cotton cloths in checks or stripes for summer lunches. White always looks good and suits just about any occasion, but darker colours can create some stunning effects. If you can't find a table cloth to suit your proposed colour scheme, buy a piece of upholstery or dress fabric instead. As long as it is washable, it will do well as a table cloth.

## NAPKINS

Napkins are a necessary element of all table settings, however informal. Whether you use starched damask napkins at a formal dinner party or disposable paper napkins for a barbecue lunch, it is worthwhile putting a bit of thought into their presentation. Try to give your napkins an individual touch by folding them in different ways, tying them with ribbon and fresh flowers or using your favourite napkin rings to enhance the table setting.

## CANDLES

No outdoor party after dark is complete without candles or flares. Naked flames cast magical light and flicker gently in the night air; candlelight is also very flattering and will make your guests look more attractive! Use candles on a dining table as part of the centrepiece or use nightlights in lanterns or jars around the deck, perhaps hanging from the pergola or surrounding trees. Garden flares cast good light too and can be placed in flower beds or containers.

TOP: *An afternoon tea table is transformed by embroidered jampot covers, apple blossom and strawberry flowers – the essence of summer.*

ABOVE: *Rather than having a single centrepiece on a dining table, why not make a series of little arrangements to put next to each place setting.*

LEFT: *Fresh flowers are suitable for any occasion but have a particular relevance gracing a table in the garden.*

# apricot centrepiece

A mound of luscious apricots, creamy flowers and leaves makes a pretty centrepiece for a summer lunch party. Your guests can enjoy the delicious apricots at the end of the meal.

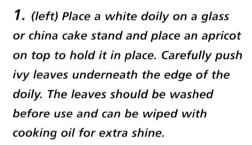

*1. (left) Place a white doily on a glass or china cake stand and place an apricot on top to hold it in place. Carefully push ivy leaves underneath the edge of the doily. The leaves should be washed before use and can be wiped with cooking oil for extra shine.*

## CARVED MELON

*2. Next arrange the apricots in a mound on top of the doily. Avoid letting them touch the ivy leaves which are poisonous. Then arrange a few sprays of cream freesias around the pile of apricots.*

*3. Finally, slot a few flowers into the gaps between the apricots. Any small cream or white flowers will do – these are miniature narcissi. Check with the florist that the flowers are not poisonous.*

This centrepiece not only looks scrumptious but can be served for dessert at the end of the meal. Mix the cubed melon flesh with a selection of other fruits and use to fill the melon case. Garnish with mint leaves and fruit slices.

# sumptuous summer jugs

For a summer table decoration, nothing can surpass the beauty of flowers, especially if you have picked them in your own garden. This display uses a small number of different flowers in shades of white, pink and red, so most gardens could supply enough. The secret of successful flower arranging is a careful choice of containers and a harmonious colour scheme to complement them.

## CENTREPIECE

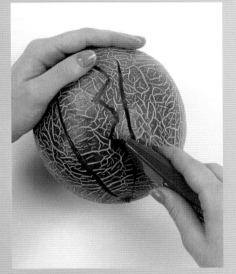

Use a sharp knife to cut strips out of the melon skin to create a pattern. Take care not to cut the skin too deeply or it will break. When the pattern is complete, slice off the top of the melon, discard the seeds and scoop out the flesh.

*1. Choose a selection of pretty jugs in a variety of different shapes. These have contrasting forms but similar colours to hold the display together.*

*2. This fat, rounded jug has a wide neck and is ideal for full-blown roses which look good clustered together. A few sprigs of aster break up the mound.*

*3. The tall jug contains a mixture of anemones, ranunculus, schizostylis and white asters, the mixture of shapes providing variety. The smallest jug contains a tiny narcissus, ranunculus and anemones and a few sprigs of love-in-a-mist (Nigella). The deep red anemone at the front serves as a focal point. Arrange the jugs together on the table.*

# net napkin rings

For a touch of frivolity, tie up your napkins with lengths of colourful net to make pretty napkin rings. You will need three lengths of net for each napkin, so choose three different shades which look good together and go well with the napkin. You will also need to take into consideration the colour of your table cloth and any other table linen you are using to make sure the overall effect is right.

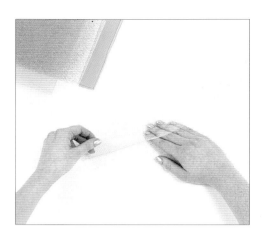

*1. For each napkin ring, cut three rectangles of net 45x35cm (18x14in). They should be different colours for maxiumum impact.*

*2. Fold a napkin into quarters to form a square, then fold it in half diagonally to form a triangle. Finally, roll it up lengthways into a tube.*

*3. Fold the three pieces of net crossways into three equal sections to form a long rectangle. Position the three lengths of net on top of each other and tie them round the napkin. Separate out the ends of the net.*

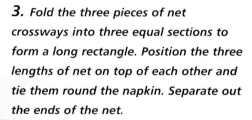

RIGHT: *For a really special occasion, an all-white scheme is most striking. This table has been decorated for a wedding with a pure white cloth and white netting swags around the edge. The swags have been enhanced by sprigs of white asters tied with white ribbon for a romantic effect. Your guests will definitely know it is a special day.*

# fun fairy cakes and candles

These individual cakes, each with its own candle, make an unusual alternative to a large birthday cake and form an attractive centrepiece for a birthday tea table.

*1.* *Decorate each little cake with a pattern, or use icing to pipe each guest's name onto one. Find a pack of long birthday candles in mixed colours.*

*2.* *Stick a candle into each cake and arrange the cakes on a large plate. Do not allow the candles to burn for too long or they will drip wax on the cakes.*

# clever containers

This charming informal centrepiece is perfect for a sophisticated dinner al fresco and proof that flowers can be arranged effectively in all sorts of containers. In fact, an unusual container often adds interest to a simple flower arrangement. The two shown here are a pretty floral mug and a wide breakfast cup and saucer.

*1.* *Tulips are usually arranged in a tall vase but here they are to be grouped in the mug. White freesias and red anemones have been chosen for the cup.*

*2.* *Cut the tulip stems short and arrange the flowers and leaves in the mug. Partially fill the cup with freesias, then add a few anemones as spots of colour.*

# quilted table mats

Use these pretty placemats to liven up your table. They are quick to make and easy to launder if you make them from a washable fabric and synthetic wadding. The backing fabric is brought to the front to make an attractive self-binding. You will need checked top fabric, some 56g (2oz) wadding cut to the finished size plus 1.25cm (½in) all around, and a piece of backing fabric cut to size, plus 3.5cm (1⅜in) all round.

**1.** *Place the backing fabric, wrong side up, flat on the work surface. Centre the wadding on top of it, and place the main fabric, right side up, centred on top. Pin the layers together with several rows of pins running diagonally across the mat to hold them together securely for quilting.*

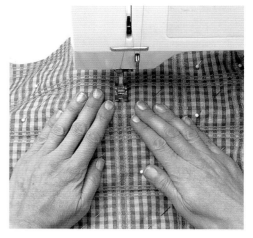

**2.** *Starting from the centre, work machine quilting across to one edge, then go back to the centre and quilt in the other direction. Make vertical rows of quilting as desired (here the lines follow the pattern of the fabric), then work horizontally across the mat in a similar way.*

**4.** *At each corner, fold the point of the backing fabric over the main fabric as shown. Fold the backing in half along the sides so the raw edge lies along the raw edge of the main fabric. Turn the backing again to enclose the raw edge of the main fabric and pin along the fold. The folded edges will make a mitre at each of the corners.*

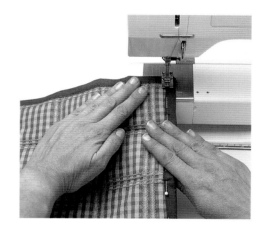

**5.** *Topstitch the inside folded edge of the backing all around, turning sharply at the corners. The small mitres should be held in place by the stitching, but slipstitch to secure them if you prefer.*

**3.** *Remove the pins and trim away the edges of the wadding around all edges of the table mat.*

# pressed leaf candle

Candles are available in numerous colours and textures and are a must for a romantic table setting. Many are very attractive, particularly the hand-made varieties with a mottled finish which can be enhanced with some fresh leaves from the garden. The leaves have been pressed to make sure they lie flat on the candle sides. They are held in place with wax which is painted onto the leaf backs when molten and will set to stick them into position on the candle.

*1. Press the leaves in a flower press or between the pages of a heavy book. When they are ready, select a number of a similar size and shape to use around the base of the candle.*

*2. Melt a little wax in a bowl over a saucepan of hot water. Working quickly, brush the leaf backs with wax and press into position on the candle. If the wax hardens on the brush, dip it in hot water.*

*3. Continue the design right round the base of the candle to make a border. When all the leaves are in position and you are happy with the design, tie a length of raffia around the leaves.*

# side plate posy

With one placed on every guest's side plate, these pretty posies will scent a summer table and can be taken home by the guests after the meal as a memento. Choose scented flowers such as roses, freesias, lilies or lily-of-the-valley to bring the perfume of the garden to the dinner table.

ABOVE: *Pretty pink-tinged ornamental cabbage heads have been used around a candle to make an instant centrepiece.*

*1. Group together five or six flowers to form a neat posy, aiming for a selection of shapes and colours. Tie the stems firmly together with fuse wire.*

*2. Fold the smaller of two paper doilies in half and set aside. Use scissors to snip a hole in the centre of the larger doily and push the stems of the posy through the hole about half way up.*

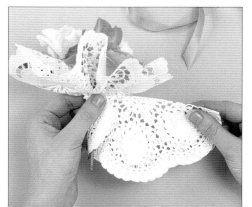

*3. Gather the large doily together round the flower stems and hold in place. Wrap the folded doily round the stems to hold the bottom of the large doily in place. Tape together and tie with ribbon.*

# simple square cushions

Cushions are straightforward to make and will make hard wooden or stone seating really comfortable. Pads can be purchased to fill standard-sized covers, but they are simple to make in almost any shape.

**1.** Cut two pieces of fabric to the final size plus seam allowances. Mark a seamline 1.25cm (½in) from the edge on the wrong side of one piece. Use a zip 5cm (2in) shorter than one side of the finished cushion.

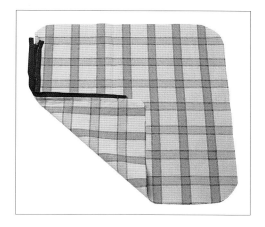

**2.** On one edge of the marked piece, pin, baste and stitch the zip into position. Centre the zip on the seam as shown. Backstitch at both ends to secure it in place.

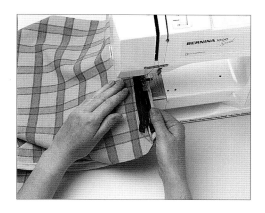

**3.** If you are using piping or another trim, apply it to the edge of the second, unmarked piece. Baste and stitch the other side of the zip to one edge of the trimmed piece with the teeth resting against the trimming.

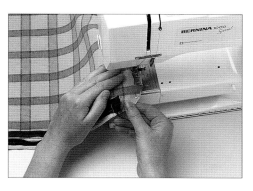

**4.** Open the zip, and pin and stitch the two pieces, with right sides together, around the sides. Begin and end just short of the zip, using backstitch to secure it. Zigzag-stitch the seam allowance.

**5.** Trim the seam allowance without cutting through the stitching. Turn the cover right side out through the open zip and insert a cushion pad.

## HINTS AND TIPS

● Gently rounding the corners of a square cushion cover will give a more attractive finish on covers that have a decorative edge such as piping or ruffles.

# barbecues

There can be few more relaxing pastimes than sitting on the deck, a glass of wine or a long cool drink in your hand, and the scent of barbecued food wafting through the air. Not only is food at its best and most flavoursome when grilled, it is also very healthy – barbecuing avoids the need for extra fat and allows the food to retain all its nutrients. It's also a great way to entertain as everyone loves a barbecue.

## CHOOSING A BARBECUE

There are many different types of barbecue on the market, from simple disposable ones to highly sophisticated gas and electric types, and it is quite possible to make your own. If you are new to barbecuing, or about to invest in a new barbecue, it's worth taking a few minutes to consider the different options to decide which would suit you best.

Assuming you would want to use something more than once, the cheapest and simplest option is a shallow metal bowl on a frame. There is no venting or cover but it is easy to light and simple to control.

The kettle barbecue has its own hood, often with adjustable ducts, and is suitable for all types of barbecuing. There are several advantages to having a hood on the barbecue; if the weather turns bad, it helps to protect food while it's cooking, and it also prevents spattering of fat and billowing of smoke.

If you like regular barbecues, you might want to consider building your own – you can use your own materials, or buy a ready-to-assemble pack. Either way, the barbecue should have three walls with bars built into the brickwork. Make sure there is enough space for it as a permanent structure in the garden, and think carefully about where you site it. It should be far enough away from the house not to be a fire hazard, in a convenient position for people to gather round, and shielded from strong breezes if possible.

Gas barbecues contain either vaporiser bars or lava bricks, which heat in the gas flame and absorb juices dripping from the food as it cooks, thus creating flavour. These barbecues ignite almost instantaneously and require no starter fuel. They retain an even heat and it is possible to have hot coals on one side and moderate on the other if the model has twin switches. Some are very sophisticated wagon models, but all have a gas bottle, which is cumbersome. However, the advantage of this type of barbecue is that you can use it at any time of year.

Electric barbecues are more popular in some countries than in others. As with gas barbecues, they depend on lava bricks to produce an even heat – they take about 10 minutes to heat – and are usually uncovered. Electric barbecues must not be used in the rain, but the more sophisticated models can be used indoors with suitable ducting.

## FUEL

Unless you are using a gas or electric barbecue, you will also need to buy suitable fuel. There are two types of coal fuel that can be used: lumpwood charcoal is cheaper, easier to light and burns more hotly than its alternative, pressed briquettes. However, once lit briquettes last longer. Wood can also be used as a fuel, but it is more difficult to start. If you do want to use wood, choose hardwoods, which burn longer. Allow the flames to die right down before cooking.

Aromatic wood chips are available for use on barbecues to impart flavours to the food. Oak and hickory wood chips are especially popular for this purpose, but you may also wish to try out more unusual ones, such as mesquite and cherry. It is important that you soak the woodchips for about 30 minutes in cold water, then drain them before you place them on the ashen coals.

Firelighters, jelly starters or lighting ignition fluid are also essential to start the barbecue. Make sure you follow the manufacturer's instructions carefully if you are using ignition fluid, and never use petrol, paraffin or other similar flammable liquids for this purpose – apart from affecting the taste of the food they are highly dangerous.

## SAFETY

If you are going to cook out of doors, you should think about it carefully. First of all, it is important to consider all the safety aspects. Do not site the barbecue too close to buildings, fences or plants, particularly precious plants that may suffer from scorch. Think about where the prevailing winds blow from, and do not organize your barbecue so that smoke drifts downwind over your guests. You should also try to ensure that smoke does not drift into the windows of neighbouring flats or houses.

Although it involves more fetching and carrying, a spot away from your house, and your neighbours, would be much wiser.

Some people prefer to build a permanent barbecue area out of bricks at a specific point in the garden, and this is probably very sensible if you have the room to do so. Make sure, however, that you have taken the preceding points into account when planning where to site your barbecue

as mistakes will be hard to rectify. Finally, make sure you have some kind of permanent table or sturdy trolley you can use while cooking, keep a fireblanket close by, and keep any flammable or poisonous chemicals out of reach of children and away from naked flames.

**ABOVE:** *A range of barbecues and accessories. Ask yourself how often you will use it before you decide on one.*

## LIGHTING THE BARBECUE

Before you light the barbecue, ensure that it is in the right position (a hot barbecue is difficult to shift). There is no particular mystery to starting a charcoal fire. Spread a single layer of coals over the barbecue base, pile up the coals a little and push in firelighters or jelly starters. (Don't worry about instructions to make a pyramid, as it really isn't necessary.) Light with a taper rather than matches, and as soon as the fire has caught, spread the coals out a little bit and add more as necessary.

The coals will probably take 30–40 minutes to become hot enough to start cooking over; when the flames have died down and the charcoal is covered with a white ash, it's time to commence cooking. (Lava bricks on the other hand only take a few moments to heat up sufficiently.) Charcoal will burn up to 1½ hours and occasionally pieces can be added around the edges. Use smaller pieces of charcoal to poke through spaces in the grid, if necessary.

## THE RIGHT TEMPERATURE

Barbecuing can be done over high, medium or low heat, depending on the type of food. It is easy to adjust the heat on gas and electric barbecues, but more difficult with the open grid types unless you have a kettle barbecue with adjustable vents. To test the temperature of the barbecue, place your open hand over the coals. If you can keep your hand a few inches above the coals for as long as 5 seconds, the temperature is too low; for 3–4 seconds it is medium hot, and for only 2 seconds it is hot. The right height for cooking is about 5–7.5cm (2–3in) above the grid. On a lidded barbecue the heat will be greater when the lid is lowered. If you want to cook over medium heat and the coals have become too hot, either place the food away from the centre of the barbecue and when cooking is completed push it right to the edges to keep it warm, or push the coals aside to distribute the heat. To make the fire hotter, poke away the ash, push the coals together and gently blow (you can use a battery-operated fan for this – it is invaluable and inexpensive).

**ABOVE:** *For barbecuing chunks of meat, fish, vegetable or fruit, use long skewers with either square edges or ridges.*

**LEFT:** *Food can be wrapped in silver foil to retain the juices, or to cook it in the coals themselves.*

## BARBECUE ACCESSORIES

The right equipment is a great help for barbecuing, and there are a few tools which are worth investing in:

● *Wooden block or table – useful for keeping implements and food close to hand*

● *Long tools, including tongs and forks; ordinary kitchen tools are not long enough to keep the hands away from the heat source*

● *Wire baskets, such as rectangular, hinged ones, to support the food*

● *Skewers – square, metal, long wooden or bamboo ones are best*

● *Brushes for basting food with oil or marinade as it cooks*

● *Heavy-duty aluminium foil for wrapping food to cook in the coals or on the grill rack*

● *Tapers – better than short matches for lighting*

● *Oven gloves, but not the double-handed kind*

● *Apron – a thick one with pockets is ideal*

● *Metal griddle plates for cooking certain fragile foods*

● *Water sprayer for dousing the flames if they become too unruly*

● *Stiff wire brush and metal scrapers for cleaning the barbecue after use*

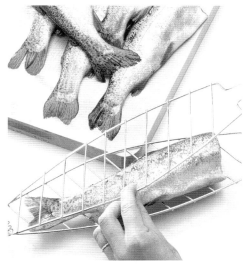

**TOP:** *Your guests will love a selection of chargrilled vegetables to accompany their meat, or even on their own.*

**ABOVE:** *Fish-shaped baskets enable whole fish to be turned half way through cooking without damage.*

# drinks parties

Drinks parties allow the host to invite plenty of friends without the need to worry about where everyone is going to sit. Another bonus is that you are not expected to spend hours in the kitchen producing a full meal, though nibbles are required. Serve the usual crisps and peanuts, plus some warm cheese straws or sausage rolls.

## GLASSES

Although there are many styles and shapes of glasses and although there are some classic pairings of glasses and cocktails, such as a dry Martini in a cocktail glass, or an Old-Fashioned in an old-fashioned glass, in general the style and shape of glass used is not really critical.

However, whatever the glass, it should be spotlessly clean and free from detergent or odour. When stored upside down, air can be trapped and affect the smell and taste of a drink. If glasses have been stored upside down, rinse and dry them before using. Coloured or heavily patterned glasses can detract from the appearance of some drinks, so choose carefully. Be sure to choose a glass that will suit the quantity of the drink, especially if it is served on ice.

## BAR EQUIPMENT

Although the right equipment makes preparing drinks and garnishes a lot easier and looks professional, not much is essential. Most drinks can be made with a small selection of utensils found at home. If you intend to entertain extensively, it is worthwhile and fun to invest in special items. The selection below is a basic list.

● **Measure** The standard bar measure varies between countries, but is usually about 3 tablespoons or 45 ml. If you do not have a standard bar measure, use a shot glass, liqueur glass or an egg cup instead.

● **Cocktail shaker** A standard stainless steel cocktail shaker consists of two parts that fit together with an integral strainer. More elaborate silver cocktail shakers are available if you plan on serious home cocktail serving. Alternatively, a wide-necked screw-top jar can be used. To use, add the stipulated ingredients and a scoop of ice to the larger bottom bowl, cover and, depending on the style of the shaker, twist together and hold the two parts together with both hands. Shake vertically and briskly (don't 'roll') until the shaker is ice cold and frosty on the outside.

● **Strainer** A classic bartender's strainer is made of stainless steel; it has springy wire coil around the edge and the flat surface has holes. Another type is a spoon-shaped strainer; it is attractive, but sometimes allows extra ice to slip in.

● The following items are also useful, but generally ordinary kitchen

## HINTS AND TIPS

● *Keep all drinks in a cool place; keep mixers, wines and juices in the fridge*

● *Make sure there are plenty of non-alcoholic drinks for those who are driving*

● *Use chilled glasses; to chill quickly, fill with cracked ice for a few minutes*

● *Handle glasses by the stem or base and never put your fingers inside or near the rim*

● *Prepare drinks on a water-proof surface, so water marks and spills will not spoil other surfaces*

● *Always add ice to the cocktail shaker, but remember the more ice, the more dilute the drink*

● *Do not put fizzy ingredients into a cocktail shaker as they will fizz up and spill*

● *For clear ice, use mineral water; tap water can some-times make cloudy ice cubes*

● *Do not use the same ice in the shaker for different types of drinks*

● *Wash equipment between preparing different types of drinks*

● *Keep a bowl of warm water close by for rinsing equipment*

● *When serving drinks with lots of ice or frosted rims, add straws for neater drinking*

equipment can be substituted: mixing glass; long-handled spoon for stirring tall drinks; toothpicks (or cocktail sticks) for decorations; drinking straws; teaspoon and tablespoon; stainless steel vegetable knife; small chopping (or cutting) board for cutting lemons; fruit juicer or squeezer; heatproof glass or measuring cup (jug) to hold hot water in which to rinse spoons used for mixing drinks; clean dish towel and dish cloth; paper towels; corkscrew; bottle opener; closure for sparkling wines; ice bucket; scoop; and drink mat.

**ABOVE: *The tools of the trade. These pieces of bar equipment are enjoyable to use and worth the investment if you hold lots of drinks parties.***

**LEFT: *Cocktails seem to make any occasion more enjoyable than plain wine or beer – have fun!***

# deckside plants

# shrubs

## ABELIA
### *Abelia x grandiflora*
h 1.5m (5ft) s 1.8m (6ft)

Semi-evergreen. This shrub is valuable as it fills the gap between late summer and autumn when there are few shrubs in flower. It has pretty small tubular flowers which are pink and white. The leaves are olive-green, often with a reddish tint. Some fall in autumn. It makes a good background shrub and can be fan-trained against a wall. About a third of the older stems should be removed in early spring each year. It will grow on any good garden soil.

## TRAILING ABUTILON
### *Abutilon megapotamicum*
h 1.8m (6ft) s 1.8m (6ft)

Semi-evergreen. A loose, open shrub which makes an excellent container subject for a small deckside garden. The stems are black and stand out well against the foliage. The flowers are bell-shaped with a red, balloon-shaped base and yellow petals and are well set off by the mid-green, heart-shaped leaves. This shrub is slightly tender but often hardy enough to be left outside in sheltered town gardens. Remove up to a third of the older wood every spring to thin it out. Any good garden soil will be suitable.

## SPOTTED LAUREL
### *Aucuba japonica*
h 4m (13ft) s 4m (13ft)

Evergreen. This is a very solid-looking shrub with large glossy leaves. It is too massive for many small gardens, but makes a very useful, dense screen on the boundary of a garden if one is required. There are varieties with spotted leaves which lighten the plant and make it appear less solid, especially when grown in shade. It has clusters of pale yellow flowers in spring, followed by berries on female plants. No pruning is necessary but the plant can be cut back hard if it gets big. Any soil is suitable and it grows happily in dense shade.

## BARBERRY
### *Berberis*
h 4m (13ft) s 4m (13ft)

Deciduous/evergreen. There are a large number of berberis that are suitable for the small garden. Most have small leaves, some evergreen others deciduous, with colour varying from green to purple. Most have stiff prickly spines on the stem which make them good to plant under vulnerable windows or on the garden boundary to form an impenetrable hedge to deter intruders. The flowers vary from pale yellow to orange and are fragrant in some species. No pruning is required but they can be cut back to restrict size or keep them neat. Any soil will be suitable.

## BUTTERFLY BUSH
### *Buddleja*
h 4m (13ft) s 4m (13ft)

Deciduous. There is a wide selection of buddlejas that are suitable for the small garden although most will become too large for the smallest of gardens. The flowers, which appear in summer, are in long or round clusters and vary in colour from lilac to purple and from pale yellow to near orange. Butterflies and insects love them. They are best planted as a background plant in a border. Many common varieties should be hard pruned early each spring, almost to the ground. Any soil, even dry ones, will be suitable.

## BOX
### *Buxus sempervirens*
h 5m (16ft) s 5m (16ft)

Evergreen. Box can be allowed to grow freely like any other bush but it is usually clipped tight and used to form a hedge or a topiary shape. The form 'Suffruticosa' is useful for miniature or dwarf hedges around beds and borders and along paths. As topiary, box can be clipped to virtually any shape you require. It is slow-growing and has small oval, dark green leaves and insignificant flowers. Box only needs clipping over once a year and as a shrub needs no pruning at all. It will grow in any well-drained soil and tolerates situations from full sun to deep shade.

## CAMELLIA
### Camellia japonica
h 10m (33ft) s 6m (20ft)

Evergreen. Superb flowering shrub that varies in height from low growing to almost tree-like proportions. The foliage is dark green and glossy and offsets the flowers beautifully. The flowers can be single, semi-double or double and vary from light pink through to very dark pink and red; there are also white forms. It flowers in late winter and spring and may be caught by the frost. It needs no pruning, but requires a neutral to acid soil and light shade. Plant away from early morning sun.

## CALIFORNIAN LILAC
### Ceanothus
h 4m (13ft) s 4m (13ft)

Evergreen/deciduous. Although this can be grown free-standing, it makes an excellent wall shrub. The evergreen varieties are dense and tightly packed and generally have small, dark green, oval leaves, which perfectly set off the clusters of blue flowers that appear between spring and autumn. The looser, deciduous shrub tends to have larger leaves. The evergreen needs no pruning but deciduous varieties need the previous year's growth cut back by at least half. Good soil in full sun.

## ORNAMENTAL QUINCE
### Chaenomeles
h 3m (10ft) s 3m (10ft)

Deciduous. This can be grown as a free-standing shrub or a wall shrub. If grown as a free-standing specimen, it usually becomes loose and straggly and too big for a small space. However, as a wall shrub it can be kept cut back and be very compact and decorative. It flowers in spring and often through the winter as well. The flowers can be single or double and vary in colour from orange through red to pink and white. In autumn it has very hard, pear-shaped fruits, often with a decoratively coloured skin. It needs pruning hard, but likes any soil, and sun or shade.

## MEXICAN ORANGE BLOSSOM
### Choisya ternata
h 1.8m (6ft) s 1.8m (6ft)

Evergreen. A rounded shrub with glossy foliage that sets off the clusters of white flowers that appear in late spring or early summer. There is often also a second flush of flowers. The flowers are deliciously fragrant so it is worth planting this near a sitting area or a window that is often open. Remove up to a third of the old wood every year after flowering to help the plant rejuvenate. Plant in any good garden soil. It will be happy in either sun or shade.

**LEFT:** *Camellia japonica* 'Tricolor'.

LEFT: *Cotoneaster horizontalis.*

## ROCK ROSE
### *Cistus*
h 1m (3ft) s 1m (3ft)

Evergreen. A large group of beautiful shrubs, most with soft hairy leaves, grey or green. The flowers are like single roses made of crumpled tissue paper and appear only for a day, but there is a continuous supply of them. The basic colour varies from white to various shades of pink, and there are often purple or chocolate blotches on the petals. Some rock roses have resinous buds which produce a delightful aroma. Little pruning is needed except for light trimming, but this plant requires a well-drained soil and full sun.

## SILVERY CONVOLVULUS
### *Convolvulus cneorum*
h 45cm (18in) s 60cm (24in)

Evergreen. A stunning shrub with silvery foliage that appears to shine in the sun. This is complemented by white trumpet flowers throughout

LEFT: *Cotoneaster horizontalis.*

the summer. Unlike the more weedy convolvuluses this one does not spread and is not a rampant weed. It is short-lived but will last several years or more if it has a well-drained soil and a warm, sunny position. It grows particularly well on walls. No pruning is required.

## COTONEASTER
### *Cotoneaster horizontalis*
h 1m (3ft) s 1.5m (5ft)

Deciduous. Low, spreading shrub which will grow flat against a wall or fence. The main branches have sub-branches arranged in a neat herringbone fashion, which are clothed with tiny oval leaves. In summer small white flowers are produced on the plant, followed by bright red berries. The berries last well into the winter and often through to the following summer. No pruning is required and this plant will grow in any garden soil in either sun or medium shade.

## DAPHNE
### *Daphne tangutica*
h 75cm (30in) s 1m (3ft)

Evergreen. This is one of the easiest of daphnes to grow as well as being one of the longest lived. It forms a dense, rounded shrub, with dark green, oval foliage and pink starry flowers. These appear mainly in

spring, but it often flowers intermittently for the rest of the summer and into the autumn. The flowers are very fragrant and are followed by orange-red berries which are poisonous. No pruning required, but plant in any good, reasonably well-drained garden soil, in light shade.

## ELAEAGNUS
### *Elaeagnus pungens* 'Maculata'
h 3.6m (12ft) s 4m (13ft)

Evergreen. A brightly coloured shrub that has bright golden leaves with dark green margins. The undersides of the leaves are duller silvery-green. The young stems are a light brown dusted with gold. It does not require pruning but its size can be contained by regular trimming and any branches that revert to green foliage must be cut out. It can even be used to make a hedge. It will grow in any soil and can be planted in sun or shade.

## HEATHER
### *Erica*
h 30cm (12in) s 45cm (18in)

Evergreen. There are a wide variety of heathers which are compact and easy to maintain. The foliage is small and needle-like, usually green but there are also golden forms. The flowers vary from white, through pink to purple and red. It mixes well with conifers and other permanent subjects of a more subdued nature, rather than with annuals and colour-ful perennials. It needs neutral to acid soil (although there are a few that can be grown on chalk) and does well on sandy soils. Full sun is best.

## ESCALLONIA
### *Escallonia*
h 3m (10ft) s 4m (13ft)

Evergreen. This is an attractive shrub with small glossy leaves that are oval and light to dark green. These are a perfect foil for the small, bell-shaped flowers that appear in late spring and early summer and continue intermittently for the rest of the growing season. The flowers vary in colour from light to dark pink and through to red, as well as white. Prune out about a third of the old wood each year after flowering. It will grow on most garden soils, in either sun or light shade.

## EUONYMUS
### *Euonymus fortunei*
h 60cm (24in) s 3m (10ft)

Evergreen. Excellent shrub for the small garden, especially for filling odd gaps or as ground cover. Although only low-growing, it will scramble up through other shrubs or up walls and fences. The best forms are the variegated ones which are available with gold or silver variega-tions. These are bright and cheerful and are especially useful in shady

ABOVE: *Helianthemum cupreum.*

areas as they lighten them consider-ably. No pruning is required. It will grow in any good garden soil and can be planted in situations with full sun to moderate shade.

## FUCHSIA
### *Fuchsia*
h 1.2m (4ft) s 1.5m (5ft)

Deciduous. There is a vast quantity of different fuchsia varieties to choose from and nearly all are suitable for a small garden. There is one important distinction. Some are hardy and can be left in the garden all year round, while others are tender and need to be given protection during the winter months. All fuchsias have very attractive flowers featuring pink, white, red and purple which appear over a very long season. The hardy

varieties can be left unpruned, in which case they will flower earlier, or cut back hard in early spring. Fuschias prefer sun or light shade.

## SUN ROSE
### *Helianthemum*
h 30cm (12in) s 75cm (30in)

Evergreen. A superb plant for the deckside garden. It forms low hum-mocks and carries colourful flowers for a long period. There is a great number of varieties varying from bright brash oranges and reds, to soft, subtle pinks, whites and yellows. Some are double, others single. The leaves are small, sometimes grey and sometimes green. It is perfect for the front of a border or for growing on a rock garden, raised bed, wall or cascading down a bank. Trim over after flowering. Full sun and well-drained soil are required.

## HORTENSIA HYDRANGEA
### *Hydrangea macrophylla*
h 3m (10ft) s 3m (10ft)

Deciduous. This is a wonderful, old-fashioned shrub with large, rounded heads of flowers over a very long period from midsummer onwards. The flower heads can be dried for flower arrangements. Their colour varies from pale to dark pinks and reds and also in shades of blue and white. They tend to be pink if the plant is grown on alkaline soils, red on neutral and blue on acid soils. No pruning is required, but remove any old flowerheads in spring. Any moisture-retentive soil will be suitable but light shade is preferred.

## LAVENDER
### *Lavandula angustifolia*
h 1m (3ft) s 1m (3ft)

Evergreen. This shrub is grown for its foliage and flowers, especially the fragrance that is given off by both. The leaves are silvery-grey in colour. The flowers, which form on short spikes carried on stiff stems, are lavender-blue, although there are some varieties with purple, pink or white flowers. This is an excellent plant for a container or for lining the edges of a deck in a formal or cottage garden. Trim over the plants in spring to keep them compact and tidy and remove old flowerheads in autumn. Any well-drained soil in full sun will be suitable.

## LAVATERA
### *Lavatera* 'Rosea'
h 3m (10ft) s 3m (10ft)

Deciduous. An airy shrub that has masses of large pink, saucer-shaped flowers. These showy flowers appear over a long period, from summer onwards. If left unpruned the plant will start flowering much earlier, but pruning will help to produce more flowers overall during the summer months. In exposed positions it can suffer from wind rock, and it can die in very wet winters. Frosts will cut it back, but it will usually regenerate. Cut back the previous year's growth each spring, almost to the base. Any free-draining soil will be suitable, but it should be planted in a sheltered and sunny position.

ABOVE: *Thymus* 'Doone Valley'.

## MOCK ORANGE
### *Philadelphus* 'Manteau d'Hermine'
h 75cm (30in) s 1m (3ft)

Deciduous. This is a miniature philadelphus that is eminently suitable for a deckside garden. It flowers in summer with double flowers that are creamy white and extremely fragrant with a typical philadelphus scent. Being small this shrub can be tucked away among other shrubs or among herbaceous plants in a mixed border. Once established, cut out up to a third of the old wood straight after flowering each year. It will grow in any good garden soil and can be planted in any situation between full sun and light shade.

## SHRUBBY CINQUEFOIL
### *Potentilla fruticosa*
h 1.2m (4ft) s 1.2m (4ft)

Deciduous. Very useful shrub for containers and small borders. It makes neat rounded hummocks and is covered with simple pink, yellow or white flowers over a long period in the summer. It fits in well with other shrubs or perennials. Although pruning is not strictly necessary, without it the amount of flowers will decrease. Once established it is best to prune out some of the old wood each year to rejuvenate the bush continually. Any soil will do, although it prefers a sunny position.

## RHODODENDRON
### *Rhododendron yakushimanum*
h 1.2m (4ft) s 1.2m (4ft)

Evergreen. Many small rhododendrons and azaleas are suitable for containers and the deckside, but this really is one of the best. It has very dark, glossy foliage that sets off the flowers beautifully. The large, handsome flowers are held in tight clusters and consist of dark pink buds that open into lighter pink bells, which age to white. On a healthy plant, the flowers will literally cover the shrub. No pruning is necessary. This plant needs a neutral to acid soil and dislikes any alkalinity. If the soil is moist enough it will grow in the sun, but otherwise it prefers a lightly shaded position.

## COTTON LAVENDER
### *Santolina chamaecyparissus*
h 50cm (20in) s 1m (3ft)

Evergreen. A very decorative shrub with finely cut silver foliage. It is a very useful colour for mixing in a border or container with very soft-coloured flowers such as pale blues and pinks. It is also useful for linking colours that might otherwise clash. This plant produces yellow flowers, but most gardeners remove these as they spoil the foliage effect. Trim the plant over lightly in spring when new growth starts. It will grow in any well-drained soil. Like all silver plants, it needs a sunny position otherwise it will grow very leggy.

## SKIMMIA
### *Skimmia japonica*
h 1m (3ft) s 1m (3ft)

Evergreen. Attractive, glossy-leaved bush that has clusters of fragrant white flowers in late spring. These flowers are followed in autumn by large shining red berries which remain on the plant all winter. Unfortunately it is necessary to have both a male and a female plant in order to produce fruit, so ensure that you buy one of each. No pruning is required. This plant needs to have a neutral or acid soil to thrive and dislikes alkaline conditions. It can be grown in containers, if the containers are large enough. It will grow in either sun or light shade.

## THYME
### *Thymus*
h 10cm (4in) s 50cm (20in)

Evergreen. A compact shrub that is ideal for containers or small borders around the deck. It is a valuable herb for kitchen use as well as an attractive garden plant. It can be grown in the front of a border or herb garden, or it can be grown on a rockery bed or allowed to tumble down a wall. It is perfect for growing in cracks in paving and will stand the passage of feet. It has small, fragrant leaves and clustered heads of pink flowers. It requires no pruning and will grow in most soils, but it prefers sun.

## VIBURNUM
### *Viburnum carlesii*
h 1.8m (6ft) s 1.8m (6ft)

Deciduous. There are a number of handsome viburnums that are suitable for small gardens, some of which are evergreen. This one has the advantage of being small and also carrying the most deliciously scented flowers. The pretty domed heads of the small flowers are white, opening from soft pink buds, and they appear in spring. The softly hairy leaves turn an attractive orange-red in autumn. Plant this shrub with other shrubs, or at the back of a deckside border. It needs no pruning. It will grow in any reasonable garden soil but prefers a light sunny position.

# climbers

### CLEMATIS
### *Clematis montana*
h 12m (40ft) s 12m (40ft)

Deciduous. A strong climber that can easily fill a tree or cover a garage or shed. However, it can be controlled by pruning to fill a much smaller space. The flowers are pink or white and they have a creamy vanilla scent, stronger on warm days. Although it will scramble through trees and bushes it may need tying to other supports. No pruning required except to restrict size and remove dead wood. Any good garden soil will do. Plant with the roots in the shade but the top preferably in sun.

### CLEMATIS
### *Clematis viticella*
h 4m (13ft) s 4m (13ft)

Deciduous. This is a group of small-flowered clematis that are particularly valuable as they flower from mid-summer onwards and are suitable for growing through shrubs and trees. The flowers vary from white through to blue, pink, red and purple. They are produced in great profusion. Prune back each spring to a pair of buds not far above the ground, removing all the old wood above them. Any good soil will do. Plant with the roots in the shade and top in sun or light shade.

### CLEMATIS
### *Clematis* large-flowered forms
h 4m (13ft) s 4m (13ft)

Deciduous. A large group of some of the most decorative clematis, with flowers up to 25cm (10in) across. They vary in colour from white through pink, red, purple and blue, and in time of flowering from spring to autumn. They can be grown up trellis, poles, walls or through shrubs and trees. Prune each year by removing some growth, cutting back to a pair of strong buds, although some late-flowering cultivars need to be more heavily cut back to remove most of the previous year's growth. Any good soil is suitable, but with the roots in shade, and the top in sun.

### CATHEDRAL BELLS
### *Cobaea scandens*
h 10m (33ft) s 10m (33ft)

Evergreen. This is a perennial but it is usually treated as an annual in colder areas. It has large, perfectly shaped bells which are creamy green turning to purple with age. It can be trained up any form of support. It is grown each year from seed and planted out after the frosts into a rich soil that does not dry out too much. It needs a sunny position to flower well. No pruning is required; discard the dying plant in autumn.

### CHILEAN GLORY FLOWER
### *Eccremocarpus scaber*
h 3m (10ft) s 3m (10ft)

Evergreen. Not a vigorous climber but one that is very useful for growing through other plants, including other, early-flowering climbers. It has small tubular flowers that are a flame-red on the outside and orange on the inside and appear from spring until autumn. It can be treated as an annual and grown from seed each year. Alternatively, in warmer areas against walls, it can be left in the ground from one year to the next. No pruning is required. Any soil and a sunny position.

### IVY
### *Hedera*
h 5m (16ft) s 5m (16ft)

Evergreen. There are a large number of ivies available. Nearly all are grown for their foliage rather than flowers or fruit. The foliage varies in size and to some extent in shape. Colour also varies, sometimes with strong gold or silver variegation to create very striking plants. They make an excellent wall-covering and can also be used to cover the ground. They need little attention and no pruning other than cutting stems back from gutters where they have become a nuisance. Ivy is a self-clinging climber so no training is required. Any soil and situation is suitable, from full sun to deep shade.

## GOLDEN HOP
### *Humulus lupulus* 'Aureus'
h 5m (16ft) s 5m (16ft)

Deciduous. A perennial climber that dies back to the ground every autumn. The hop is a twisting climber and readily attaches itself to poles, wires, string or trees and bushes. The stems are very rough and can cause skin burns if rubbed against. It is mainly grown for its beautiful golden foliage, but it also develops hops, which are at their best in late summer. Since it starts from ground level it does not attain any great height until midsummer. Any good soil and a sunny position.

**BELOW:** *Clematis* 'Nelly Moser'.

## CLIMBING HYDRANGEA
### *Hydrangea anomala petiolaris*
h 12m (40ft) s 12m (40ft)

Deciduous. A strong-growing wall climber which can also be grown through trees. It can sometimes grow rather too large and strong and may need cutting back regularly to prevent it invading gutters and roofs. The leaves are light green turning to an attractive yellow in autumn. In the summer months it carries large and airy heads of pretty, lacy flowers, typical of lace-cap hydrangeas. It is self-clinging and needs no training or tying in. It will grow in any garden soil although it prefers rich and moist. It is happiest in full sun or in medium shade.

## MORNING GLORY
### *Ipomoea tricolor*
h 3m (10ft) s 3m (10ft)

Deciduous. Although this climber is a perennial it is usually grown as an annual, especially when planted outside, where it will not survive the winter. The flowers are very attractive funnels or shallow trumpets. The flared part of the trumpet is a rich and vivid blue or purple, inside which is a band of bright white with a final touch of yellow right in the base. This plant is grown from seed and it should be planted outside only after the last frost of the spring. It needs a rich, moist soil and a warm position in the sun.

## JASMINE
### *Jasminum officinale*
h 12m (40 ft) s 12m (40ft)

Deciduous. A climbing shrub that is grown for its deliciously scented flowers, which are white and appear from midsummer onwards. They are particularly fragrant in the evening and it is worth planting this climber near open windows or close to your table and chairs on the deck. The plant itself is not overly attractive if it becomes restricted and over dense. To start with, tie the stems in to their supports. After the plant reaches a reasonable size, prune out dead and surplus wood to stop it forming a dense mass. Plant jasmine in a rich, moisture-retentive soil in sun.

## SWEET PEA
### *Lathyrus odoratus*
h 2.1m (7ft) s 2.1m (7ft)

Deciduous. An annual that is sown from seed every winter. It is hardy and can be planted out when it is large enough. It is grown entirely for its wonderful flowers; many cultivars are distinctly fragrant. The flower colours vary from white through pink and red to purple and blues. It should be grown in a rich, moisture-retentive soil and allowed to climb through peasticks, trellis or some other support. It needs a sunny position to grow and flower well.

## HONEYSUCKLE
### *Lonicera periclymenum*
h 10m (33ft) s 10m (33ft)

Deciduous. A twining plant that naturally grows through trees and bushes. In the deckside garden, it can be trained over a pergola, trellis or any other form of support. It is grown for its heads of yellow tubular flowers, which are highly and sweetly scented, especially around dusk. Good for planting near windows and close to a table and chairs. It flowers mainly in spring but is often repeat flowering. No pruning required except for removing any dead wood. Any moisture-retentive soil will do, but with the roots in shade and the top in sun.

## VIRGINIA CREEPER
### *Parthenocissus*
h 10m (33ft) s 10m (33ft)

Deciduous. A wonderful climber for covering walls around the deck. There are several species, each reasonably vigorous and creating a dense cover. The leaves are attractive in the summer, but it is the rich, fiery autumn colour that makes them so appealing. The flowers are insignificant and rarely noticed, but they do attract many bees and other insects. This plant is self-clinging and needs no supports. No pruning is required except to keep it back from windows and gutters. It will grow on any soil and can be grown in shade, although it prefers sun.

## PASSION FLOWER
### *Passiflora caerulea*
h 6m (20ft) s 6m (20ft)

Deciduous. A slightly tender climber that is best grown on a warm wall in a sheltered spot. It is grown for its curious but very attractive flowers, which are a mixture of creamy-white and bluish-purple. In autumn these are followed by egg-like orange fruits. There are other species and cultivars, but these are more suitable for indoor cultivation except in very warm areas. No pruning is needed. although the plant can be heavily cut back every few years to restrict its size. A rich, moisture-retentive soil is required and it prefers a warm, sunny position.

## POTATO VINE
### Solanum crispum 'Glasnevin'
h 4m (13ft) s 4m (13ft)

Semi-evergreen. A vigorous but very attractive climber with large clusters of blue flowers through the growing season. It can be grown as a rather sprawling, free-standing shrub, but it is best trained against a wall, trellis, pergola or tall fence. It is not self-supporting and will need to be tied in to the support. It requires regular pruning; a third of the old wood should be removed to the ground each spring. It can be grown in any good garden soil and should be planted preferably in a warm, sunny position against a wall.

## WHITE POTATO VINE
### Solanum jasminoides 'Album'
h 5.5m (18ft) s 5.5m (18ft)

Semi-evergreen. A delightful climber that has clusters of white flowers set against handsome dark green leaves. The flowers are very fragrant and they appear in summer and through into the autumn. This climber is on the tender side and should be grown against a warm wall, although in warmer areas it can be trained over a pergola, trellis or tripod. It works well in a white garden as the flowers are very bright. Up to a third of the old wood should be removed each spring to rejuvenate the plant. Plant in a rich, moisture-retentive garden soil, in full sun.

## BLACK-EYED SUSAN
### Thunbergia alata
h 1.8m (6ft) s 2.4m (8ft)

Deciduous. A perennial climber that is usually treated as an annual and grown from seed sown each spring. The flowers are a bright golden yellow-orange with a distinctive black spot in the centre. It is not self-supporting and will need tying in unless it is scrambling through a bush. It can be grown up any form of support and is suitable for borders or container displays. No pruning is required. Black-eyed susan should be planted in a rich, moisture-retentive soil and should be kept well watered, especially in containers which are liable to dry out. It requires sun or light shade to grow well.

## NASTURTIUM
### Tropaeolum majus
h 1.5m (5ft) s 1.5m (5ft)

Deciduous. An annual climber with very distinct, trumpet-shaped flowers in bright oranges, reds and golds. These are set off beautifully by the dense, light green, round foliage. It should be grown from seed each spring and planted out after the frosts. It can be trained to climb up any support or allowed to spread out across the ground, and is also suitable for containers. It needs no pruning. Grow in a moisture-retentive soil and preferably in light shade, although it will grow in full sun.

## VINE
### Vitis
h 6m (20ft) s 6m (20ft)

Deciduous. There are a number of vines that are worth cultivating, some ornamental others producing grapes. They can be used on vertical surfaces such as walls or trellis but come into their own when grown across pergolas or arbours to create shady seating areas over decks. The leaves are large and usually in varying shades of light green, but there are purple-leaved forms. The flowers are insignificant. No pruning is required except on vines grown for fruit. Plant in a good free-draining, but moisture-retentive soil. Try to choose a site in sun, although vines will grow in light shade.

## WISTERIA
### Wisteria
h 15m (50ft) s 15m (50ft)

Deciduous. A very attractive climber with long pendant clusters of mauve or white pea-like flowers. The flowers appear in the late spring and occasionally later in the year as well. It is a vigorous climber and should be kept under control in smaller gardens. It can be grown up a wall but looks its best when trained over pergolas and trellis. It is important to keep new growth cut back to just a few buds, unless the spread is being extended. A rich soil and sunny position is preferred.

# roses

## ROSE
### *Rosa* 'Abraham Darby'
h 1.5m (5ft) s 1.5m (5ft)

Shrub rose. A delightful rose that does not get too big. It has good dark glossy leaves which set off the apricot-pink flowers beautifully. The flowers are large, double and delightfully scented. They appear over a long period from summer into the autumn. This handsome rose looks good planted with yellow roses such as 'Graham Thomas'. Prune side shoots back by about half in early spring and on older bushes remove up to a third of the old wood. It can be planted in any rich garden soil, but is best in sun.

## ROSE
### *Rosa* 'Aloha'
h 3m (10ft) s 3m (10ft)

Shrub or climbing rose. This is an excellent rose with masses of flowers over a long period. The flowers are double pink, getting darker towards the centre, and have a wonderful scent. It flowers from summer well into autumn, and goes well with other flowers of pinks and reds. It can be pruned as a shrub rose or allowed to grow and tied in as a climber. Plant in any soil that has been enriched with manure or compost, but it grows best in sun.

## ROSE
### *Rosa* 'Cécile Brunner'
h 1m (3ft) s 1m (3ft)

China rose. A low shrubby rose with arching stems carrying beautiful pale pink flowers that are set off by glossy dark green leaves. The flowers are double and highly scented. They appear continuously from summer into the autumn. This rose works well with deeper pink roses. Prune the side shoots back by about half in early spring and on older bushes remove up to a third of the old wood. 'Cécile Brunner' can be planted in any garden soil that has first been enriched with compost or manure. It is best grown in full sun.

## ROSE
### *Rosa* 'China Doll'
h 45cm (18in) s 45cm (18in)

Miniature rose. This is a dwarf Polyantha rose with clusters of small double flowers. These are pink and set off against mid-green leaves. It is continuously in flower from summer well into the autumn months, making it valuable in the garden. Being a rather small plant it is ideal for the smaller garden, where it can be used at the front of a border or can be grown successfully in a container. Prune the stems back by about a third. It will grow in any garden soil but it will do best in soil enriched with garden compost or farmyard manure and positioned in full sun.

## ROSE
### *Rosa* 'Dublin Bay'
h 3m (10ft) s 3m (10ft)

Climbing rose. The glory of this climbing rose is its beautiful deep crimson flowers that darken towards the centre with a wonderful velvety quality. They are double blooms and have a long season, flowering from summer well into the autumn. The foliage is a good glossy dark green. This is really a marvellous rose for the small deck garden and can be grown against a wall or up a tripod or trellis. Once established, prune back the main shoots to maintain its shape and size, and side shoots by a third. Plant in a good garden soil in sun.

## ROSE
### *Rosa* 'Gertrude Jekyll'
h 1.5m (5ft) s 1.2m (4ft)

Shrub rose. A beautiful, award-winning (AGM) rose with foliage of mid-green and double flowers of a most pleasing dark pink. These are fragrant and appear over a very long period from summer into autumn. It goes well with pale pink roses. Prune side shoots back by about half in early spring and on older bushes remove up to a third of the old wood. It can be planted in any garden soil enriched with garden compost or farmyard manure, but is best grown in full sun.

RIGHT: *Rosa* 'Iceberg'.

ROSE
## Rosa 'Graham Thomas'
h 1.2m (4ft) s 1.5m (5ft)

Shrub rose. A very attractive rose with long arching stems carrying rich yellow flowers. These flowers are perfectly double and are carried in some quantity over a long period from summer, right into the autumn. The dark glossy foliage sets the flowers off beautifully. This lovely rose mixes well with apricot and pale yellow roses. Prune side shoots back by about half in early spring and on older bushes remove up to a third of the old wood. It can be planted in any rich garden soil but is best grown in a sunny spot.

ROSE
## Rosa 'Iceberg'
h 1m (3ft) s 75cm (30in)

Floribunda bush rose. This is one of the best white-flowered roses, with its clusters of double, pure white flowers with the occasional red spot. It flowers from summer though to the autumn and also occasionally in the winter. It is an award-winning plant (AGM). Although mainly grown as a bush rose, there is also a climbing form. It is especially good for a white garden or border. Prune back stems by about a third. It will grow in any garden soil but does best in soil enriched with garden compost or farmyard manure, and in sun.

ROSE
## Rosa 'Little White Pet'
h 45cm (18in) s 60cm (24in)

Miniature. A gem of a rose that should be in every smaller garden. It forms a low, rounded bush and is continually in flower from summer right through to late autumn. The flowers are relatively small but they are produced in abundance, making a fine showy display. They are double and coloured very pale pink. As well as being suitable for borders, this rose is small enough to fit onto a rock garden. Prune back stems by about a third each year. It will grow in any garden soil but does best in soil enriched with garden compost or farmyard manure and planted in sun.

ROSE
## Rosa 'New Dawn'
h 3m (10ft) s 3m (10ft)

Climbing rose. A wonderful climbing rose with pale pink flowers that are well set off against dark green, glossy foliage. The flowers are double and strongly perfumed and appear continuously from summer into autumn. One of the great benefits of this rose is that it will flower in the shade of a north-facing wall. Once the rose is established, prune back the main shoots to maintain its shape and size, and side shoots by a third. Grow in any garden soil, preferably enriched with good garden compost. It can be planted in either sun or light shade.

# perennials

### BUGLE
***Ajuga reptans***
h 15cm (6in) s 60cm (24in)

Evergreen perennial. A spreading perennial with dark green foliage and upright stems of dark blue flowers in spring. There are also variegated forms, as well as ones with white or pink flowers. The foliage is pressed to the ground and so, when out of flower, it has virtually no height. It spreads without becoming a nuisance and makes a good ground cover. Remove the flowering spikes when they have faded. It prefers a moist soil and will grow in either sun or light shade, preferring the latter.

### LADY'S MANTLE
***Alchemilla mollis***
h 60cm (24in) s 1m (3ft)

Herbaceous perennial. A wonderful plant that is too often dismissed as common. It has sprays of yellow-green flowers in early summer, and again late in the year if the old stems are removed. The leaves are round and heavily pleated giving an attractive appearance, especially when wet with dew. Plant in the front of a border or beside water. Shear the plant over once the flowers begin to fade. Any garden soil will be sufficient and it will grow in shade, although a sunny position is better.

### JAPANESE ANEMONE
***Anemone x hybrida***
h 1.2m (4ft) s 1.8m (6ft)

Herbaceous perennial. The Japanese anemone is an important part of any late summer border. It has single or double flowers, usually in shades of pink although there are also white versions. The flowers are carried on stiff stems that do not need staking. It spreads, some forms almost invasively, but can be easily kept in check by digging round the clump. It works very well with the rich blue of late agapanthus. It does not like to be too dry, so a rich, moisture-retentive soil is best. It will grow in sun or in light shade.

### WOOD ANEMONE
***Anemone nemorosa***
h 15cm (6in) s 30cm (12in)

Herbaceous perennial. Delightful plant for the early spring. The flowers are pure white with a yellow central boss of stamens and are carried on nodding stems above a finely cut, filigree foliage. There are some cultivars with blue flowers. This is a woodland plant, appearing in early spring and retiring below ground again by the time leaves have appeared on the trees above. In the garden it can also be planted under deciduous shrubs, where little else

**ABOVE:** *Armeria juniperifolia* 'Bevan's Variety'.

will grow, and it will soon spread to form a colony. This plant needs a moist, leafy soil and grows best in dappled shade.

### THRIFT
***Armeria***
h 30cm (12in) s 30cm (12in)

Evergreen perennial. Hummock-forming plant from which leafless stems rise carrying rounded clusters of pink or white flowers. These appear in late spring and early summer. The leaves are narrow and make a tight bun or hummock in many species and cultivars. This is a plant of rocky cliffs and is perfect for use on the rock garden or raised bed. It can also be used at the front of borders, perhaps bordering the deck. It likes a well-drained soil and should be planted in a sunny spot.

### ELEPHANT'S EARS
*Bergenia cordifolia*
h 45cm (18in) s 60cm (24in)

Evergreen perennial. This is a good all-year-round plant. In spring and early summer it produces thick stems carrying clusters of pink or white flowers. These appear above large rounded leathery leaves which are glossy and mid to dark green in colour. It is these leaves that give the plant its attraction for the rest of the year. In winter the leaves on many cultivars turn a rich red colour. It is an excellent ground cover plant and contrasts well with irises and other strap-leaved plants. It will grow in any soil and either sun or shade. Useful for a difficult spot.

### BELLFLOWER
*Campanula*
h 1.2m (4ft) s 1m (3ft)

Herbaceous perennial. A large and varied genus of lovely plants with many species and cultivars varying from ground-hugging plants suitable for containers and gravel beds, to tall ones that are suitable for herbaceous or mixed borders. Although the shape of the plant varies, the flowers all have a characteristic bell shape. They are usually blue although there are white and pink cultivars and a few rarer yellow forms. Many will grow in either sun or light shade and are not too fussy about their soil as long as it is not too dry.

### BLUE CUPID'S DART
*Catananche caerulea*
h 60cm (24in) s 45cm (18in)

Herbaceous perennial. Attractive plants which have distinctive 'ever-lasting' flowers. The flowers are corn-flower-shaped and are blue with a deeper purple-blue centre. They appear in summer and are carried on stiff stems above a fountain of narrow, grass-like hairy leaves that are a silvery grey-green colour. The flowers can be dried for indoor arrangements. This plant is perfect for the front of a border, especially when mixed with soft pink flowers, or for contrast bright yellow flowers. It will grow in any well-drained soil but needs a sunny position to thrive.

### LILY-OF-THE-VALLEY
*Convallaria majalis*
h 25cm (10in) s 30cm (12in)

Herbaceous perennial. Much-loved old-fashioned perennial with arching spikes of tiny white bells. These are very fragrant and wonderful for scenting a room when they are cut. The flowers are wrapped as in a posy within a pair of elliptical, mid-green leaves. The plant can be invasive but can easily be controlled. It grows in shade and is ideal for planting under shrubs as ground cover around a deck. It can be planted in any soil, but prefers a moist woodland-type soil. It will grow either in a sunny or shaded position.

### YELLOW CORYDALIS
*Corydalis lutea*
h 30cm (12in) s 30cm (12in)

Evergreen perennial. This is a low, mound-forming perennial with a hummock of finely cut, filigree foliage. Over this, spikes of lemon-yellow flowers appear over a long period from spring to autumn. This is a plant for rock gardens or the fronts of borders, although it has the habit of sowing itself in just the right kind of odd corners and crevices (including in walls). Although it self-sows, it is rarely a nuisance. It grows in any soil, but prefers a well-drained one, and a sunny or shady position will be most suitable.

BELOW: *Bergenia cordifolia*.

## DELPHINIUM
**_Delphinium_**
h 2.1m (7ft) s 60cm (24in)

Herbaceous perennial. Although these are quite big herbaceous plants they are not spreading and are suitable for a deck garden with small borders. Indeed they are perfect for adding height to any border. Most produce tall spires of blue flowers, although there are also pink and white cultivars. The flowers appear in summer. This plant needs staking and slugs must be kept at bay. It also needs a deep rich soil that does not dry out, and a sunny position.

## PINKS
**_Dianthus_**
h 36cm (14in) s 45cm (18in)

Evergreen perennial. Wonderful old-fashioned plants. The flowers are carried on stiff, arching stems in summer and in modern varieties into autumn. There are a variety of colours from pink to red, and purple and white. Many of the older varieties and some of the modern ones are scented, some highly so. They make good cut flowers. Out of flower they make good foliage plants with their silver leaves. They are ideal for cottage garden borders and for edging paths. They prefer·a well-drained soil and live longer on non-acidic soils. They need a sunny position.

**RIGHT: _Diascia cordata_.**

## DIASCIA
**_Diascia_**
h 30cm (12in) s 45cm (18in)

Herbaceous perennial. Perfect plant for the small garden as it is comparatively compact and never gets out of control. It is covered with flowers from early summer through to late autumn. Most are in shades of pink, but there are some varieties with purple or white flowers. It works well as a front-of-border plant but some types are good for weaving among low shrubs and other plants, tying the border together. It looks as if it needs dry soil, but in fact prefers a moist one to perform well, and a sunny position.

## MEXICAN DAISY
**_Erigeron karvinskianus_**
h 45cm (18in) s 60cm (2ft)

Herbaceous perennial. A delightful plant that should be in every garden. The white and pink flowers are very similar to lawn daisies except that they are carried on thin stems. The plant forms a large airy hummock, which is in flower from late spring

through to late autumn. It self-sows, often in the most delightful places. It looks most at home in gravel gardens and raised beds. It will grow in any soil but does best in sun.

## SPURGE
**_Euphorbia dulcis_ 'Chameleon'**
h 60cm (24in) s 45cm (18in)

Herbaceous perennial. There are so many good garden spurges, many of them suitable for the deck garden. This one is especially good as it does not grow too big and is attractive for most of the growing season, from spring until autumn. Its big attraction is its purple-bronze foliage, which is speckled with tiny yellow flowers. It is a very good foliage plant and fits in with many different colour planting schemes. It is not long-lived, but supplies enough replacements by gently self-sowing. It likes any soil and a sunny position.

## HARDY GERANIUM
**_Geranium_ 'Patricia'**
h 45cm (18in) s 60cm (24in)

Herbaceous perennial. An extremely good plant for a deck garden. It is extremely floriferous over a long period and never gets too big. The flowers are magenta but not too harsh a colour. The ground beneath the plant is often also coloured magenta with fallen petals. It mixes well with softer colours or against a

RIGHT: *Helenium* 'Pumilum Magnificum'.

green or silver background and forms a neat dome. It will grow in any good garden soil and prefers a sunny position, although it will grow in the shade of other nearby plants.

## HARDY GERANIUM
### *Geranium* x *riversleaianum* 'Mavis Simpson'
h 30cm (14in) s 1m (3ft)

Herbaceous perennial. A wonderful geranium with a very long flowering season from midsummer onwards. It has pale pink flowers with a paler, almost white centre. These are set off beautifully by soft, greyish-green leaves. Each year the plant sends out stems in all directions which weave in and out between other plants and unite them all beautifully. It works especially well with silver foliage plants. The stems die back in winter. Plant in any good garden soil and give it a sunny position towards the front of a border.

## SNEEZEWEED
### *Helenium*
h 1.5m (5ft) s 1.2m (4ft)

Herbaceous perennial. Attractive, upright-stemmed plants that carry lots of daisy-like flowers in summer and autumn. The flowers vary in colour from golden and yellow single colours to mixtures of yellows, browns and oranges. They have a cheerful disposition and are perfect for the summer border. Some are perhaps too tall for the smallest borders but there are some shorter varieties. They work well in a variety of settings, but look best with other hot colours: reds, oranges and golds. They like a rich moist soil and sun.

## HELLEBORE
### *Helleborus orientalis*
h 45cm (18in) s 45cm (18in)

Evergreen perennial. Many of the hellebores make good small garden plants but the Oriental hybrids are some of the most useful. These have the widest range of flower colours varying from white to a deep purple that is almost black. Some have spots, others have picotee edging. There is an increasing number of doubles.

They flower in the spring and should be planted at the backs of borders where they can be seen in spring but are covered with more interesting plants in summer. Plant in a rich soil in a lightly shaded position.

## DAY LILIES
### *Hemerocallis*
h 1m (3ft) s 1m (3ft)

Herbaceous perennial. These have exotic-looking flowers and make a good contrast to many other herbaceous perennials. Tall, stiff stems of flowers are produced above a fountain of strap-like leaves. The flowers only last a day but there is a sufficient stream of buds for continuous flowering over a long period in the summer. The colour of the flowers varies from yellow to mahogany red. Plant in a moist soil in sun or light shade.

## CORAL FLOWER
**Heuchera micrantha var diversifolia 'Palace Purple'**
h 45cm (18in) s 45cm (18in)

Evergreen perennial. There are many heuchera but this one is particularly noteworthy because of its superb foliage which is a beautiful purple. Tall thin stems of tiny white bells airily float above the foliage in summer. Since this plant is usually grown from seed there is variation in the quality of the foliage so choose one when in growth so you can get a good leaf colour. Many of the modern cultivars have silver markings on the leaves. Give it a rich soil and a sunny position.

## HOSTA
**Hosta**
h 1m (3ft) s 1m (3ft)

Herbaceous perennial. Hostas are some of the best foliage plants for any garden; even the smallest deck can accommodate them in containers. The plants form clumps with

**RIGHT**: *Kniphofia* **'Little Maid'**.

**LEFT**: *Hosta* **'Tall Boy'**.

strongly shaped and marked leaves. They come in all shades of green and also include blues and yellows. There are also many variegated forms from which to choose. The flowers, usually pale blue or white, are attractive and lily-like on tall stems. Hostas make good ground cover. Give them a moist soil in sun or shade; they will tolerate much drier conditions if they are grown in shade.

## IRIS
**Iris**
h 1.5m (5ft) s 45cm (18in)

Semi-evergreen perennial. A very large genus of plants varying from small bulbs to tall herbaceous plants, all with the typical iris-type flower of three drooping petals (falls) and three upright ones (standards). They come in a wide variety of colours either singly or mixed. The foliage is usually stiff and sword-like, making a

good contrast to many other herbaceous plants, especially round-leaved ones. Those with thick rhizomes should have these exposed above the soil. Plant in any good garden soil. They should be in a sunny position.

## RED-HOT POKER
### *Kniphofia*
h 2.4m (8ft) s 1.5m (5ft)

Semi-evergreen perennial. A genus of plants from very tall to small miniatures that are perfect for the deckside garden. The flowers are carried on tall stems above the fountain of thin, strap-like leaves. The flowerheads consist of a cylindrical spike varying in colour from yellow to orange-red, and sometimes green. Some flower early in the year, others much later. They contrasts well with more rounded clumps of herbaceous plants and mix well with other hot colours. They need a rich soil and a sunny position to thrive.

## DEAD NETTLE
### *Lamium maculatum*
h 30cm (12in) s 1m (3ft)

Evergreen perennial. A valuable ground-covering plant with small nettle-like leaves. These usually have a central silver stripe; sometimes the majority of the leaf is an attractive silver. The flowers vary in colour from pink to purple and appear in late spring and early summer, with flush-

es later in the season. This plant can become straggly and need replanting after two or three years. It grows on most soils in sun or light shade.

## LILYTURF
### *Liriope muscari*
h 30cm (12in) s 45cm (18in)

Evergreen perennial. A valuable perennial for its late flowering. Spikes of tiny round flowers appear in autumn and often continue into winter. They are a rich blue, a valuable colour for that time of year. The spikes of flowers rise out of tufts of grass-like foliage. These tufts are dense and several plants together create a good ground cover. It will grow in most soils (but prefers acid) and likes a shaded position. However, it will grow in a sunny spot if the soil is moist enough.

**LEFT:** *Liriope muscari.*

## CATMINT
### *Nepeta* x *faassenii*
h 45cm (18in) s 60cm (24in)

Herbaceous perennial. An excellent plant for any size of garden. The grey-green leaves and small lavender flowers carried on airy, arching spikes create a wonderful misty effect, ideal for romantic or cottage-style gardens. It mixes very well with other soft colours, especially pinks, silvers and yellows. The plant begins to look untidy in late summer and is best cut to the ground so it will reshoot for an autumn flowering. Any well-drained soil will be suitable, but a sunny position is needed.

## MARJORAM
### *Origanum laevigatum*
h 45cm (18in) s 45cm (18in)

Herbaceous perennial. A spreading plant grown for its foliage and flowers. Its leaves are scented when crushed, so plant it next to a path if possible. The flowers grow on tall thin stems that appear above the mat of ground-hugging foliage. They are carried in clusters and are pink, purple or white. They create a slightly misty effect and are perfect for the front of a border. Cut off the flowerheads before they seed. This plant mixes well with pink and blue flowers. It will grow on any soil but needs a sunny position.

## PENSTEMON
### *Penstemon*
h 60cm (24in) s 60cm (24in)

Evergreen perennial. Very valuable plant for any deckside garden as it is available in a wide range of colours and flowers over a long period. The long flowers are tubular and come in a variety of pinks, reds, purples, whites and blues. The larger-flowered ones tend to be less hardy, but many will come through winter, some even flowering in mid-winter. Cut back hard in the spring as growth restarts. It will grow in any type of soil and should be planted in a sunny position

## PERSICARIA
### *Persicaria affinis*
h 30cm (12in) s 60cm (24in)

Evergreen perennial. A spreading, mat-forming plant which has something to offer in all seasons. It forms a tight mat of bright green foliage, which turns red in autumn and then brown, maintaining its colour throughout the winter months. The flowers are pink, opening from red buds and forming short, cylindrical spikes held well above the foliage. They turn rust red in autumn and are still attractive right throughout the winter months. The dense foliage makes a good ground cover. This handsome plant will grow in any type of soil and is happy in either sun or light shade.

## JACOB'S LADDER
### *Polemonium caeruleum*
h 1m (3ft) s 30cm (12in)

Herbaceous perennial. This is an attractive plant with tall, upright stems that carry bright blue flowers in spring and early summer. There is also a white form. The leaves are made up from a number of parallel leaflets, which give rise to the ladder in the name. It works well as a clump in an herbaceous or mixed border, and fits in well with a green foliage background or with other bright early flowers such as doronicum. It will grow in most garden soils but does best on a moisture-retentive one. It can be planted in either sun or light shade.

## PRIMROSE
### *Primula vulgaris*
h 15cm (6in) s 20cm (8in)

Evergreen perennial. One of the best-loved of spring flowers. Soft yellow blooms are carried on thin stems above a rosette of light to medium green leaves. The flowers have the most delicious scent. This is a plant of light woodland, and in the garden it is best placed under deciduous shrubs or trees around the deck, preferably informally mixed with other spring flowers. A lot of its charm will be lost if it is planted formally or in serried ranks as a bedding plant. It must have a moisture-retentive soil if it is to do well.

## LUNGWORT
### *Pulmonaria*
h 30cm (12in) s 45cm (18in)

Evergreen perennial. A pretty spring-flowering plant that is useful for the rest of the year as a foliage plant. The flowers are carried in clusters on rising stems. Many have flowers that open from pink buds, and then mature to blue of varying shades, giving the plant an unusual mixture of colours. Some remain pink or almost red, others are white. The foliage is rough with bristly hairs, sometimes plain green but often spotted or blotched with shiny silver. Shear the plant over after flowering to get fresh foliage for the summer. Plant in shade in a moist soil.

## SAGE
### *Salvia x sylvestris*
h 75cm (30in) s 60cm (24in)

Evergreen perennial. A shrubby plant with spikes of small flowers in the summer. The flowers come in various shades of blue or purple, depending on the cultivar, of which there are a number available. The foliage is a mid-green and softly hairy. This is a plant for well-drained soils and is perfect for use in gravel gardens or Mediterranean beds. It will mix well with pink, blue and purple-red flowering plants. It must have a sunny position to thrive, but it will grow well in any soil as long as it is free-draining.

## STONECROP
### Sedum 'Ruby Glow'
h 25cm (10in) s 45cm (18in)

Herbaceous perennial. Many of the sedums would be suitable for the deckside garden, but this is one of the best. It does not get too tall nor spread too far. It has flat-topped heads of deep red flowers from mid-summer onwards, set against fleshy leaves of a rich reddish-green colour. This plant can be used at the front of a border or it can be planted on a rock garden or raised bed. Any free-draining soil will be suitable, but grow in a sunny position.

## HOUSELEEK
### Sempervivum
h 10cm (4in) s 30cm (12in)

Evergreen perennial. Although this little plant does produce flowers, it is mainly grown for its foliage. This is fleshy and is produced in whorled rosettes, giving it a very graphic look. Most have a glaucous bloom on the leaves and some are distinctly hairy, as if covered with spider's webs. The colour of the foliage varies from many shades of green to bronze, purple and almost red depending on the variety. The houseleek is very good for gravel gardens and raised beds. It also does very well in containers, including bird baths or other shallow receptacles. Try mixing several different varieties together. It likes any soil in full sun.

## SISYRINCHIUM
### Sisyrinchium striatum
h 1m (3ft) s 60cm (24in)

Evergreen perennial. Striking, architectural fans of iris-like foliage are produced by this plant, from which rise tall stems of flowers in summer. These are pale yellow and are only fully open in the sun, when they have a star-like quality. The leaves are a handsome pale green, but they suffer from brown tips that die back in late summer. It is a beautiful plant that mixes well with a wide variety of other plants, especially soft-coloured ones. Remove the flower stems before they set seed as they self-sow prodigiously. Any good garden soil and a sunny position is required.

## VERBENA
### Verbena bonariensis
h 1.8m (6ft) s 45cm (18in)

Semi-evergreen perennial. An incredible plant in that it is very tall and spindly with thin, wiry stems that carry small clusters of purple flowers for a very long period from summer until the first frosts of autumn. The stems are rough to the touch. In spite of the plant's height it appears almost transparent and can easily be seen through, making it one of the few tall plants that can be planted at the front of a border where it can grow up through other plants. It is not a long-lived plant, and needs a well-drained soil and a sunny spot.

## VERONICA
### Veronica spicata
h 30cm (12in) s 45cm (18in)

Herbaceous perennial. A very beautiful plant with erect spikes of usually blue flowers set off against green or bluish foliage. There are several cultivars with different shades of blue flowers, some of pink, and others of white. The flowers appear in summer. These veronicas look good with other soft-coloured flowers. They are mat-forming and perfect for the front of a mixed border, although they will also work well in containers. Remove the flower spikes as they fade. Plant in any well-drained soil in a sunny position.

## VIOLA
### Viola riviniana 'Purpurea'
h 15cm (6in) s 20cm (8in)

Evergreen perennial. There are many violas that will grow in a deckside garden, some being easier to grow than others. This is one of the easiest. It has bronze-coloured foliage which sets off the violet-purple flowers that appear in spring and again later in the year. Unfortunately, it is not scented. It is a vigorous self-sower and needs to be kept under control if it becomes too prolific. It makes a wonderful edging to a path or deck, especially round a bed of roses. It will grow in any soil, and although it will survive in shade, it loses its delightful purple colouration.

# bedding plants

### SNAPDRAGON
### *Antirrhinum majus*
h 45cm (18in) s 30cm (12in)

Hardy annual or biennial. This is grown for its distinctive tubular flowers, which when gently pressed open like a dragon's mouth hence the common name. They come in a wide range of colours and each plant can have single-colour flowers or bicoloured ones. It can be used in borders, bedding displays or in containers and can be bought as plants, or grown from seed sown under glass or directly in the soil. Any good garden soil is suitable, but plant in a sunny position.

### SEMPERFLORENS BEGONIA
### *Begonia semperflorens*
h 30cm (12in) s 30cm (12in)

Tender perennial. This is a popular plant, both for its foliage and flowers during the summer and autumn. It has a waxy foliage in various shades of green and bronze. The flowers are white, pink, red or orange and often appear in profusion. It is mainly used as a bedding or container plant. Although perennial it is usually bought afresh each year, or grown from cuttings or from seed. It should not be placed outside until the frosts have passed. It likes any good soil and light shade or moderate sun.

### BIDENS
### *Bidens ferulifolia*
h 30cm (12in) s 45cm (18in)

Tender perennial. An attractive, sprawling plant that can be used as a bedding plant but is more frequently used as a container and hanging basket plant. It has daisy-like flowers with yellow petals and a bronze central disc. The flowers appear all summer and well into autumn. The foliage is very finely cut and delicate. It works well with orange or flame red-flowered plants. It is bought afresh each year or grown from seed or cuttings. Do not plant outside until the likelihood of frosts has passed. Any good soil and sun are required.

### SWAN RIVER DAISY
### *Brachycome iberidifolium*
h 45cm (18in) s 45cm (18in)

Annual. This is a tender plant that is grown for its profusion of small blue flowers. These are daisy-like with vivid blue petals and a yellow central disc. There are also strains that have white, pink or purple flowers. It is used as a bedding plant or in containers of various sorts. It can be purchased as a plant or grown from seed sown in the spring under glass. Do

**RIGHT**: *Calendula officinalis*.

not plant it out in the garden until after the threat of frost is over. It will grow in any good garden soil, but should be given a warm and sunny position to thrive.

### POT MARIGOLD
### *Calendula officinalis*
h 60cm (24in) s 45cm (18in)

Annual or biennial. These have yellow or orange daisy-like flowers and can be single or double depending on variety. They are used in borders and as bedding and can also be grown in herb gardens. They are usually grown from seed, but can be found as plants in nurseries. They will also self-sow, but the resulting plants tend to have basic single flowers. Being brightly coloured, it looks good in hot-coloured borders. Plant in any good garden soil, but choose a bright, sunny position.

RIGHT: *Cosmos bipinnatus* 'Candy Stripe'.

## COSMOS
### *Cosmos bipinnatus*
h 1.5m (5ft) s 45cm (18in)

Annual. An attractive annual that is good for filling gaps at the back of a border. The flowers are flat saucers with white or pink petals and a yellow central disc. The foliage is light green and very finely cut so it has a filigree appearance. The flowers can be planted in mixed-colour groups but look more attractive when planted as a single colour. The white forms are superb for white gardens and borders. It is grown from seed and needs a good garden soil, preferably moist, and a sunny position.

## FOXGLOVE
### *Digitalis purpurea*
h 2.1m (7ft) s 45cm (18in)

Biennial. The wild plant is very elegant, with a tall spire of purple or white 'gloves' arranged up one side of the stem. It self-sows and rarely needs to be replanted. There are also cultivated varieties, which have larger flowers that are arranged all around the stem. These come in a wider range of colours including apricot. The cultivated ones are best planted as a group, but the wild species works well when dotted through a border to add a romantic, old-fashioned air. It likes any soil and sun or light shade.

## WALLFLOWER
### *Erysimum cheirii*
h 35cm (14in) s 30cm (12in)

Biennial. An old-fashioned bedding plant with erect stems of single- or multicoloured flowers. The colours are mainly in the yellow-orange-red range. Most forms have a wonderful evocative scent. It is very colourful and can be used as a spring bedding plant to be replaced once the flowers fade. It is grown from seed sown in spring, and planted out in its flowering position in autumn to flower in the following spring. Avoid planting it in the same soil two years running. To do well, wallflowers need a good garden soil and a sunny position.

## CALIFORNIAN POPPY
### *Eschscholzia californica*
h 30cm (12in) s 30cm (12in)

Annual. A beautiful annual with poppy-like, tissue paper flowers. The basic colour is rich golden yellow but there are also orange, red and white forms. These fragile flowers are set off by a mid-green foliage that is very finely cut. It will flower all summer and into autumn and can be used as a bedding plant or mixed into a general border. It looks especially good with other hot colours, such as orange and flame reds. It needs a well-drained soil and must be sited in a sunny position. Remove the seedheads as they form to prevent invasive self-seeding.

## BUSY LIZZIE
### *Impatiens*
h 35cm (14in) s 45cm (18in)

Tender perennial. Colourful perennial, that when grown outside is treated as an annual. The flat-faced flowers come in a wide range of colours mainly based on red and pink, but including white. As well as single-colour flowers there are also varieties with bicoloured flowers. It is mainly used as a bedding and container plant. This plant is valuable as it is among the few really colourful subjects that can be grown in the shade. It looks good when grown as a single colour in a large container. Plant in rich, moist soil and partial shade.

## POACHED EGG PLANT
### *Limnanthes douglasii*
h 15cm (6in) s 25cm (10in)

Annual. This plant gets its curious name from the fact that the flowers are white with a bright yellow centre, rather like a poached egg. It makes very colourful edging to a path, as well as being useful to create drifts between other plants. It can also be used as a bedding plant. Its flowering time is early summer, or sometimes a bit later. Although it is grown from seed sown in spring, it will also freely self-sow, so once planted it will grow again year after year. It is very attractive to honey bees. Plant in any soil and give it a sunny position.

## LOBELIA
### *Lobelia erinus*
h 15cm (6in) s 25cm (10in)

Annual. A versatile plant that is available in varieties that form hummocks or as loose sprawling plants that are useful for hanging baskets or window boxes. The flowers are usually various shades of blue with a white spot, but there are an increasing number of pinks, purples, reds and white. Lobelia can be grown from seed or bought as a small plant ready for planting out. It can get rather leggy and so is worth clipping over when this happens to rejuvenate it. It will grow in any moist soil and in either sun or partial shade.

## STOCK
### *Matthiola incana*
h 75cm (30in) s 30cm (12in)

Perennial. This perennial is usually treated as an annual. There are several different types of stock, but they all have closely packed spikes of highly scented flowers. The flowers are double, varying in colour depending on cultivar from white

LEFT: *Nicotiana* 'Crimson Rock'.

through pink to purple, often in soft colours. The leaves are softly hairy and grey-green. This plant is usually grown from seed but can be bought as young plants. It is mainly used for bedding or in a mixed border. Any good soil will suffice but it should have a sunny position.

## TOBACCO PLANT
### *Nicotiana*
h 1.5m (5ft) s 60cm (24in)

Annual and biennial. There are several species varying in height from 30cm (12in) to the tall *N. sylvestris* at 1.5m (5ft). The trumpet-shaped flowers are common to all species, as is the range of colours from white to red, including pinks and purples, as well as green. Most are deliciously scented. The foliage is softly hairy and sticky. It is used as a bedding plant, with the taller ones suitable for the back of mixed borders. It can be grown from seed or bought as a young plant. It likes any good soil, in sun or light shade.

## LOVE-IN-A-MIST
### *Nigella damascena*
h 45cm (18in) s 45cm (18in)

Annual. These hardy annuals are delightful plants with flowers surrounded by filigree bracts which create the 'mist' in the name. The flowers are generally a soft creamy blue but there are also white and pink forms. The seed pods are also very beautiful. It is grown from seed but will usually self-sow for the following year. It will grow in any soil but prefers a sunny position.

## OSTEOSPERMUM
### *Osteospermum*
h 60cm (24in) s 60cm (24in)

Tender perennial. This plant has daisy-like flowers in a wide range of colours including multicoloured ones. Some have curious, but attractively distorted petals. Most of them only fully open in sunshine. In milder areas it may be hardy, but in most it is best to overwinter cuttings and

BELOW: *Nigella damascena.*

start again the following year. It can also be bought as a young plant, ready to go out. It can be used as a bedding plant or planted in groups towards the front of a border. It will grow in any good soil but needs a sunny position to thrive.

## OPIUM POPPY
### *Papaver somniferum*
h 1.5m (5ft) s 45cm (18in)

Annual. Tall, upright plant with beautiful papery poppy flowers in a variety of colours from pink through red to purple and white. There are double forms as well as some with cut petals. The foliage is a light grey-green. The dried seed pods are useful for indoor decorations. The opium poppy is grown from seed and will usually self-sow, making it unneces-

sary to resow the following year. It can be planted in any situation in the deckside garden, as long as it is sunny, and in any garden soil.

## PELARGONIUM
### *Pelargonium*
h 45cm (18in) s 45cm (18in)

Tender perennial. Often also called geranium. This is a colourful plant that is used in containers or as a bedding plant. Some form a bushy plant while others are sprawling and are useful as a trailing plant for hanging baskets and window boxes. The flowers are mainly reds, pinks and white. The foliage in some varieties is also very colourful. It is usually started afresh each year from cuttings. It will grow in any good soil and should be given a sunny position.

## PETUNIA
### *Petunia*
h 40cm (16in) s 1m (3ft)

Annual. Very colourful plant that is popular for containers, especially hanging baskets, as well as bedding. It has funnel-shaped flowers which are often delightfully scented. The range of colours is extensive, some being a single colour while others are bicoloured, sometimes with stripes or spots. It can be grown from seed or cuttings or bought as a young plant in spring. Grow in any good soil in a sunny position.

# moisture-loving plants

## ASTILBE
### *Astilbe x arendsii*
h 1.2m (4ft) s 60cm (24in)

Perennial. A delightful plant with vertical, feathery plumes of flowers in mainly creams, pinks, purples and reds. The plumes are held well above the deeply divided foliage, which is attractive in its own right. The flowers appear in summer and the brown, dead flowers look attractive in winter. This plant can be grown in a bog garden next to the deck or beside water, preferably in drifts. The soil should be moist but not water-logged. It grows in light shade but can be grown in sun as long as the soil is moist enough.

## MARSH MARIGOLD
### *Caltha palustris*
h 30cm (12in) s 1m (3ft)

Perennial. Also known as kingcups and one of the glories of the spring. It has large buttercup-like flowers that are a shining gold, set off against shiny green leaves. There are also double-flowered varieties. It will grow in bog gardens or beside water, and it will also grow in water as long as it is not too deep. It tolerates shade but shines out best in sunshine. It also grows in ordinary borders, as long as the soil is moist enough. Any good garden soil will do.

## WATER HYACINTH
### *Eichhornia crassipes*
h 15cm (6in) s infinite

Tender perennial. This can become invasive but in colder areas it is kept in check by the winter. It has handsome spikes of blue flowers above rosettes of shiny green leaves. It quickly forms a large mat on the water but is cut back by frosts and pieces should be overwintered in a bucket in a greenhouse. The water hyacinth floats on any depth of water. No soil is required but it should be given a sunny position.

## CANADIAN PONDWEED
### *Elodea canadensis*
h submerged s indefinite

Perennial. This pond weed has the potential to become a nuisance in that it spreads rapidly and can choke a pond. On the other hand it is a very good oxygenating plant, essential for a pond with fish in it. In spite of its rapid growth it is easy to pull out and areas of the pond should be kept clear of it. The narrow leaves spiral out from the branching stems and it has insignificant white flowers. To start it off, tie a bundle of the weed stems with a strip of lead or other weight and drop it into the pond where it will sink to the bottom. It needs sun to thrive.

## WATER VIOLET
### *Hottonia palustris*
h submerged s indefinite

Perennial. A submerged plant that produces tall flower spikes above the surface of the water. These airy spikes carry whorls of pretty small white or lilac flowers, which appear during the summer. The foliage stays below water and is finely divided and bright green. The plant will grow in up to about 60cm (24in) of water, so is suitable for shallow ponds alongside the deck. Plant cuttings in a basket or tie a bundle with a strip of lead or other weight and drop it into the pond. It needs a sunny position.

## HOUTTUYNIA
### *Houttuynia cordata* 'Chameleon'
h 30cm (12in) s 1m (3ft)

Perennial. This is an excellent moisture-loving plant for the edge of a pond. It will grow in wet conditions, including shallow water. It has a variegated foliage, coloured in dull green, yellow and red. The stems are also red. During the spring it produces cone-like flowers surrounded by white, petal-like bracts. It tends to sprawl, sending out long trails of colourful foliage between other plants. It will grow in any moist soil in sun or light shade. There are green-leaved and double-flowered forms.

ABOVE: *Astilbe* x *arendsii* 'Hyazinth'.

## CORKSCREW RUSH
### *Juncus effusus* 'Spiralis'
h 45cm (18in) s 45cm (18in)

Perennial. This is a curious rather than beautiful plant, although it does have some charm. It forms a tufted plant with very thin, needle-like stems and no leaves (the stems act as leaves). These stems are contorted and grow in spirals, producing a rather bizarre curly-headed plant. Its flowers are insignificant. It will grow either in a bog garden or beside a pond and contrasts well with decking. It will also grow in shallow water on the margins of the pond. Any soil will do, but it will grow best in sun or light shade.

## CARDINAL FLOWER
### *Lobelia cardinalis*
h 1m (3ft) s 30cm (12in)

Perennial. This handsome plant is called the cardinal flower because of its bright red flower, reminiscent of a cardinal's robes. The scarlet flowers appear on tall spikes over a long period in summer and well into autumn. The flowers are like larger versions of the bedding lobelia, with their distinctive trumpet shape. The foliage is green and offsets the flowers beautifully. There are excellent cultivars such as 'Queen Victoria' with purple foliage and 'Cherry Ripe'. It will grow well as a bog garden plant or beside water. Any garden soil and a sunny position is required.

## ASIATIC WATER IRIS
### *Iris laevigata*
h 1m (3ft) s 30cm (12in)

Perennial. An excellent iris for either growing in a bog garden or in shallow water. It produces typical iris-like flowers with three hanging petals and three erect ones. The basic colour is blue but there are many to choose from including white and purple. The foliage is sword-shaped and upright, making it look good when planted in association with water. It will spread to form a large clump, but is not invasive. It will grow in any good soil as long as it does not dry out. It needs a sunny spot.

## PURPLE LOOSESTRIFE
### Lythrum salicaria
h 1.2m (4ft) s 45cm (18in)

Perennial. This is a colourful plant for the bog garden or for planting beside a pond. It is a slowly spreading, clump-forming perennial with upright stems carrying spires of purple-red flowers. It flowers in the summer and into autumn. It is a very useful plant for adding strong blocks of purple-red beside a pond. The narrow foliage provides a good background to the flowers. It can be grown in any soil, preferably a moist one, but it should not be waterlogged or actually standing in water. It needs a sunny position to do well.

## YELLOW MONKEY FLOWER
### Mimulus luteus
h 30cm (12in) s 60cm (24in)

Perennial. A wonderful perennial for growing round the margins of ponds or through other plants at the front of a bog garden. The flowers look a bit like cheeky faces and are yellow with red spots. The plant is sprawling, with trailing stems that scramble up through other plants in a rather delightful way. It will grow either in moist soil or in shallow water on the edge of a pond. The questing stems will root, eventually covering a large area, but it is not invasive and is easy to remove if you want to. It needs sun to do well.

## WATER LILY
### Nymphaea
h floating s indefinite

Perennial. There are hundreds of different water lilies of varying colours and shapes. The leaves also vary in shape and colour, many having bronze markings. They also vary in their vigour – some spread rapidly across the pond while others are much slower. Some are more hardy than others and they may also grow in different depths of water. So, when buying, check that you are getting a plant which is really suitable for your needs. In a small garden it is best to avoid vigorous water lilies. They will grow in any aquatic compost and need a sunny position.

## WATER MINT
### Mentha aquatica
h 1m (3ft) s 1m (3ft)

Perennial. An upright plant with running underground stems that spread to create a large patch. The plant can be invasive but is good for a wildlife or a natural pond. It has roundish flower heads of lavender pink flowers in summer. The foliage is very aromatic with a distinct mint fragrance. It can be grown in a bog garden or beside a pond. It will tolerate most soils as long as they are moist and will even grow in shallow water, but should be given a sunny position. In limited space plant it in a container to prevent it spreading into the other plants around it.

## WATER FORGET-ME-NOT
### Myosotis scorpioides
h 30cm (12in) s 30cm (12in)

Perennial. Like the ordinary garden forget-me-not this has small, vivid blue flowers which open in a spiral. They appear in early summer and spangle the waterside plants with dots of bright blue. It is a plant for both the bog garden and for the edges of ponds. It will grow in shallow water (up to 15cm/6in deep) at the edge of the pond as well as on the banks beside the pond. Unlike the garden forget-me-not this plant is perennial and continues without replacement. It will grow in any soil as long as it is moist, and needs a sunny position.

## BISTORT
### Persicaria bistorta 'Superba'
h 1m (3ft) s 1.8m (6ft)

Perennial. A fresh-looking plant for the bog garden or the edge of a pond or stream. It has tall stems which carry tight, cylindrical heads of pink flowers. These hover above the dense mat of large leaves that makes an excellent ground cover. It comes into flower in early summer when it has its main flush, and then it continues intermittently until autumn. It mixes with many of the other bog plants and works well with contrasting plants such as grasses and hostas. It will grow in any moist soil and in either sun or light shade.

## PICKEREL WEED
### *Pontederia cordata*
h 1m (3ft) s 75cm (30in)

Perennial. This is a rather beautiful plant for growing in the pond. It produces long stems above the surface of the water that carry tight cylindrical heads of pale blue flowers. They flower during the summer and early autumn months. The foliage is a glossy green and lance-shaped, both forming a good background to the flowerheads and decorative in its own right. The plant will grow in moist soil, but it looks best growing in water. It will thrive in any soil, as long as it is moist, and needs to be planted in a sunny position.

## JAPANESE PRIMROSE
### *Primula japonica*
h 45cm (18in) s 36cm (14in)

Perennial. Many of the primulas are happy to grow near water, but this is one of the easiest and most attractive of them all. The flowers appear in handsome whorls up the stem in shades of either rich reddish-purple or white. It comes into flower in late spring and early summer, when the tall spikes appear from a rosette of typical primula leaves. This plant is not very long-lived, but it happily self-sows so that it is always present once planted. It will grow in any moist soil in a bog garden or beside a pond or a stream, although it prefers light shade or sun.

## GREATER SPEARWORT
### *Ranunculus flammula*
h 1.2m (4ft) s 1m (3ft)

Perennial. This is a plant for bog gardens and the margins of ponds. It is just like a giant buttercup with shiny golden cup-like flowers borne on tall, slender stems. The long, strap-like foliage grows on separate stems to the flowers. The leaves are blue-green. The plant forms a clump and the tall stems often weave through nearby plants. It grows in moist soil or in shallow water, up to 15cm (6in) deep and should be planted in a bright sunny position to do well.

## CHINESE RHUBARB
### *Rheum palmatum*
h 2.4m (8ft) s 1.8m (6ft)

Perennial. A spectacular plant for the bog garden or for planting beside water. It has giant rhubarb-like leaves with jagged margins, making a very architectural statement in the garden. The undersides of the leaves are a rich purple. In early summer it throws up very tall, bright red flowering stems, that are covered with clusters of cream or red flowers in a very eye-catching way. Even when the flowers are dead, the brown stems are still a sight to see. This plant will grow in any moist but not waterlogged soil. A sunny position is needed. For the smaller garden, *R.* 'Ace of Hearts' would be a better option, as it is half the size.

## GLOBEFLOWER
### *Trollius europaeus*
h 75cm (30in) s 45cm (18in)

Perennial. A colourful plant for the spring in the bog garden or waterside border. As its name suggests, the flowers are spherical but are really a larger form of a buttercup flower. They are usually a rich gold, although there are also paler varieties. This plant flowers from late spring into early summer. The foliage is deeply divided, again like the leaves of many buttercups. The plant forms a rounded clump and grows in any moist soil. Plant in either a sunny or lightly shaded position.

**BELOW:** *Lythrum salicaria* 'Feuerkerze'.

# bulbs

### AFRICAN BLUE LILY
### *Agapanthus*
h 1m (3ft) s 60cm (24in)

A perennial but often considered to be a bulb because of its fleshy roots. This is a very attractive plant with round heads of blue or white trumpet flowers carried on a tall stem. The flower stems arise from an elegant fountain of strap-like leaves in summer. It goes well with so many other plants, especially pinks and reds. It likes a moisture-retentive but well-drained soil and should be planted in a sunny position.

### ORNAMENTAL ONION
### *Allium*
h 1m (3ft) s 30cm (12in)

There are many ornamental onions for the deckside garden. The various species and cultivars flower at differing times in spring and summer. The flowers are carried in heads on the top of a leafless stalk. In some species the heads are spherical and make good dried decoration. The flower colours are mainly in shades of pink or purple, but also include white, blue and yellow. The foliage is strap-like and comes from the base of the plant. It often looks rather tatty so the bulbs are best planted between other plants to hide it. Plant in any soil in a sunny position.

### GLORY OF THE SNOW
### *Chionodoxa*
h 20cm (8in) s 5cm (2in)

This plant is named because it often flowers through the retreating snow. It is a small bulbous plant that usually has star-like flowers with blue petals and a white centre, although there are also white and pink varieties. The short leaves are strap like. It can be planted in odd places between other plants, where it will shine out in spring before much else is in flower. It looks particularly effective in drifts and can also be grown in containers. Plant in autumn in a free-draining soil in a sunny position.

### NAKED LADIES
### *Colchicum*
h 30cm (12in) s 15cm (6in)

The flowers of this bulb appear in the autumn directly from the soil, without any foliage (hence the name 'naked ladies'). They are shaped rather like crocuses and appear when there is little other colour in the garden. They come mainly in shades of soft pink and purple, but there are also white forms. The shiny foliage appears in the late spring and has disappeared again by the time the flowers emerge. It is usually planted between other plants so that the flowers can be seen easily in the autumn but the leaves are covered up and out of sight. Plant in any good garden soil in a sunny position.

ABOVE: *Agapanthus* Headbourne hybrid.

### CROCUS
### *Crocus*
h 15cm (6in) s 2.5cm (1in)

There are a large number of these well-loved bulbs. The majority flower in spring, appearing in a wide range of colours, especially blues, purples, yellows and white. The flowers are goblet-shaped and have a ruff of very narrow leaves. The larger crocuses can be naturalized in grass and there are some species that flower in autumn, when blue predominates. There is also another group of more difficult bulbs which are usually grown in containers. The crocus will grow in any well-drained soil in a sunny position, which includes under deciduous trees and bushes.

## CYCLAMEN
### *Cyclamen hederifolium*
h 10cm (4in) s 30cm (12in)

This delightful bulb is completely hardy. It flowers in late summer and into autumn, producing pink or white flowers held above the bare soil. As the flowers fade so the leaves appear and remain until the following year. The foliage has decorative markings and is ornamental in its own right. The tuber should be planted with the top above the soil and it will eventually grow very large. It readily self-sows to produce a colony. It prefers any well-drained soil and light to medium shade and is very good for difficult areas.

## DAHLIA
### *Dahlia*
h 1.5m (5ft) s 60cm (24in)

A decorative plant for the border but also useful for cut flowers for the house and exhibition. It flowers in summer and autumn and there are a wide variety of shapes, sizes and colours. It is one of those plants to which people can be addicted and collect many different varieties. It can be used in borders or grown in separate beds but taller varieties need staking. It is tender and the tuber is usually lifted each autumn and stored in a cool frost-free place. Plant in a rich soil in a sunny position.

## WINTER ACONITE
### *Eranthis hyemalis*
h 7.5cm (3in) s 7.5cm (3in)

A delightful little plant that acts as a harbinger of spring; once seen, warmer days are not far away. It has buttercup-like flowers with shiny golden petals, that are surrounded by a ruff of deeply cut green leaves, making each into an individual posy. Once planted it will naturalize and spread, forming a carpet of gold. It is useful under deciduous trees and shrubs, where little else will grow once there is a leaf cover. It will grow in any type of garden soil and can be planted either in a sunny position or in light shade.

**BELOW:** *Fritillaria imperialis*.

## DOG'S TOOTH VIOLET
### *Erythronium dens-canis*
h 15cm (6in) s 15cm (6in)

This is so-called because the small bulbs look like a dog's tooth. The flowers are exquisite and it is a plant that ought to be more widely grown. The nodding flowers come in shades of pink with narrow petals bent back and look very dainty and graceful. They appear on leafless stems floating above the foliage, which is attractively mottled brown over a bluish-green background. Once planted it will spread to form a clump. This is a woodland plant and needs a moist fibrous soil. It should be planted in light shade so under deciduous trees is ideal.

## FRITILLARIES
### *Fritillaria*
h 45cm (18in) s 25cm (10in)

There are a number of species of fritillary, of which a few are suitable for the open garden and a large number more suited to containers. They range from low-growing species with solitary bells to taller ones with multiple flowers. The colours vary, with blue being the only one missing. The snake's head fritillary (*F. meleagris*) is one of the most beautiful and easiest to grow. It needs a moist soil and a sunny position. Most of the other species are best grown in a well-drained soil on a rock garden or raised bed in a sunny position.

ABOVE: *Galanthus nivalis* 'Straffan'.

## SNOWDROP
### *Galanthus*
h 20cm (8in) s 5cm (2in)

One of the delights of the winter months. Although they are all alike to the untutored eye, there are over 300 species and varieties, but the common ones are just perfect for most gardeners. The white nodding flowers hang over green, strap-like leaves. The bulbs clump up quickly and should be divided every three years, immediately after flowering. In this way the colony is kept healthy and an attractive drift can be created. Buy growing plants rather than dried bulbs. Plant them in any garden soil, preferably in a lightly shaded position, such as under deciduous shrubs or trees.

## GLADIOLUS
### *Gladiolus*
h 1.5m (5ft) s 25cm (10in)

A very distinct plant, this cormous bulb produces tall, slightly arching stems of funnel-shaped flowers. The flowers appear down one side of the stem. There is a wide range of colours of which soft ones predominate, although there are some fiery reds and oranges. The leaves are stiffly erect and sword-like. This plant can be grown in the open border, but some gardeners get addicted to them and prefer to have a separate bed, growing for cutting and for exhibition. Lift the corm in autumn and store until the following spring. Any free-draining soil in sun is suitable.

## BLUEBELLS
### *Hyacinthoides non-scripta*
h 30cm (12in) s 30cm (12in)

The bluebell is one of the glories of the springtime woodland scene. The blue bells hang from leafless stems surrounded by arching, strap-like leaves. It spreads rapidly by seed and should be planted with caution. *H. hispanica* is very similar, although with paler bells, but has the advantage that it does not spread so rapidly and is a better choice for a more formal garden. This species includes pink varieties. Plant in any good garden soil. It will grow in sun, but is useful for unused spaces under deciduous shrubs or trees.

## HYACINTH
### *Hyacinthus*
h 30cm (12in) s 10cm (4in)

This is a wonderful plant for spring, either grown in the open garden or in containers. It produces dense flower spikes of bell-like flowers. There is a very wide range of colours and the flowers are usually heavily scented with a distinctive fragrance. The flower spike rises from stiff strap-like leaves. A good way of proceeding is to plant a few bulbs in containers for one spring and then plant them out in the garden for subsequent years. They can be forced for indoor use. Plant in any good garden soil in sun or light shade.

## RETICULATA IRIS
### *Iris reticulata*
h 15cm (6in) s 10cm (4in)

There are a number of other species and several hybrids of winter bulbous irises besides this one. It flowers in late winter and early spring. The flowers are typically iris-shaped, with three hanging petals and three upright ones, but they are on a much

BELOW: *Nerine bowdenii*.

smaller scale than most. The leaves are very narrow and shorter than the flowers, but extend well above them after the blooms have faded. The colours are mainly based on blue or purple with yellow often a secondary colour. Plant in a well drained soil in a sunny position.

## LILY
### *Lilium*
h 1.5m (5ft) s 60cm (24in)

Few gardeners can resist growing lilies for the touch of the exotic that they add to the border. There are hundreds of different species and varieties to choose from, with several different basic flower shapes and colours varying from white to bright red and including yellow and orange. They can be grown in the border with other plants or kept in containers. Plant in a well-drained but moisture-retentive soil. Some prefer an acid to neutral soil, while others tolerate or prefer an alkaline one. The majority prefer a sunny position but some like light shade.

## GRAPE HYACINTH
### *Muscari armeniacum*
h 20cm (8in) s 5cm (2in)

This is a small plant with a conical head tightly packed with round, bell-like flowers. The bells are blue with a small pale lip. They rise above narrow foliage that is rather lax and floppy.

Although the flowers are very attractive the foliage can look very untidy, especially after flowering. The bulbs rapidly clump up, producing a carpet of leaves and flowers. There are other similar species, some with white or pink-purple flowers. They should be grown in moisture-retentive, but well-drained soil and given a position in the sun.

## DAFFODIL
### *Narcissus*
h 50cm (20in) s 15cm (6in)

One of the best-loved groups of bulbs. There are very many species and cultivars, all with flowers roughly based on the same shape of a trumpet emerging from a flat disc. The colour is basically yellow with a few white and orange variants. The flowers are held singly or in groups on stems above the stiff, strap-like foliage and they appear in spring. Daffodils can be grown in borders or containers or can be naturalized in grass. They can be grown in any good garden soil and can be used in either the sun or dappled shade.

## NERINE
### *Nerine bowdenii*
h 36cm (14in) s 7.5cm (3in)

A delightful plant that flowers late in the year. The flowers are carried in heads on tall, leafless stems. They are pink and trumpet-shaped with nar-

ABOVE: *Tulipa praestans*.

row petals. The foliage is strap-like and much smaller than the flower stems. The flowers look good when growing through silver foliage. Nerine bulbs clump up quite quickly to form a small colony. They should be planted in a free-draining soil in full sun to do really well.

## TULIP
### *Tulipa*
h 60cm (24in) s 20cm (8in)

These are favourite plants of the late spring or late winter. The goblet- or cup-shaped flowers come in a wide range of colours and the leaves are quite broad. Some tulips are tall but some, especially the species, are very short and more suited to the rock garden or containers than to the border. They can be used as bedding and should then be lifted after flowering. Plant in any good garden soil in a sunny position.

# acknowledgments

*The publishers would like to thank the following for the kind loan of photographs in this book.*

**HILLHOUT**: pages 5, 6, 8, 9, 11, 14 bottom right, 14 bottom centre, 20, 23 top, 26, 32, 41, 43, 44, 45, 47, 79 bottom left, 101, 103, 169 top, 174, 177, 179, 189 top, 191 bottom, 197 top, 201 bottom, back of jacket. Hillhout manufacture quality wooden garden products to suit all tastes and budgets. To find out more, please contact Rosemary McIlwham on +44 (0) 1502 718091.

**DECKSDIRECT** (photography by Ben Grant): pages 1, 3, 14 top, 15 centre, 19, 24, 25, 27, 46 bottom, 49, 50 left. DecksDirect offer a comprehensive deck design and construction services to the domestic and commercial marketplaces. Telephone +44 (0) 1296 718620.

**FOREST GARDEN**: pages 12–3, 15 left, 40, 42, 46 top, 48 left, 50 top right, 51, 52 top, 53 centre, 61 top, 61 bottom left, 61 bottom centre, 78 top right.

**ARCHADECK**: page 48 right.

**RICHARD BURBIDGE**: pages 166 top, 172, 187 top.

**INDIAN OCEAN LIGHTS**: pages 167 right, 188.

**UNWINS SEEDS LTD**: pages 90 top, 91 bottom left, 93 top left, 93 bottom right, 94, 95 bottom right, 107 bottom.

**ELM HOUSE NURSERY**: pages 91 bottom right, 93 bottom left, 95 top left.

**SUTTONS**: page 95 bottom left.

**THOMPSON & MORGAN**: pages 90 bottom, 91 top, 92 bottom, 106 top, 110.

**GARDEN PICTURE LIBRARY**: pages 2, 10, 97, 115, 190 top right, 198, 202 top, 218 top, jacket top, jacket bottom left.

*All other photographs © Chrysalis Books.*